UFO

Government Informants

Keyhole Publishing Company
P.O. Box 92188
Rochester, New York 14692
USA

Copyright © 1991 and 2013 by T. Scott Crain, Jr. and Grant Cameron
Second Edition, 2013, Published by Keyhole Publishing Co.

Library of Congress Cataloging-in-Publication Data

Cameron, Grant and Crain, T. Scott
        UFOs, Area 51, and Government Informants: A Report on Government Involvement in UFO Crash Retrievals / by Grant Cameron and T. Scott Crain.
        300 p.   cm.
        Includes Appendices and index.
        ISBN 978-1482069389
        1. Unidentified Flying Objects
        2. History—United States—Armed Forces—Intelligence.
        I. Cameron, Grant and Crain, T. Scott II. Title

First published in the United States by Keyhole Publishing Company

First Printing: January 2013

Cover design by Keyhole Publishing Co. (http://keyholepublishing.com)

All photographs and illustrations in this book were reproduced with the kind permission of their owners, or else are in the public domain.

Manufactured in the United States of America.

UFOs, Area 51, and Government Informants

A Report on Government Involvement in UFO Crash Retrievals

Grant Cameron

and

T. Scott Crain, Jr.

KEYHOLE PUBLISHING CO.
ROCHESTER, NEW YORK

This book is an expanded, updated version of *UFOs, MJ-12, and the Government: A Report on Government Involvement in UFO Crash Retrievals*, by Grant Cameron and T. Scott Crain, Jr. Originally published by the Mutual UFO Network, Inc., 1991.

Contents

Introduction

It has been over twenty years since *UFOs, MJ-12, and the Government* was first published by the UFO research group called the Mutual UFO Network. It was the first book MUFON had ever published. Unfortunately, it did not get wide distribution, because it was not offered in stores and Amazon.com was still a twinkle in the key of computer programmers and businessmen.

UFOs, MJ-12, and the Government became a book that was sold strictly within the UFO research community. Despite this limited distribution, it did bring comments and leads from many of the key players in the UFO world. It also set up a historical chronology of related UFO developments, starting in Canada in 1950 and moving up to Area 51 and the modern black world that has been tasked with the UFO problem. That chronology remains as valid as it was when we first proposed it in 1991, and we have been able to add new evidence to support it.

Many things have changed in the world since *UFOs, MJ-12 and the Government* was released, and much has remained the same. So, too, within the world of UFOs and its related research. This is why we feel it is so important to release a new updated version of the book, which we have retitled *UFOs, Area 51, and Government Informants*. There were so many changes, in fact, that the final version of the book was held back many times as new developing material was added.

As to those things that have remained the same, the UFO mystery remains as elusive as it was in 1991. Researchers are still busy filing and cataloguing sightings from around the world. Meanwhile the governments of the world, particularly the United States government, which seems to be at the core of so much UFO research, still plays dumb as to what is going on. In November 2011, the White House went so far as to release an official statement declaring, "The U.S. government has no evidence that any life exists outside our planet, or that an extraterrestrial presence has contacted or engaged any member of the human race. In addition, there is no credible information to suggest that any evidence is being hidden from the public's eye."[1]

Then, as if to prove that the government is bipolar and totally dysfunctional, President Obama stood up after a visit to Roswell and, mentioning the rumored recovery of an alien spaceship in 1947 said, "We will keep our secrets here."[2]

Similarly in the dual world of UFOs, we spelled out in our earlier book strong and direct evidence from high ranking, reputable witnesses that there was indeed a government cover-up of the UFO evidence—despite denials by key government agencies such as the Air Force, NSA, and CIA. The new, updated edition adds to the evidence of a government UFO cover-up. Like the original book, we use actual names instead of relying on secret unknown witnesses.

The new edition also adds evidence to a theory that we advanced earlier, namely that there appears to be a leaking of the UFO story to the public in some sort of bizarre disclosure action. This slow release of this information appears to be regulated by a mixture of disinformation. In this way, the basic story is told, but the actual facts are impossible to prove.

The evidence we presented over twenty years ago has held up very well over time. Our research on Wilbert Smith and the Canadian government UFO investigation, Dr. Eric Walker and his disclosures about the UFO cover-up, and the story of Area 51 remain as relevant today as when we originally conducted it. What has changed is that more evidence continues to surface. It is this flow of new material that has supported the idea for an updated version of the book.

Dr. Walker, a key witness, died a few years after the initial book release. Henry Victorian, who did many of the Walker interviews and exposed the story of the Aviary, wrote a book on mind control and then disappeared from the face of the Earth.

Despite the disappearance of both men, many new facts have been added to the updated version. Dr. Walker's son came forward with information that confirmed Walker's key role in UFO history and his father's possible role in UFO crash recoveries. A new key interview done by Victorian just as the original book went to press was added. Members of the Aviary, whose names Victorian first publicized, were confirmed to be important men with important information on the UFO mystery. The new updated version looks at these men and what we can learn from them.

One thing that continues to elude us is a breakthrough into the all-encompassing secrecy that permeates the world of UFOs. We have tried as much as possible to untangle the secrets and to educate the reader regarding what truths have been learned by those in charge of the UFO topic. Understandably, the government retains its secrets, claiming a defense of national security, leaving researchers with much unresolved despite all the new discoveries. Moreover, secrecy among researchers remains a problem, like a second wall of defense that further hampers any movement toward a true disclosure on the UFO issue.

One secret that did break, however, was the identity of Bill Moore's key government contact. Moore, one of ufology's leading researchers of the 1980s, had become connected to a mysterious informant whose code-name was Falcon. This man played a major role in the surreptitious release of the MJ-12 document and many other inside tales of the government UFO cover-up. His true name—Harry Rositzke—confirms our original research and shows that he was a very high-level intelligence agent.

In our updated book, we explore who hired Rositzke. This in turn shows how such knowledge changes one's assessment of the MJ-12 document, as well as various other UFO-related leaks that have come from the government over the past three decades. It is a fascinating spy thriller of lies, misdirections, and disclosure.

The name of the book was changed to highlight the stunning popularity of Area 51. This Top Secret base outside of Las Vegas has not only captivated the mind of the public; it has become as well known as the Pyramids of Giza and the Great Wall of China.

It even captivated the minds of many in the Clinton administration to the point that Bill Clinton felt pressured to send someone to the base to see if there were indeed recovered flying saucers and a live alien. In 1998, 1999, and 2000 there were demonstrations of up to 150 people at the entrance of the base, demanding openness and help for workers who had been injured by base activities. The Clinton administration was forced to take more land around the base to prevent the eager public from viewing activities on the base, and they were forced to remove a sign that warned of the "use of deadly force" against those who tried to get on the base.

We feel lucky that we were among the first investigators to report this story as it unfolded in the late 1980s. What we wrote then turned out to be accurate years later. Now, after every major news outlet in the world has scrambled to cash in on the Area 51 on the story, we present the new evidence we have gathered. All of it supports our original investigation. John Lear, one of the key players in the Area 51 story, called our new investigative report "the best recap I have ever read."

We dropped the term "MJ-12" from the title because, while

this rumored UFO control group was a big topic of discussion for UFO researchers in the late 1980s, we have targeted this updated book more for the general public. But dropping MJ-12 from the title does not mean that the research was lacking, or that it is not worth further inquiry. The concept of MJ-12 has remained alive and well. This mysterious group still pops up from time to time, as it did when the phrase "Top Secret MJ-12" mysteriously appeared on the cover of James Bamford's 2008 book, *The Shadow Factory: The Ultra Secret NSA from 9/11 to the Eavesdropping on America.* Bamford is a best-selling American author widely noted for his investigations into United States intelligence community, especially the National Security Agency. As with all things related to UFOs and MJ-12, Bamford said he had no idea how "Top Secret MJ-12" had ended up carefully hidden in plain view on his book cover.

Bill Moore, a key figure in the original MJ-12 document saga, left the field in the early 1990s. Although many accused him of being behind a giant MJ-12 hoax, many new MJ-12 surfaced after Moore left, and after the initial publication of our book. In the updated book, we discuss where these MJ-12 documents may have originated and look at the overwhelming evidence which shows that government elements, and not Bill Moore, were behind the initial MJ-12 document release.

We conclude that there was indeed a powerful group known as MJ-12. It may well exist today, regardless of what its name may actually be. This group probably oversees the UFO mystery for the U.S. government and perhaps the world. Our new evidence also indicates that there was a clear government role in the release of the MJ-12 document and other similar documents that were leaked into the UFO community in the 1980s and 1990s.

In our original book, we examined Area 51 as the story itself was breaking. Looking back, to our surprise, we find that we had captured all the main components of the story. Yet we have added much in this new edition that points strongly to the reality of back-engineered saucers and even a live alien at Area 51, just as Robert Lazar was claiming at the time.

In this new updated book, we add all the new evidence that has surfaced in the ensuing years. That evidence strongly suggests that all of this information was part of a slow, deliberate release of information by the government. However, the government lost control of the process, mainly due to a long investigation by Las Vegas investigative reporter George Knapp. This had not been in the plan. Unlike other UFO stories that the media ignored, Area 51 turned out to be one story that the media could not get enough of.

This leads us to another story that the media could not get enough of: Chase Brandon. In 2012, a 40-year CIA veteran of the CIA gave interviews to several major media outlets, declaring that the Roswell crash was real and that there were extraterrestrial bodies. Brandon stated that he saw the evidence supporting his claim in an archive box at CIA headquarters, despite an official CIA statement that the Agency could not find the files to back up Brandon's claims.[3]

As we suggest, it is simplistic to argue whether Brandon is telling "the truth" or is "lying." Reality is certainly more complex than this. In this case, as also seems likely with the claims fifteen years earlier by the late Philip J. Corso, we are most probably dealing with pieces of truth that are allowed to leak to the public, but in just such a way that the information is deniable by the agency in question, and the public receives another tidbit bringing it that much closer to the ultimate truth that the UFO phenomenon is indeed a reality. We provide much more analysis on the Chase Brandon saga in Appendix 1.

A major theme that appears in this book is that of disclosure, but of a limited and careful sort. Government agencies, at various times, perceive a need to release some UFO information to the public. Some, definitely not all. How do they do it?

Always via avenues that leave no one at risk. That means ensuring there is no direct connection between the agency and whoever is doing the actual releasing. It also means the necessity of mixing in some false information. It means, ultimately, to tell the truth, but tell it *slant*. Until there is a full disclosure of the UFO/ET reality, deniability will remain paramount to those in possession of this great secret.

Chapter 1:

Prologue

In the summer of 1987, news media from around the world published details concerning the release of the Majestic-12 Document, which pinpointed twelve men who had supposedly orchestrated the cover-up of a crashed flying saucer in July 1947.

When Canadian UFO investigator Grant Cameron read that Dr. Vannevar Bush, a top U.S. Government scientist and alleged Majestic-12 member, was directly involved, he concluded that his ten years of investigating the flying saucer research of Canadian scientist Wilbert B. Smith were about to pay off.

Scott Crain, Jr., then State Section Director in Pennsylvania for the Mutual UFO Network (MUFON), listened carefully to the presentation of information regarding that document as it was proffered to the public at the June 1987 International UFO Symposium held in Washington, D.C., by MUFON. He wondered, "Could this be the smoking gun we have been looking for?"

Cameron and Crain teamed up in the fall of 1987 to (A) determine if a group known as "Majestic-12" really existed, (B) study how the Canadian and American governments interacted on the subject of "flying saucers," (C) determine if any scientists would admit that they were involved in UFO-crash retrieval operations, and (D) study how "think tanks" financed by the U.S. Government and U.S. Government agencies might have approached the UFO problem.

With the assistance of researcher William S. Steinman, co-author of *UFO Crash at Aztec*, Cameron and Crain located an informant who acknowledged the existence of Majestic-12 and who admitted to having attended secret meetings at Wright-Patterson Air Force Base concerning UFO phenomena. Through a number of Canadian letters and documents, they gained some indication of just how deeply involved Canada and the United States actually were in examining flying saucer evidence. In addition, they tried to find out what government mechanisms would most likely be put to use in the event that the U.S. Government was, in fact, analyzing a "flying saucer."

It all began in 1947, when something very unusual happened near Roswell, New Mexico. When and where it will end remains a mystery.

Chapter 2:

A Majestic-12 Informant

Since the time of the public release of the Operation Majestic-12 Document at the 1987 Mutual UFO Network Symposium in Washington, D.C., UFO researchers have been looking for evidence to determine whether the material is legitimate or not.

The material was clearly marked "TOP SE-CRET/MAJIC/EYES ONLY," and was designated as a "Briefing Document: Operation Majestic 12/Prepared for President-Elect Dwight D. Eisenhower: (Eyes Only) 18 November, 1952." The putative briefing officer was Admiral Roscoe H. Hillenkoetter (MJ-1), who happened to be the first Director of the Central Intelligence Agency (CIA), which itself, interestingly, had been established under the National Security Council by the National Security Act on July 26, 1947.

According to the document, following Kenneth Arnold's famous June 24, 1947 sighting of nine "flying discs" over Washington State, little was learned about the source of UFOs. That is, until a ".. local rancher reported that one had crashed in a remote region of New Mexico located approximately seventy five miles northwest of Roswell Army Air Base (now Walker Field)."

The infamous press release issued so precipitously by Roswell Army Air Force Base public relations officer, 1st Lt. Walter Haut, in July 1947 appeared, among many other places, in the *San Francisco Chronicle* on July 9, 1947, and runs as follows:

> The many rumors regarding the flying disc became a reality yesterday when the intelligence office of the 509th Bomb Group [allegedly the only nuclear-armed bomb group in the world operational at that time] of the Eighth Air Force, Roswell Army Air Field, was fortunate enough to gain possession of a disc [i.e. flying saucer] through the cooperation of one of the local ranchers and the sheriff's office of Chaves County.
>
> The flying object landed on a ranch near Roswell sometime last week. Not having phone facilities, the rancher stored the disc until such time as he was able to contact the sheriff's office, who in turn notified Major Jesse A. Marcel of the 509th Bomb Group Intelligence Office.
>
> Action was immediately taken and the disc was picked up at the rancher's home. It was inspected at the Roswell Army Air Field and subsequently loaned by Major Marcel to higher headquarters.

A front-page story entitled "RAAF [Roswell Army Air Field] Captures Flying Saucer On [sic] Ranch in Roswell Region [sic]" appeared in the July 8, 1947 issue of the Roswell Daily Record and runs (in part) as follows:

> The intelligence office of the 509th Bombardment group at Roswell Army Air Field announced at noon today, that the field has come into possession of a flying saucer.
>
> According to information released by the department, over authority of Maj. J. Marcel, intelligence officer, the disc was recovered on a ranch in the Roswell vicinity, after an unidentified rancher had notified Sheriff Geo. Wilcox, here, that he had found the instrument on his premises.
>
> Maj. Marcel and a detail from his department went to the ranch and recovered the disc, it was stated.
>
> After the intelligence officer here had inspected the instrument it was flown to "higher headquarters."
>
> The intelligence officer stated that no details of the saucer's construction or its appearance had been revealed.

Regarding the aftermath of Roswell, the "Eisenhower Briefing Document" has more to say:

On 07 July 1947 a secret operation was begun to assure recovery of the wreckage of this object for scientific study. During the course of this operation, aerial reconnaissance discovered that four small human-like beings had apparently ejected from the craft at some point before it exploded. These had fallen to Earth about two miles east of the wreckage site. All four were dead and badly decomposed due to action by predators and exposure to the elements during the approximately one week time period which had elapsed before their discovery. A special scientific team took charge of removing these bodies for study. (See Attachment "C".) The wreckage of the craft was also removed to several different locations. (See Attachment "B".) Civilian and military witnesses in the area were debriefed, and news reporters were given the effective cover story that the object had been a misguided weather research balloon.

According to the Document:

OPERATION Majestic-12 is a TOP SECRET Research and Development/Intelligence operation responsible directly and only to the President of the United States. Operations of the project are carried out under control of the Majestic-12 (Majic-12) Group which was established by special classified executive order of President Truman on 24 September, 1947, upon recommendation by Dr. Vannevar Bush, and Secretary James Forrestal.(See Attachment "A".) Members of the Majestic-12 Group were designated as follows:
Adm. Roscoe H. Hillenkoetter
Dr. Vannevar Bush
Secy. James V. Forrestal
Gen. Nathan F. Twining
Gen. Hoyt S. Vandenberg
Dr. Detlev Bronk
Dr. Jerome Hunsaker
Mr. Sidney W. Souers
Mr. Gordon Gray
Dr. Donald Menzel
Gen. Robert M. Montague
Dr. Lloyd V. Berkner

Since it was clearly indicated in the document that Operation Majestic12 was a "TOP SECRET Research and Development / Intelligence operation," it became clear to us that efforts
to locate members of the military's R&D Board active in the
late 1940s and early 1950s might well shed some light on the
matter.

After a member of the Research & Development Board who
fit the criteria was identified, researchers William Steinman,
Grant Cameron, and Scott Crain initiated a concerted effort to
uncover what he knew about UFOs.

The text and inserts that follow review William Steinman's
investigation (commenced in 1983) and Grant Cameron and
Scott Crain's investigation (commenced in 1987). To put things
into perspective and explain how we became involved with our
informant, some preliminary information is supplied.

On September 15, 1950, a meeting to discuss matters of
national security was held in the Washington office of Dr.
Robert I. Sarbacher with members of the Canadian Embassy
staff. Dr. Sarbacher, an American physicist, was then a Science
Consultant in the U.S. Defense Department's Joint Research
and Development Board and a member of the Guidance &
Control Panel. He specialized in problems associated with
guided missiles.

Dr. Sarbacher's credentials were impressive: he was a
graduate of the University of Florida (B.S., 1933), Princeton
University (M.S., 1934), and Harvard University (Sc.D., 1939).
He served as a Harvard instructor in physics and communications engineering (1936-40) and was a professor of electrical
engineering at the Illinois Institute of Technology (1940-42).
Sarbacher was a professor at Harvard in 1941, a wartime
science consultant for the U.S. Navy from 1942-45, and dean of
the graduate school of the Georgia Institute of Technology from
1945-49. He was an inventor and helped author such technical
works as Hyper and Ultra-High Frequency Engineering (1944).
In the 1980s he was President of the Washington Institute of

Technology.

At this particular 1950 meeting, the Canadians expressed curiosity over a recent best-selling book (i.e. *Behind the Flying Saucers*) by columnist Frank Scully. This book claimed that the U.S. Government had in its possession a crashed flying saucer along with its occupants. Amazingly, Sarbacher responded that Scully's claims were "substantially correct."

Indeed, this meeting had been arranged by one of the Canadian scientists, one who had had an interest in flying saucers since the late 1940s. This was Wilbert B. Smith, the senior radio engineer with the Canadian government's Department of Transport. Smith had read Scully's book and had made some interesting discoveries.

Smith saw similarities in the magnetic power propulsion described by Scully and the work being done in the Canadian Department of Transport to create a power source using the magnetic field surrounding the Earth. "I feel," wrote Smith in a Top Secret memo to the Department of Transport, "that the correlation between basic theory and the available information on the saucers check too closely to be mere coincidence."

It was because of these similarities that Smith used the Canadian Joint Staff in Washington, D.C., to set up a meeting with Sarbacher and others in order to exchange information.

The following is a transcript of the interview conducted by Smith with Sarbacher. The handwritten transcript notes were found in Smith's personal files following his death.

> Sept 15, 1950
> Notes on [an] interview through Lt/C. Bremner with Dr. Robert I. Sarbacher.
> *WBS:* I am doing some work on the collapse of the Earth's magnetic field as a source of energy, and I think our work may have a bearing on the flying saucers.
> *RIS:* What do you want to know?
> *WBS:* I have read Scully's book on the saucers, and I would like to know how much of it is true.
> *RIS:* The facts reported in the book are substantially correct.

WBS: Then the saucers exist?

RIS: Yes, they exist.

WBS: Do they operate as Scully suggests-on magnetic principles?

RIS: We have not been able to duplicate their performance.

WBS: So they come from some other planet?

RIS: All we know is, we didn't make them, and it's pretty certain they didn't originate on the Earth.

WBS: I understand the whole subject of saucers is classified.

RIS: Yes, it is classified two points higher than the H-bomb. In fact, it is the most highly classified subject in the U.S. Government at the present time.

WBS: May I ask the reason for the classification?

RIS: You may ask, but I can't tell you.

WBS: Is there any way in which I can get some information, particularly as it might fit in with our own work?

RIS: I suppose you could be cleared through your own Defense Department, and I am pretty sure arrangements could be made to exchange information. If you have anything to contribute, we would be glad to talk it over, but I can't give you any more at the present time.

Note: The above is written out from memory following the interview. I have tried to keep it as nearly verbatim as possible.

After the meeting with Sarbacher, Smith requested clearance from the "appropriate service" inside the United States. Other material indicates he was successful.

Analysis of Interview with Sarbacher

What is worth noting about the interview is that Sarbacher implied that Smith would not necessarily get the information he sought from the United States. Sarbacher seemed to imply that Smith would only be helped if he had something to contribute to the Americans.

Smith had approached the Americans on a solely technical mission. He was offering the Canadian work done on geomagnetic energy in exchange for what he could use from the American analysis of flying saucers.

Sarbacher indicated that Smith must first be properly

cleared to receive information; this step was taken. Dr. Sarbacher stated that the Americans had Smith file for his clearance. (See Image 2-01.)

Once Smith's credentials were in order, the Americans gave him more information. Some of this included the fact that there was a small group headed by the World War Two czar of weapons development, Dr. Vannevar Bush, that was studying the flying saucer mystery. Smith also learned that the American authorities (1) were interested in mental phenomena associated with the saucers and (2) sought Canada's help.

Smith was impressed enough by what the Americans told him that he proposed a special project be set up. Calling it "Project Magnet," it was to study the relationship between geomagnetic energy and flying saucers. Smith wrote out his proposal to the Controller of Telecommunications, G.P. Edwards, on November 21, 1950. The Deputy Minister of Transport for Air Services.

Edwards approved the program on December 2, 1950. He

TOP SECRET

Mr. Edwards should write to the Dept of National Defence Ottawa

requesting that clearance may be obtained for Mr. W. B. Smith to visit

the appropiate Service in the United States to discuss the use of
terrestial magnetic forces in relation to   aerodynamic problems
associated with saucer shaped objects .

In the covering request, the Department of Transport should relate in as

much detail as possible the objects of this study and also detail the

work which has been carried out in the geophysical field in Canada.

Information unofficial- obtained from Dr. Robert I Sarbacher , dean of

the Graduate school, Georgia University.

Top Secret memo indicating that clearance was necessary "to discuss the use of terrestrial magnetic forces in relation to . . . saucer shaped objects."

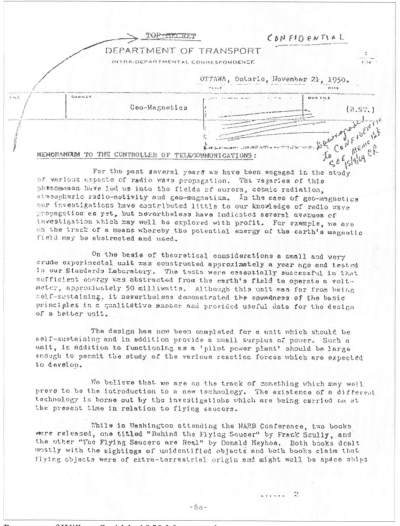

Page one of Wilbert Smith's 1950 Memorandum.

wrote on the document, "OK, go ahead with it, and keep me posted from time to time."

A copy of Smith's famous "Geo-Magnetics" document was classified TOP SECRET until September 15, 1969, when the Canadian government accidentally downgraded it to confidential.[4] Ottawa UFO researcher Arthur Bray obtained a copy of Smith's memo from the Canadian government in 1978 when it

from another planet. Scully claimed that the preliminary studies of
one saucer which fell into the hands of the United States Government
indicated that they operated on some hitherto unknown magnetic
principles. It appeared to me that our own work in geo-magnetics
might well be the linkage between our technology and the technology
by which the saucers are designed and operated. If it is assumed that
our geo-magnetic investigations are in the right direction, the theory
of operation of the saucers becomes quite straightforward, with all
observed features explained qualitatively and quantitatively.

I made discreet enquiries through the Canadian Embassy
staff in Washington who were able to obtain for me the following
information:

a. The matter is the most highly classified subject in the United
    States Government, rating higher even than the H-bomb.

b. Flying saucers exist.

c. Their modus operandi is unknown but concentrated effort is being
    made by a small group headed by Doctor Vannevar Bush.

d. The entire matter is considered by the United States authorities
    to be of tremendous significance.

I was further informed that the United States authorities are investigating
along quite a number of lines which might possibly be related to the saucers
such as mental phenomena and I gather that they are not doing too well since
they indicated that if Canada is doing anything at all in geo-magnetics they
would welcome a discussion with suitably accredited Canadians.

While I am not yet in a position to say that we have solved
even the first problems in geo-magnetic energy release, I feel that the
correlation between our basic theory and the available information on
saucers checks too closely to be more coincidence. It is my honest opinion
that we are on the right track and are fairly close to at least some of the
answers.

Mr. Wright, Defence Research Board liaison officer at the
Canadian Embassy in Washington, was extremely anxious for me to get in touch
with Doctor Solandt, Chairman of the Defence Research Board, to discuss with
him future investigations along the line of geo-magnetic energy release.

••••••• 3

Page two of Wilbert Smith's 1950 Memorandum.

was finally declassified.

Bray, author of the book, *The UFO Connection*, was also the
researcher responsible for finding a copy of the Smith-
Sarbacher interview among Smith's personal papers. Bray
announced his discovery to UFO investigator Leonard
Stringfield in a letter on July 3, 1980. Bray wrote:

> The noted Canadian Ufologist, Wilbert B. Smith, conducted
> an interview with a top American scientist involved in the
> UFO business in the early days, who confirmed to Smith

I do not feel that we have as yet sufficient data to place before Defence Research Board which would enable a program to be initiated within that organization, but I do feel that further research is necessary and I would prefer to see it done within the frame work of our own organization with, of course, full co-operation and exchange of information with other interested bodies.

I discussed this matter fully with Doctor Solandt, Chairman of Defence Research Board, on November 20th and placed before him as much information as I have been able to gather to date. Doctor Solandt agreed that work on geo-magnetic energy should go forward as rapidly as possible and offered full co-operation of his Board in providing laboratory facilities, acquisition of necessary items of equipment, and specialized personnel for incidental work in the project. I indicated to Doctor Solandt that we would prefer to keep the project within the Department of Transport for the time being until we have obtained sufficient information to permit a complete assessment of the value of the work.

It is therefore recommended that a PROJECT be set up within the frame work of this Section to study this problem and that the work be carried on a part time basis until such time as sufficient tangible results can be seen to warrant more definitive action. Cost of the program in its initial stages are expected to be less than a few hundred dollars and can be carried by our Radio Standards Lab appropriation.

Attached hereto is a draft of terms of reference for such a project which, if authorized, will enable us to proceed with this research work within our own organization.

(W.B. Smith)
Senior Radio Engineer

WBS/cc

- 6c -

Page three of Wilbert Smith's 1950 Memorandum.

that the facts in Scully's book were "substantially correct." I have Smith's personal notes recording this interview on September 15, 1950. The interview was conducted through the Canadian Embassy in Washington. I reported this information on page 59 of my recent book, "The UFO Connection." The name of the American scientist was Dr. Robert I. Sarbacher, who was Director of Research, National Science Laboratories, Inc.

2-05. Page one of letter from Robert Sarbacher to William Steinman.

While attending the MUFON Symposium in Toronto, Canada, in July 1982, Bray, along with Mrs. Wilbert Smith, confirmed to Stringfield that the "Geo-Magnetics Memo" was an official government document. Stringfield was impressed with Bray's findings and mentioned them in his monograph *UFO Crash/Retrievals: Amassing the Evidence-Status Report III*, released in September 1982.

California UFO investigator William Steinman read of Sarbacher's connection to Smith. He then wrote to Bray, asking for a copy of the interview notes, and Bray complied. Steinman decided to look for Sarbacher. He found him in Palm Beach, Florida and wrote to him on September 12, 1983.

On November 29, 1983, Sarbacher responded. He confirmed that high-level discussions involving UFOs and their recoveries had indeed been held. Unfortunately, he wrote, although he had been "invited to participate in several discussions associated with the reported recoveries," he had not personally attended the meetings.

At least one of these discussions appeared to have taken place at Wright-Patterson Air Force Base, in Dayton Ohio. Sarbacher said that he had been invited to attend a meeting there. There, officials were to report on their findings to scientists connected with the Defense Department's Research and Development Board. Sarbacher had other commitments at the time and could not attend.

He did, however, name several others who had, including Dr. Vannevar Bush and the noted mathematician John von Neumann of Princeton University. These men were listed in

2-06. Page two of Sarbacher's letter to Steinman.

Sarbacher's letter to Steinman. However, researcher Gordon Creighton reported something else that Sarbacher added, namely that the scientists at the meeting had been told that the vehicles "appeared to be spaceships from another solar system."[5]

Despite Sarbacher's impressive letter, researchers wondered if he might be able to remember more. Could he identify any others who might have attended any meetings on crashed UFOs? In a letter to Canadian UFO investigator Grant Cameron, William Steinman wrote:

> Back in 1983, Stan Friedman called Dr. Robert I. Sarbacher via telephone. During the conversation, Sarbacher stated, "I did not attend the meetings at Wright Field concerning the recovered saucers; but there was one person who attended all of the meetings. I can't remember his name, he wrote a book on electrical engineering, was a member of the RDB, [i.e. Research and Development Board] and was head of the electrical engineering department at a university in Pennsylvania."

Grant, I did some research and found that this man was Dr. Eric A. Walker. I called Dr. Sarbacher, who verified that Walker was the man who did attend all those meetings at Wright-Patterson A.F.B.

I wrote to Stan Friedman on March 21, 1984, telling him that Dr. Eric A. Walker was our man. Friedman wrote back to me on May 25, 1984 (exactly 7 days prior to his "Access to Information Request" of June 2, 1984) telling me that he was sure that Walker was the right man and that he had contacted Walker. Friedman stated that Walker knows something but is not talking.

This was Dr. Eric A. Walker began to be connected to the UFO crash retrieval phenomenon. A copy of Steinman's March 21, 1984 letter to UFO investigator Stanton Friedman appears in the next insert.

Dr. Fred Darwin served as Executive Director of the Guided Missile Committee for the Department of Defense's R&D Board from 1949 to 1954. Darwin stated that if there had been a crash, Dr. Vannevar Bush and Dr. Lloyd V. Berkner would be probable candidates. As it happened, both men appeared on the list of original MJ-12 members. Darwin also named Dr. John von Neumann, whom Sarbacher had written "was definitely involved" in the recoveries.

Significantly, Darwin also named Dr. Eric A. Walker. Considering that Sarbacher had just told Steinman that Walker had been present at UFO-recovery meetings at Wright-Patterson Air Force Base, this was intriguing, to say the least.

Friedman's response to Steinman, dated May 25, 1984, elaborated on a telephone conversation he had with Walker. Friedman thought that Walker knew a great deal more than he was saying. Friedman wrote:

I checked telephone information in State College, PA—home of Penn State after checking with the library re Walker. There was no listing so I called the University. I was eventually given a location in South Carolina, Hilton Head. I got his number there and called. He was out. I left my name and said that I would call back the next night when according to his wife he would be in. I did so. He was cagey and careful. There was no admission whatsoever of any involvement with UFOs at all.

He did say that the subject had been discussed by everybody back then. He did admit to having read the Roswell Incident and threw in some cracks. There is absolutely nothing that can be used in a court of law. He certainly will not respond to pressure. My reaction to how he responded to the various questions was that he knew a great deal.

Enter Dr. Eric A. Walker

Through the 1980s, Dr. Walker's name was kept secret by a small group of investigators—the authors of this book included—in the hopes that he would discuss his past association with MJ-12, the research and development hierarchy it directed, and more.

Dr. Eric A. Walker

Researcher Stanton Friedman said that Walker had "all the credentials." They were indeed impressive. Born in England in 1910, he received his B.S. in Engineering in 1932, his M.B.A. in 1933, and his D.Sc. in 1935—all from Harvard University.

Walker taught mathematics and electrical engineering and, for two years, was chairman of the Department of Electrical Engineering at Tufts College (now Tufts University). He later joined the University of Connecticut, where he taught electrical engineering and initiated courses for a special War Training Program. It was there that he met the rumored czar of the UFO program, Dr. Vannevar Bush.

Once the Americans had entered World War Two, Walker joined the Underwater Sound Laboratory at Harvard University. He was promoted to Assistant Director and then to

Associate Director, whereupon he found himself in charge of ordnance (specifically, weapons).

Dr. Walker had studied the industrial use of acoustics. His studies were applied to the "homing torpedo," which was developed at the Underwater Sound Lab and was successfully used against Axis submarines. For his work, Dr. Walker was awarded the Naval Ordnance Development Award and also a Presidential Certificate of Merit.

In 1944, Dr. Walker was a civilian employee of the Office of Scientific Research and Development. In 1945, he was persuaded by the Dean of Engineering at Penn State to become Department Head of the Penn State Department of Electrical Engineering. Interestingly enough, the ordnance section of the Harvard Underwater Sound Laboratory was transferred to Penn State at the same time, whereupon it became the "Ordnance Research Laboratory," with Dr. Walker as Director.

Meanwhile, in 1947, President Harry S Truman took steps to oversee military defense programs by creating a combined Department of Defense. Former Secretary of the Navy Secretary James V. Forrestal was appointed Secretary of Defense. Weapons-research expert Dr. Vannevar Bush, and Forrestal then worked together to establish a board to oversee R&D for the different arms of the military. The two men saw eye to eye on the need to open all promising avenues of military research while avoiding wasteful duplication. President Truman approved the plan and, on Forrestal's recommendation, appointed Vannevar Bush as chairman of the Research and Development Board, activated in July 1947. Incidentally, all of this was explained by Walker explained in his book, *Now It's My Turn.*[6] The hope was that a new research and development board could continue the many leading edge technologies that had been developed during World War Two.

Two months later, according to the MJ-12 Document, President Truman approved a Top Secret Research & Development operation called "Majestic Twelve." This, too, was based on the recommendation of Dr. Bush and Secretary Forrestal. The briefing document stated that Operation Majestic-12 concerned itself with retrieving UFOs and analyzing the crafts and occupants.

Certainly, if one were to find credence in Sarbacher's statement, this could well have been the case. After all, as he claimed, meetings were held at Wright-Patterson Air Force Base, where the military Research and Development Board discussed UFO crash/retrieval data.

As we have seen, while Sarbacher did not personally attend those meetings, he had learned of about them from those who had.

One of those people was Dr. Eric Walker, who sat on the R&D Board in 1950, and who also served as Executive Secretary from 1950-52. Walker was in exactly the right place at the right time to have been in attendance at government meetings discussing UFO recoveries.

As an interesting sidelight, the Pentagon office that Walker occupied during his term on the R&D board was the office that Bush had occupied before leaving the Pentagon in 1950.

All very interesting, indeed.

Another document uncovered by Stanton Friedman was from the early 1950s, from the Department of the Army to the Chairman of the United States Communications Intelligence Board (USCIB). The subject of the document is "Indoctrination for Special Intelligence for Mr. Eric Arthur Walker."

In a telephone conversation from 1989, Friedman told Grant Cameron that, "I was going through the records of the Office of the Secretary of Defense, and they're badly managed and badly arranged, but there was one sheet that talked about a briefing for Eric Walker from [the] CIA or some such person."[7]

Friedman was able to locate only the cover page of the document, not the actual article that followed it. The document was originally stamped "Secret," but appears to have later been declassified.

Of course, there was no indication one way or the other as to whether Walker's indoctrination was about UFOs. However, the early 1950s time-frame did fit well with the UFO-related scenario then being pieced together. The meetings at Wright-Patterson AFB, where the Research and Development Board supposedly discussed UFO retrievals/recoveries, was said to have occurred during this time, exactly when Walker served as the Board's Executive Secretary.

In 1951, Dr. Walker became Dean of Engineering and Architecture at Penn State, where he directed the construction of Breazeale Research Reactor on Penn State's University Park campus. In 1956 Penn State President, Dr. Milton Eisenhower (brother to the President), named Dr. Walker as Vice President of Penn State. Part of Dr. Walker's job was to coordinate and stimulate research at the university. In fact, Dr. Walker's term as Vice President would actually be minus two days, as he became President due to the immediate resignation of Dr. Eisenhower, who moved to John Hopkins University.

Walker went on to involve himself in many government projects. Among these was Project Jennifer, the CIA effort to recover a sunken Soviet submarine with two nuclear torpedoes on board from the Pacific ocean floor.

Dr. Walker's first public reference to UFOs came in a speech he made in 1969 at the Franklin Lectures.

> We will soon spend millions to probe the atmosphere of Venus and Mars, while here on Earth it remains polluted with dust and heat with which we cannot cope. Indeed, it may be a good thing that ships from another planet are not sampling our atmosphere - the conclusion might be that life cannot possibly exist on Earth.[8]

William Steinman had not received Walker's phone number from Stanton Friedman, so his first attempt to contact Eric Walker came in the form of a letter dated March 19, 1984.

He received a response, but not what he expected. Steinman explained how Dr. Walker responded in a letter to Grant Cameron:

1950 "Indoctrination for Special Intelligence for Mr. Eric Arthur Walker."

The answer to my correspondence was very strange; it stated, "STOP! DON'T TRY TO FIND ME I CAME ON THAT MACHINE I WILL LEAVE MAY 15 ERGOT QUIET QUIET QUIET." The above was typed on the lower portion of my letter that I sent to Walker, as evidenced by my signature and "very sincerely yours." My return address was cut from the upper portion of my own letter to Dr. Walker and was taped to the front of his stamped envelope to me![9]

Steinman stated that he made a second attempt to contact Dr. Walker in a letter dated May 31, 1984. According to Steinman, Walker did not respond to this letter at all.

1987: A Turning Point

Steinman gave up and pursued other leads. Stanton Friedman filed a Freedom of Information request for correspondence between Wilbert B. Smith, Dr. Robert Sarbacher, and Dr. Eric Walker. When the request yielded nothing, Friedman, too, went on to other leads.

When the MJ-12 document was released in 1987, Cameron renewed his hunt for what Smith had been learned.

He sent out a list of about ten names, including Dr. Walker's, to various researchers, asking them if they knew of a Smith connection. Some researchers did not respond, while others said they knew of no connection. Steinman, however, wrote back immediately. "How did you find the name Dr. Eric A. Walker concerning this subject matter?" he asked. "I was the one who discovered this particular connection and only mentioned it to Stanton Friedman."

Not realizing that Cameron had not yet talked to Dr. Walker, Steinman now felt a renewed interest in him. Perhaps Walker was talking now, he wondered, so thirteen days after receiving Cameron's letter, Steinman again attempted to contact Dr. Walker.

This time it was by phone to Dr. Walker's winter residence in Hilton Head, South Carolina. According to Steinman's handwritten notes, the following telephone interview took

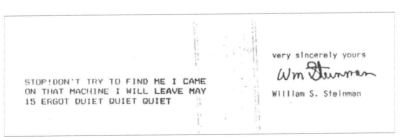

STOP! DON'T TRY TO FIND ME I CAME ON THAT MACHINE I WILL LEAVE MAY 15 ERGOT QUIET QUIET QUIET

very sincerely yours

William S. Steinman

Image 2-11. Eric Walker's message to William Steinman.

William S. Steinman
15043 Rosalita Dr.
La Mirada, Calif.
90638

Dr. Eric A. Walker

May 31, 1984

Dear Dr. Walker:

Allow me to introduce myself. My name is William S. Steinman, I am a free-lance investigator into the subject matter pertaining to Ufology, Physical Evidence.

For the past several years, I have been investigating into those cases that involve the recovery of crashed and/or disabeled Flying Saucers by the United States Military between 1947 and 1953. One case in particular that fascinates me above all the others, is that Flying Saucer that was recovered 12 miles north-east of Aztec, New Mexico, during the week of March 25, 1948.

Portions of and/or the complete craft (disassembled) arived at the Foreign Material Division of the Air Technical Intelligence Center of Wright-Patterson Air Force Base during the end of 1949 or the beginning of 1950.

I understand, that while you were acting in a consultant capacity to the National Research Council (N.R.C.) in 1949 and/or 1950, you were invited to attend meetings at the Foreign Material Division at the above mentioned Air Force Base, pertaining to the subject matter concerning these recovered Flying Saucers.

During those meetings, Dr. Vannevar Bush, Dr. John Von Neumann, and Most likley Dr. Eric Henery Wang allowed you, and the others who were invited, to view the recovered craft(s), read over the analysis reports, examine the craft(s) for yourselves, and etc.. Probably each of you were only assowed to see what you needed to know, at the time, related to your own specialties.

Dr. Walker, can you please give me a detailed description of the recovered Flying Saucers, especially that one that came down near Aztec, New Mexico during the week of March 25, 1948? Do you have access to the original Government reports that describe the recovery operations, the Flying Saucers, and the occupants thereof? Also, do you have access to the photographs of the Flying Saucers and the occupants, both at the crash-site(s) and in the Laboratory(ies)? If So, please forward copies of the reports and the photographs to me; I will gladly re-imburse you of the expenses.

The ultimate reason for my interest into those recovered Flying Saucer cases is as follows:

1. I believe that these very important pieces of hardware should be turned over to the total scientific community for the proper analysis that they deserve. Eventually, through this analysis, these Flying saucers can be duplicated, and other more advanced technology can be drawn there from.

Steinman letter to Walker, page one.

place on August 30, 1987, between Steinman and Dr. Walker:

Walker: Hello.
Steinman: Hello, this is William Steinman of Los Angeles, California. I am calling in reference to the meetings that you attended at Wright-Patterson Air Force Base in/around 1949-1950, concerning the military recovery of Flying Saucers and bodies of occupants. Dr. Robert I. Sarbacher (now deceased) related this to me. You and Sarbacher were both consultants to D.R.B. in 1950; you were Secretary

2. I believe that the United States Government wants to do this, but feels that it cannot release this information directly to the general public after holding it back for so long, even to the extent of denying the very existence of these Flying Saucers. I believe they are gradually releasing this information through investigators such as I.

Dr. Walker, please get in touch with me as soon as you possibly can, concerning this very important subject matter.

very sincerely yours

Wm Steinman

William S. Steinman

PS: Due to the death of Dr. Eric Henry Wang on December 4, 1960, there is now a huge gaping hole in the Flying Saucer Duplication Program at Kirtland Air Force Base in Albuquerque, New Mexico. This makes the above mentioned suggestions all the more urgent !!

Image 2-13. Steinman letter to Walker, page two.

1950-51.

Walker: Yes, I attended meetings concerning that subject matter; why do you want to know about that?

Steinman: I believe it is [a] very important subject. After all, we are talking about the actual recovery of a flying saucer (spacecraft) not built or constructed on this Earth! And furthermore, we are talking about bodies of the occupants from the craft who were analyzed [to be] human-like beings not of this world!

Walker: So, what's there to get all excited about? Why all the concern?

Steinman: I am not excited, just very concerned. Here we are talking about a subject that the U.S. Government officially denies, even going to the extent of actually debunking the evidence and discrediting the witnesses. Then you sit there and say, "What's there to get all excited about" and "Why all the concern?" Dr. Vannevar Bush, Dr. D. W. Bronk, and others thought it was very important and were concerned enough to classify the subject ABOVE TOP SECRET, in fact the most highly classified subject in the U.S. Government!! Did you ever hear of the "MJ-12 Group" and their "Project Majestic12" which was classified as TOP SECRET/MAJIC? I have a copy of President Elect D. D. Eisenhower's briefing paper on that project dated November 18, 1952.

Walker: Yes, I know of MJ-12. I have known of them for 40 years. I believe that you're chasing after and fighting with windmills!!

Steinman: Why do you say that?

Walker: You are delving into an area that you can do absolutely nothing about. So, why get involved with it or all concerned about it? Why don't you just leave it alone and drop it? Forget about it!!

Steinman: I am not going to drop it. I am going all the way with this!!

Walker: Then, when you find out everything about it. What are you going to do?

Steinman: I believe that this entire matter has to be brought to the public's attention. The people should know the truth!!

Walker: It's not worth it!! Leave it alone!!

Steinman: Can you remember any of the details pertaining to the recovery operations and subsequent analysis of the saucers and bodies?

Walker: I am sure that I have notes concerning those meetings at Wright-Patterson Air Force Base. I would have to dig them out and read them over in order to jog my memory.

Steinman: If I write you a letter, will you please answer in as much detail as you can remember? Furthermore, could you please Xerox those notes for me and send me a copy?

Walker: I might. At least I will keep your letter, will dig out my notes, and [will] contemplate answering. That's the best I can say for now.

Steinman: Well, Dr. Walker, I will write a letter as soon as possible. Thanks for your valuable time. Good-bye.

Walker: Goodbye.

Analysis

Steinman's conversation with Walker was certainly illuminating. Dr. Walker openly admitted that he had attended meetings concerning the military recovery of a flying saucer and its occupants.

When pressed for details of the meeting at Wright Field, Dr. Walker stated that he had notes concerning the meetings. This would not be unusual, considering that he was Executive Secretary of the Research and Development Board at that time. Dr. Sarbacher had stated that the Research and Development Board was the group invited to the meetings. (These notes would later on create some bizarre rumors in research circles, when the story of their existence circulated among researchers in Canada and the United States.)

The important question came when Steinman asked Walker about Majestic-12. Walker responded that he had known of "them" for forty years. (This would agree with the date of the formation of the group as indicated by the disputed MJ-12 documents circulated by Moore, Shandera, and Friedman; moreover, we had no reason to suspect that Walker had ever previously set his eyes on the disputed documents.)

Not surprisingly, Steinman was overjoyed by Walker's revelations. He promptly forwarded a follow-up letter to Walker the next day, asking him to comment on the MJ-12 documents and requesting from him a photocopy of the "notes" mentioned on the phone.

Other Confirmations

Later there would be other confirmations of the group known as MJ-12. One confirmation came at the same time Steinman was phoning Walker. Researcher John Lear, who had just entered the UFO field, saw the MJ-12 document and asked his mother to phone her friend, four-star General James Doolittle, to ask if the group had existed.

Doolittle, an American aviation pioneer and hero, was a friend of the Lear family through John's father, William, who had designed and built the Lear Jet. Doolittle had even been a guest at the Lear house.

It took Lear's mother a few months to work up the courage to phone. When she did, she said to the general, "John has gotten interested in this UFO subject and he would like to know if there was a group known as MJ-12." The General replied, "Yes Moya there was, but that is all I can say."

Another confirmation came from Dr. Edgar Mitchell, the Commander of Apollo 14. In speaking to trusted "old-timers," Mitchell concluded, "President Truman then elected a committee of very high level military and civilian academicians and people."[10]

This description was similar to how the former commander of Wright-Patterson AFB, General Arthur E. Exon, described the rumored MJ-12 type committee. Exon said he "was aware of a UFO controlling committee made up primarily of very high-ranking military officers and intelligence people. He did not know the name of the group, but called them the "Unholy Thirteen."[11]

In July 1989, researcher Bob Oeschler provided some of the most dramatic evidence supporting the existence of a group known as MJ-12 when he taped a conversation about MJ-12 with Bobby Ray Inman. Inman had held a number of key positions, including the Director of Naval Intelligence, Director of the National Security Agency, and Deputy Director of the CIA.

At the time of the Oeschler-Inman conversation, it was rumored that Inman had been in charge of the major engineering efforts behind UFO technology. In fact, when government insider and UFO researcher John Alexander gathered together his Top Secret/SCI group, called the Advanced Theoretical Physics Group, in the mid-1980s to look into UFO technology and possible government funding, one of the main topics on their agenda was to look into the stories of what Inman and his people at SAIC might have been doing relating to UFO engineering.

During the conversation with Oeschler, Inman said "that MJ-12 meant something to him," and that "he has been aware of a program to 'indoctrinate the public in UFO matters prior to his retirement." Moreover, he had "some expertise" in the area of UFOs, but his information was now out of date.[12]

An interesting story that appears to confirm a major UFO role for Inman occurred in 1994, when Dr. Steven Greer met with Senator Barry Goldwater, former head of the Senate Intelligence Committee, to discuss UFOs. As shown by almost 180 UFO-related letters in the Goldwater collection at Arizona State University in Phoenix, Goldwater held a longstanding interest in UFOs. One of the letters in this collection showed that there had been a discussion about Goldwater's close friend, Inman. After Greer described Inman as one of the key people in the UFO cover-up, Goldwater promised to phone Inman and set up a three-way meeting.

Greer later reported, "Goldwater phoned me back and stated "I can't make any more phone calls like that,' and then his daughter Joanne Goldwater spoke on the phone and she said, 'I don't know what Bobby Ray Inman said to daddy, but he cannot make another phone call like that."[13]

Yet another person who gave some confirmation to the existence of MJ-12 was an archivist at the National Archives in College Park, Maryland. This person approached Cameron after a lecture in Eureka Springs, Arkansas, in 2005. His job was to declassify documents for release. This meant that he worked inside the classified vault and saw all government documents prior to their release. He was the person with the black felt marker who actually made the decisions to withhold documents or to withdraw sections within documents that were released.

This archivist stated that his girlfriend had an interest in UFOs, and when the MJ-12 document debate began, she showed him the articles that had been written on the authenticity of the documents. He was curious about the issue and decided to look into it.

What he discovered was that there might be some validity to the MJ-12 concept. He stated that he and a colleague had gone into the vault to look at the Cutler-Twinning memo, a key document from 1954 that made reference to "MJ-12," and which had been found in the national archives. In the aftermath of its publication, however, the archives official position was that the document was a hoax. The archivist, however, stated that the manner in which the document had been stored indicated that it could in fact be real.

The archivist stated that he had his work to do and could not do a search on government time. Therefore, he asked the members of his declassification team to alert him if they came across any document with an MJ-12 designator on it. Since "MJ-12," he said, was not a classified designator, this meant that if an archivist did come across a document marked MJ-12, and there was no other reason to withhold the document, he would release it and let everyone know.

After several years of searching, no document had been found. Yet, he stated that one of the declassification team recalled having seen the designator while working on documents for Joint Chiefs of Staff documents years earlier.

Another indication that MJ-12 might have existed, even if the MJ-12 document itself was not legitimate, came from Harold Stuart, a former member of the Truman administration. He had been listed as a member of an advisory committee for MJ-12 in Robert Collins' 2005 book, *Exempt from Disclosure.*[14]

In reply to a letter written to him by researcher Brian Parks asking about MJ-12, Stuart replied, "Thank you for your recent letter regarding the MJ-12 Project. It sounds familiar but it was a long time ago. I have a vague recollection of MJ-12, but not significantly specific to make a comment. If I can have a little more specifics, maybe I could recall something."

Parks detailed his next letter to Stuart identifying MJ-12 as a "group created by Truman to study the remains of an extraterrestrial craft and bodies from the Roswell/Corona New Mexico area in 1947. I also went on to describe the 1954 Cutler/Twining Memo from the National Archives that referenced an 'MJ-12 Special Studies Project' but did not relate what that project was about."[15]

Stuart replied, and surprisingly did not deny a group to study the remains of an extraterrestrial craft and bodies. However, he did distance himself from involvement. "I was not on the MJ-12 Advisory Board and only have a faint recollection of this project or group. I did know most of the Generals you mentioned in your letter, but sorry I cannot shed any light on your request."

The "Operation Majestic-12" Document and Its Background

American UFO research took an unusual turn on May 29, 1987, when the investigative team of William L. Moore, Jaime H. Shandera, and Stanton T. Friedman released to the public a document outlining America's involvement in flying saucer crashes and the recovery of their occupants (sometimes referred to as "Extraterrestrial Biological Entities" or "EBEs.") The document had been received by mail in 1984 in the form of undeveloped film addressed to Shandera. The investigative team made an exhaustive study of the document and concluded that it appeared to be genuine.

Skeptics of the document questioned the fact that Shandera, a Hollywood producer with no UFO background, would be the one to receive the document. A possible answer to the question could be that Shandera, unknown to anyone except Bill Moore, turned out to have an intelligence background. He therefore may have been the key to the document release. Years later, after Shandera had suddenly disappeared from the UFO field, Bill Moore described a meeting with the CIA when he learned who Shandera actually was.

> We were in a meeting with some CIA people and others. After it ended, we were standing around talking, and one of the agency guys looked at me and said "You're new here, but you [pointing at Shandera] we've known about for awhile." Obviously I couldn't wait to ask Jamie what was going on. He told me that he had done some work for the government during the Vietnam war, essentially providing expert testimony in a court-martial trial involving voice identification.[16]

One member of the research team, nuclear physicist Stanton Friedman, was awarded a $16,000 grant by the Fund for UFO Research to determine whether or not the MJ-12 Document was authentic. At the 1989 Mutual UFO Network (MUFON) Symposium in Las Vegas, Friedman reported that there was "no indication that the documents are fraudulent and a host of small details which tend towards legitimacy for MJ-12."

At the same time that Friedman, Moore and Shandera were making their document release, it became known that a second copy of the MJ-12 document had been given to British UFO researcher Timothy Good. In fact, Good had reproduced the document in his book, *Above Top Secret,* released in May 1987. When asked by researcher Lee Graham how he had obtained the document, Good replied that there was nothing he could tell him or anyone else "about how or from whom I obtained the document."[17]

There were strong indications that Good got the document from the same source that provided it to Moore, and that both men knew it. Lee Graham, for example, told of being invited to a dinner with Moore and Good at a restaurant in Tujunja, California, shortly after both men had made MJ-12 public. Not knowing what was going on, Graham reported being surprised when Good and Moore suddenly held a toast to the worldwide release of the MJ-12 document. No one bothered to explain to him what had just happened.

However, it also appeared that the MJ-12 documents had been offered in 1986 to British UFO researchers Jenny Randles and Peter Hough. An army officer named Robert met with the two researchers in a prearranged meeting in a pub. He offered them not only the document, but the various appendices (mentioned in the MJ-12 document). These appendices have never been made public. Robert claimed to have 600 pages of classified material that had come from Wright Patterson Air Force Base.[18]

Randles and Hough conducted a background check on Robert. He appeared to be who he claimed to be. However, when the two researchers showed up for a second meeting with him, he did not appear. Instead, he later phoned, stating that the material had been seized by the government. Randles concluded that their efforts to run checks had set off alarm bells, and what she perceived to be a carefully orchestrated setup was called off.

It is possible that once the Randle/Hough offer fell through that a new approach was made to Good, who ended up publishing the MJ-12 document in his best-selling book.

As expected, many criticisms about the legitimacy of the MJ-12 document surfaced, with some objections holding up under scrutiny. Probably the most troublesome objection came from UFO skeptic Philip J. Klass, who made it known on October 12, 1989, that a respected document examiner had analyzed the MJ-12 document and concluded that it was a counterfeit because it was typed using a Smith-Corona machine that was introduced around 1963, more than 15 years after the MJ-12 document's date of September 24, 1947.[19]

Four days later, Moore responded to the allegation by asserting that four document examiners had scrutinized the Truman memo and that their opinions were mixed. Moore also said that the expert Klass had used (whom Moore had also included), said to him that "although the document itself may be a fabrication, the information in it could very well be real."

"This sort of thing," the expert said, "is not uncommon in such a situation."

At the time, Moore was in regular communication with a

high-level government insider known as "Falcon" (more on Falcon in Chapter 7). The authors asked Moore if he had ever asked Falcon to comment on the authenticity of the MJ-12 document. Yes, replied Moore, and Falcon had said that the "Eisenhower Briefing" was real. According to Moore, Falcon "was correctly aware of some of the data in the document before I showed him a copy." Falcon also said that he was not the one who had sent the document to Moore's research team.

In addition, a spirited defense of the MJ-12 document was published in 1989 by French Ufologist Jean Sider.

> The group Majestic 12 seems to have had an actual existence. The Truman memo, typed with another machine, a normal date style, and provided with different classification stamps, can provide the proof. Mention of MJ-12 also figures in the Cutler memo, which has been authenticated by analysis of the original onionskin paper. The paper belongs to the right era, and has not been manufactured since the beginning of the 1970s (my information comes by a phone call from J. L. Rivera in New York in 1988, who found out from Moore). Furthermore, I have obtained two confirmations of the existence of this ultra-top-secret group dedicated to the UFO problem. One comes first hand from a retired American scientist, the other second-hand from a friend, himself an official, who received the information from a high-ranking military officer still on active duty.
> So, in ascertaining the truth about the MJ-12 document, I have been able to establish not only that it is most likely a fake, at least in part, but that Majestic 12 had an actual existence, despite the misleading clues. Here the issue stands barring further evidence to the contrary.[20]

Stronger criticisms came from UFO researchers Robert Todd, Mark Rodeghier, Barry Greenwood, and Bruce Maccabee. In their article, "A Forum on MJ-12," they gave their views on the controversy.[21] It was their consensus that the MJ-12 Document was probably not genuine. Todd went so far as to say, "If one or more of their team did not fabricate the MJ-12 document, then the document had to have been fabricated by somebody with a level of knowledge available to

Moore and Friedman."

Rodeghier pointed out, "Whoever wrote the briefing paper was reasonably knowledgeable about the early history of government involvement in UFO investigation and, especially, about the details of the Roswell UFO crash. Everything I have learned about the Roswell event matches well the details as reported in the briefing paper." Rodeghier speculated that the hypothetical forger was either (1) out to play a "joke" on ufologists or (2) motivated by a more sinister urge, namely "to confuse the UFO community" and "destroy the credibility of the Roswell event."

Greenwood reported that his group had found "numerous flaws and inconsistencies in the documents" and said that their release may have "led to a serious erosion of the credibility of UFO-document research."

Maccabee was less definitive about the matter. He concluded:

> From the mass of evidence gathered by investigators of the Roswell incident, we know that at least one UFO crash has occurred. That being the case, there would have had to be a highly compartmented, highly classified project to study the hard evidence and to develop policies and guidelines relative to the handling of information about extraterrestrial visitation. Such a project may or may not be called MJ-12. I am not certain as yet that the MJ-12 documents, which include the Aquarius Teletype message, the Eisenhower briefing document, and the Cutler- Twining memo, are factual or forged. But MJ-12 by any other name is still MJ-12.

An interesting anecdote providing some support for the MJ-12 document came from a source of T. Scott Crain. On August 3, 1990, Crain interviewed a U.S. Air Force non-commissioned officer who claimed that she had seen the briefing document Operation Majestic-12 while on duty in 1979. She was cleaning out a safe in a general's office, along with four other personnel, when they came across a briefing document describing a UFO crash near Roswell, New Mexico, in 1947.

The informant said that she had a TOP SECRET/SBI/SCI clearance* and had been on active duty at Kadena Air Force Base in Okinawa, Japan. The informant asked not to be identified, as she was still working for the government and wanted no trouble. She said that "a lot of military people" knew about the document but were not allowed to discuss it. She said the document had never been declassified. Her orders had been to shred the document, which she did.

Crain asked his informant what the circumstances were of her seeing the MJ-12-type documents. She responded, "I was cleaning out a safe. . . . I was on the general's staff. . . . Once a year you go in and you do what they call a 'classified review.' You go in and anything that's been downgraded you take out, you shred, you destroy." The informant added, "The general I was working for wasn't even there when we were doing it. I mean it's just a routine thing. Why that document hadn't been taken out before is beyond me. Actually it was found like underneath a shelf that pulls out. It might have been there for years."[22]

Another military base in Japan also appears to have harbored sensitive government UFO documents. In a 2006 copyrighted story by UFO researcher Linda Moulton Howe, naval non-commissioned officer Chief Yeoman Thomas Colman Sheppard and several other military personnel said that they had seen "MAJIC files about—and photographs of—extraterrestrial biological entities while stationed in Okinawa's White Beach Naval Base." Sheppard said that the documents were in a vault (or safe) that stored classified materials. The incident occurred on Thanksgiving night, 1976.[23]

On the advice of Falcon, Moore gave a copy of the MJ-12 document to California UFO researcher Lee Graham, who worked for the aerospace contractor, Aerojet, and held a Secret

---

* SBI stands for "Special Background Investigation," SCI for "Special Compartmentalized Information." Both of these are security levels higher than Top Secret.

clearance. Graham turned the document into his supervisor, which set off a security review of Graham and the document.

Graham spent the next number of years trying to get the U.S. Government to make a determination on the authenticity of the document. That was part of Graham's job. He would hand Moore's documents into the security department at Aerojet where he worked, and do lots of talking.

Richard Doty of the Air Force Office of Special Investigation (AFOSI), about whom we shall hear more later on, gave more advice to Moore about the documents he was getting from Falcon: "Find someone to show them to who would do a lot of talking about them to a lot of people. Show them to this person but be sure not to give him any copies. Let whoever it is talk all they want."

Moore passed on many documents and leads to Graham. Graham once recalled, "Bill called me once from Washington, D.C., asking: 'Do you know who this is? Don't say my name. Take this date down. A satellite has detected a UFO making a crop circle."

Some of the documents Moore circulated through Graham never made it to the rest of the UFO community. One of them, according to Graham, included "a Lockheed Engineering document regarding a novel flying disc propulsion system" at Area 51.

Moore provided Graham with the FOIA reply to his FBI file, which he said could be distributed. Of the 61 pages in the file, 55 were withheld in their entirety under a B1 exemption.* The fact that 90% of a UFO researcher's file was withheld, totally for reasons of national security, sends a clear message that whatever Moore was doing, it was of great interest to the government.

The first page of Moore's FBI file illustrates that most of the 6 pages that were released were also blacked out. A September 1988 appeal by Moore for the 55 withheld pages was turned

---

* (Exemption (b)(1) - National Security Information)

down completely.

Then there was the bizarre image of the alien that Moore produced for Graham. During a 1986 dinner, Moore passed a piece of paper under the table to Graham and his wife. They looked at it for a few moments then passed it back. It was a drawing of an alien head. The alien appeared to be dead. In a later dinner meeting, Moore confided that Falcon had asked Moore to let Graham see it, saying that Falcon believed it

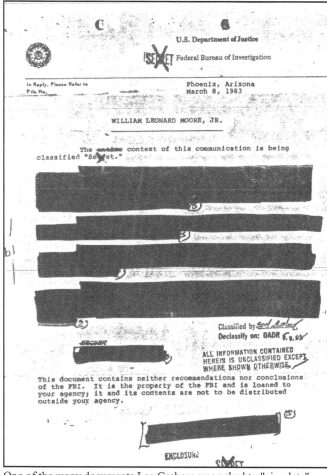

One of the many documents Lee Graham was asked to "circulate" was Bill Moore's FBI file, which had 55 of 61 pages withheld in their entirety under a B1 - National Security FOIA exception. This first page of Moore's FBI file shows that not much of the 6 released pages was readable either.

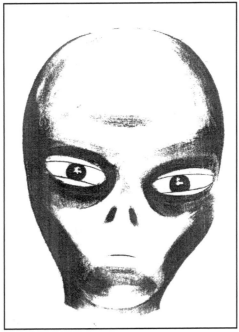

Vince DePaula's alien drawing.

"would turn Graham on."

Partly based on this drawing, Graham had artist Vince DePaula draw the alien head. This caused a great of attention from the Defense Investigative Service, which conducts security clearance investigations for the Department of Defense. Soon they photocopied it and ran an investigation. Graham was questioned by DIS officers about what he knew about the drawing. UFO researcher Ron Regehr, who worked for the same company as Graham, also had to explain his role in the drawing.

DePaula, the artist, received the most attention. According to Graham, DePaula "had to spend a week downtown with the DIS explaining how he came to make this drawing." Years later, after DePaula had died, Graham learned that DePaula's wife was furious that her husband had gotten into so much trouble over this.

Despite all this, Moore, who had caused the whole mess, and

was in possession of the original alien head drawing, was never questioned or investigated.

A Two-Star General and Colonel Come to Visit

From time to time, Graham received indications that he was on the right track, and that people inside the government were acknowledging his key role in bringing documents like the MJ-12 and others to the public.

One such positive indication came on September 15, 1987, when Graham received a personal visit at work from a two-star General from Air Force headquarters in Washington. The visit came shortly after Graham sent a letter to Vice President George Bush on UFOs and the stealth fighter.

Along with the General was a man who identified himself as FBI Special Agent William Hurley. The General, dressed in civilian clothes, was introduced only as "Mickey." Later, while reading an Air Force magazine in the Aerojet Library, Graham found a picture and identified the second man as USAF Major General Michael C. Kerby, who at the time of the meeting was Director of the Air Force Legislative Liaison Office. Kerby had previously been stationed at Nellis Air Force Base, where he appeared to "have been in command of the operational aspects of the 'stealth' fighter aircraft, as well as other very sensitive aviation activities."[24]

To Graham the meeting was further confirmation of the story that Bill Moore had told him: that Falcon had chosen Graham to be the front man for a series of leaked documents that told a secret inside story of the UFO cover-up.[25]

Graham had been filing scores of FOIAs on UFOs and on the F-117 stealth fighter program (which had not yet been declassified in 1987).[26] In 1985, Graham had undergone a "Code Red" investigation by the Defense Investigative Service because of his interest in the F-117. Aerojet had requested the security investigation, telling the Defense Investigative Service (DIS), "this facility has learned that the above subject employee has been seeking information (very sensitive) that he has no need to know and may not be in the best interest of National Security."[27]

In the 1987 meeting, the General told Graham that the code name for the stealth fighter was "Senior Trend." This turned out to be accurate. Graham was asked to sign a "certificate" by Hurley that he had received information for which he did not have a "need to know," and that he should not disclose it until it was declassified. As Graham later pointed out, this was a break from standard procedures: he should have signed a Standard Form 312 rather than a certificate.

When the stealth discussion was over, Graham pulled another leaked document out of his pocket referring to Project Snowbird, and which claimed there was a recovered flying saucer being tested at Groom Lake. Graham asked the General if he was free to distribute the document. The General looked at the document and saw the Unclassified stamp in the bottom right corner.[28] He pointed to it and asked Graham "What does that say?"

When Graham replied unclassified, Kerby told him that meant that he could do what he wanted with it

Later, Graham talked to Bill Moore about the visit. Moore said that the men who had visited him "had been sent to encourage me to circulate copies" of the MJ-12 Document. This made sense, as Moore had once told him he was the "pigeon" that was chosen for the leak, the one who would carry the message to the public.

Shortly after Graham had uncovered General Kerby's identity, he received a call from Dr. Scott Jones, who was then working as an aide to Senator Claiborne Pell on paranormal phenomena. In a report, Jones wrote to Pell that Graham had phoned him about the encounter and that he in turn had contacted General Kerby. The two then held a private meeting on the subject of UFOs and Kerby's meeting with Graham. Kerby, however, denied knowing or meeting Graham. Jones reported that Kerby simply "gave the standard Air Force line on Blue Book that established before it shut down that there was nothing of substance to UFO reports."[29]

It appears that Graham did not even know Jones and did not phone him. Jones may have instead run into General Kerby while he was in Pell's office on other business. Kerby knew Jones and his interest in UFOs. They began a conversation on UFOs and Kerby volunteered the fact that he had visited Graham incognito.

This led Jones to phone Graham. He opened the conversation by saying that he and Graham "had a mutual acquaintance." Jones was referring to Kerby, whom Jones did not realize Graham had identified. Jones promised to send information that would help Graham identify the mysterious interviewer. This he did with a letter on Senatorial letterhead, with a picture and biography of Kerby attached. Kerby had indeed admitted that he met with Graham and had discussed UFOs.

Graham also mentioned the Kerby meeting in a letter from August 6, 1989 to Vice President Dan Quayle. In the letter, Graham attached the MJ-12 and Snowbird documents and asked if he was free to circulate them. If not, he asked, would Quayle repudiate their authenticity? Unfortunately, in his letter he mentioned both the F-117 and its codename: Senior Trend. Although the existence of the F-117 had been declassified in 1988, the codename was still classified. Graham therefore came under another DIS investigation.

The final DIS Investigation report, dated April 19, 1990, seemed to confirm that the MJ-12 document and the Snowbird documents were indeed legitimate. The documents that Graham had attached for Quayle caused DIS Director William A. Hughes to initiate a Special Investigations Inquiry (SII) into their status. Indeed, an investigation was even launched into the text of the speech that Bill Moore had given to the 1989 MUFON conference—in which he outlined how government UFO secrecy had operated. During the course of the security determination, the MJ-12 and Snowbird documents were each stamped "Unclassified." Graham learned this fact when he requested and received a portion of his 1990 DIS file. According to Graham, who had worked in the world of classification his whole career, this meant that the documents had been declassified and were free to distribute to the public.[30]

The facts seemed to support Graham's conclusion, but when the Government Accounting Office (GAO) became involved in a reinvestigation of the Roswell UFO crash, it asked the head of the USAF study, Colonel Richard Weaver, about the now apparently declassified MJ-12 document. Weaver told the GAO that the document was "bogus and therefore unclassified." Weaver continued that "when the document was first sent to the "Internal Security Office for review they stamped it unclassified before they reviewed it. After they studied it and determined that it was not authentic, they returned it to the sender, however, they had already put the unclassified mark on it which to the sender meant that it was an authentic document."[31]

When Graham learned of this, he immediately filed a FOIA to the Air Force, asking for records of who stamped the documents unclassified, and when. Most importantly, realizing that the unclassified MJ-12 and Snowbird documents in the DIA report were just copies, he asked for color copies of the original documents. These would have shown the unclassified markings in red ink.

Despite the government claims that no UFO information has been withheld, Graham has yet to receive real color copies of the MJ-12 and Snowbird documents.

Graham did form a strong opinion, however, on who was involved in the declassification of the two documents. This was Colonel Weaver's friend, Colonel Barry Hennessey. Hennessey was head of USAF Special Projects security, and also had many rumored links to the world of UFOs.[32] His official job at AFOSI was to manage security of Top Secret programs, such as the F-117.

To support his case that UFOs and Hennessey were keys to the meeting with General Kerby, Graham provided another incident involving Hennessey and the subject of UFOs. This involved a second meeting that took place at exactly the same time Graham was being visited by Kerby and the FBI agent. This meeting took place in Washington at the office of Graham's aerospace friend, John Andrews of the Testor Corporation. Andrews was considered by many to be one of the best civilian aircraft researchers in history. He had become famous for his building of a Roswell model based on eyewitness descriptions, and for his F-19 (later named F-117) stealth model that became the best-selling model kit of all time. Andrews had become friends with Graham and Moore, sharing their interest in UFOs and secret stealth technologies.

Andrews was a key MJ-12 witness for Moore and Graham. That is because in 1987, when Moore, Friedman, and Shandera went public with the MJ-12 document, Andrews wrote a series of letters stating that he had known of MJ-12 for years. These are key letters from a respected aerospace figure who was clearly saying that MJ-12 was not something Moore had invented, as he was aware of the group long before Moore went public with the MJ-12 documents.

In the first of these MJ-12 letters Andrews wrote to his friend, Ben Rich at Skunkworks. "I have known of MJ-12 for many years even though, officially it 'didn't exist,'" wrote Andrews. "There was an Air Force Radar (AC&W) detachment at Sinop, Turkey . . . it was standard for the detachment to forward radar tapes of the UFOs to MJ-12. That was policy. I knew it because a man who was stationed there revealed 'MJ-12' in a conversation."

In a second letter dealing with MJ-12, Andrews told Graham that he had known of MJ-12 since early 1984, which was almost a year before Jamie Shandera received the MJ-12 document in his mailbox. Andrews stated that the man, who

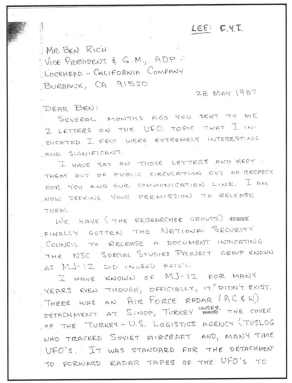

Letter from John Andrews to Ben Rich, May 28, 1987, p. 1.

was now "separated from the Air Force," was secretly producing a report for Andrews "on all codes for routing, declassification, etc."

Unfortunately, as far as we know, Andrews did not make this MJ-12 report public before his death in 1999.

In the final MJ-12 letter, written to UFO researcher and aerospace worked Ron Regehr, Andrews identified the NSA/MJ-12 unit where the UFO data was being sent. Andrews stated that the UFO material being gathered along the Turkish Soviet border was being sent to the USAF Security Command at Medina Base (Media Annex) at Kelly AFB in San Antonio Texas.. Research has confirmed that there is in fact an NSA facility at Median Annex Kelly AFB (now Lackland AFB).

Andrews also mentioned in this letter that UFO skeptic, Phil Klass, was aware that he had known about MJ-12. Klass peppered Andrews with questions, which Andrews refused to answer, hoping that the silence would drive Klass crazy.

Lee Graham filed two FOIAs with the NSC/MJ-12 Special Studies Project address at Kelly AFB that Andrews had referenced in his letter to Regehr. However, he received no reply. The letters were not returned "undeliverable" so it appeared that the address was right.

When neither letter got answered Graham took up the failure to reply in an FOIA with USAF Intelligence.

FOIA Project Manager Marzett V. McCall replied in a March 7, 2008 letter:

> In your letter you refer to two Freedom of Information (FOIA) requests, dated 23 Jul and 1 Dec 07, you forwarded to USAF Security Command Medina. I am not familiar with that office or its mission. Your FOIA requests were not forwarded to this office and I have no way of knowing

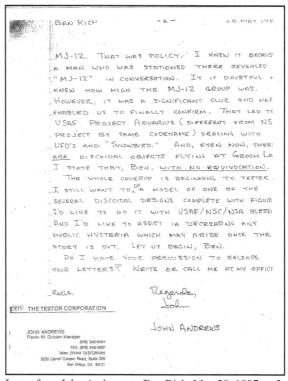

Letter from John Andrews to Ben Rich, May 28, 1987, p. 2.

who received them or where they were sent. Your request that I provide you with an address to where these two requests were sent is not a proper FOIA request as you are not seeking documents this Agency might have but attempting to locate mail that may or may not have been delivered to an address that may or may not exist. Unfortunately, I am not able to assist you in this matter.

The man who had come to visit Andrews at his office was none other than Colonel Barry Hennessey. Here too, UFOs and stealth were the topics of conversation. Andrews reported the details of the meeting to Graham, writing, "he instructed me to not use its (Stealth 117) 'F' number nor its codename. He didn't ask me how I had learned such things, and I didn't offer. He opened the conversation saying, 'I don't know anything about UFOs.' Hennessey said 'I won't lie to you.' But his comment about not knowing anything about UFOs was already a lie. He professed to not even know what NICAP was."[33]

Over the years and decades, Graham continued to pursue Hennessey, believing that he has been part of the plan to get the MJ-12 and Snowbird documents out. In his DIS file, Graham found the following statement, which showed that UFOs was Hennessey's main interest: "It has come to our attention that Subject has had frequent correspondence with the U.S. Air Force regarding UFOs. His correspondence may be reviewed by contacting Col. Barry Hennessey, USAF, office of Special Projects, at the Pentagon." Stealth was not even mentioned in the complaint.[34]

Graham wrote three FOIA requests directly to Hennessey at the Pentagon, trying to get to the bottom of the UFO connection to the mysterious Colonel. Two of the letters were returned as undeliverable. However, according to Graham, "I proved through the library that they were received. They had been opened and resealed. One of them was on paper that I had not sent. It was a different color paper and it was folded differently."[35]

In a 1990 issue of *Focus* magazine, William Moore discussed the DIS response:

> What the significance of all this may ultimately be to the
> continuing MJ-12 controversy remains unclear at this
> point, although it appears we may have a somewhat
> oblique confirmation of the documents' authenticity
> through the [DIS's] having submitted them for a security
> determination and them having been officially stamped
> "Unclassified" in the process. What seems important here
> also is the fact that nowhere in all of this is there any
> indication that the [DIS's] Special Investigations Inquiry
> found the documents to be bogus.[36]

That same year, Moore and Shandera provided their own
statement about the MJ-12 document.

> THE EISENHOWER BRIEFING DOCUMENT: This very
> controversial document has held up well under an intense
> effort to examine all aspects of it. If subjected to an inno-
> cent-until-proven-guilty standard, a verdict of 'authentic'
> must be brought in only because no evidence has come to
> light [that] would sustain any other conclusion beyond
> reasonable doubt.[37]

Regardless of what others say, Moore and Shandera pointed
out, the MJ-12 document does not stand alone. Via Falcon,
Moore also obtained a series of CIA documents dated between
June 24, 1978 and December 28, 1982 that appear to be
internal communications between members of MJ-12. In mid-
1987, Moore released a copy of one of these documents, which
is dated June 24, 1982. It refers to an "executive briefing" on
"Project A" (perhaps Project Aquarius?).* As with the Eisenhower Briefing Document, or with any government UFO
document for that matter, the recipient must consider whether
what he has is misinformation, disinformation, a possible hoax,
or a reality.

Our investigation concluded that the MJ-12 document
(whether retyped or not) contains accurate information on the
Roswell UFO crash. Moreover, that it contains some, if not all,
of the names of the members of the MJ-12 group.

---

* More on Project Aquarius appears in Chapter 7.

September 23, 1987

Mr. William S. Steinman
15043 Rosalita Drive
LaMirada, CA 90638

Dear Mr. Steinman:

Some things you have right, and some things you have wrong. The machine itself was obviously a landing vehicle only, and it had no unusual features and no power plants with which we were not quite familiar. I believe it still exists and is kept someplace near Wright Field.

Your greatest error, of course, comes in the finding of the bodies--there were no bodies; there were four very normal individuals, all male. Unfortunately, they had no memory of anything in the past (probably by design), but they were highly intelligent. They learned the English language within a few hours and it was our decision not to make public spectacles of them, but allow them to be absorbed into American culture as soon as we were sure that they did not bring any contamination with them. I believe all four have done this very successfully. One assumed a simple name and proved himself to be an expert on computers, although he had not memory of such devices. He became the president and innovator for one of the largest and most successful computer organizations.

A second one became a world famous athlete, and because of his quick reaction time, exceeded any normal person in his performances. He is still a noted professional athlete.

The third became enamored with finance at our capitalistic system. He has made himself famous as a Wall Street raider, and is very rich.

The fourth, I have lost track of and have no clues as to where he might be. However, I consider the decision to let these people meld into American life, completely justified, and I can see no point in trying to reverse that decision. I hope that you will let matters lie as they are. The results are completely satisfactory, and nothing is to be gained by further publicity.

Very truly yours,

Paul.

The "Alien Letter," from Walker to Steinman.

As mentioned above, there were many supporting statements from various people that a group known as MJ-12 had actually existed. The MJ-12 document appeared to have revealed a piece of evidence about the cover-up that had never been discussed before.

The UFO community, however, mainly focused on whether or not the MJ-12 Document was in fact legitimate. The actual situation with the document proposed four possibilities. The MJ-12 document was (1) a genuine document used to brief President Dwight D. Eisenhower, (2) a disinformation trap by U.S. intelligence, (3) a hoax by one or more of the researchers involved in its release, (4) a hoaxed document containing legitimate pieces of evidence that officials wanted disclosed.

Returning to Eric Walker

William Steinman had spoken by phone with Eric Walker on August 30, 1987. Two days later, on September 1, he wrote to Walker, and attached a copy of the MJ-12 documents. In doing so, he gave up the opportunity to secure independent confirmation (as might well have been provided by Walker) of the identities of MJ-12 members, what their function was or is, and other purported facts discussed in the document. It was a calculated risk, but Steinman had thought merely that Walker's comments upon seeing the document would help confirm or deny the authenticity of the MJ-12 document.*

Steinman also sent a transcript of his interview with Dr. Walker to Grant Cameron, to whom Steinman said:

> If Walker writes to me at all, and furthermore, if he substantiates the eight pages of MJ-12, we will have taken one more giant step forward. If he sends me the Xerox copies of his Wright-Patterson AFB meeting notes, then we will have taken several giant steps forward in our quest for the truth. That is the reason for the extreme confidentiality between you and me!

Three weeks later, Steinman received a reply to his letter. Researchers working on the Walker case referred to it as the "Alien Letter."

Perhaps it was shrewd of Walker to sign the letter as he did, merely with the initials "E.A.W.," leaving room for speculation that perhaps he did not write it. However, the content of the reply directly corresponded to the contents of Steinman's original letter. Crain and Cameron also analyzed Walker's

---

* Walker later told Henry Azadehdel he believed the document was not legitimate.

signature, which compares favorably with the initials that appear in the letter that Steinman received.* Finally, the conversation that Steinman had with Dr. Walker on August 30, 1987, illuminated the fact that Walker had been familiar with UFO recovery operations as well as Majestic-12. For these reasons, we concluded that Eric A. Walker had indeed initialed the "E.A.W." letter.

Analysis

Walker appeared to have read over the MJ-12 document enclosed by Steinman because he stated that there were no bodies found at the site, only four normal-looking males. He claimed that the object had only been a landing vehicle (lacking a power supply) and, to his knowledge, was still being stored at "Wright Field" (e.g. Wright-Patterson Air Force Base).

Interestingly enough, according to an FBI document released in 1977, parts of an unidentified disc that crashed at Roswell, New Mexico, in 1947 were flown to Wright Field. In addition, Major Jesse A. Marcel, the ranking Intelligence Officer at Roswell Army Air Force Base (RAAF) at the time, and one who handled the crash remains, also pinpointed Wright Field as the probable storage location of the remains of the saucer that had crashed.

In his letter of September 23, 1987, Walker claimed that the operation had been a success and that the aliens had found jobs in the U.S. (computer expert, athlete, Wall Street raider, and a fourth he lost track of), so there would be no point in tampering with the decision. He stated once again, as he had in his telephone conversation three weeks earlier, that Steinman should "leave it alone," that "nothing is to be gained by further publicity."

The most revealing part of the whole letter was Walker's statement "it was our decision." In the first interview, Walker said he had known of MJ-12 since 1947, and now he even

---

* That analysis appears later in this chapter.

volunteered the fact that he had participated in the decision-making process related to the crash, rather than having been merely "a cog in the wheel." The implication is that more than one group was involved in this operation.

Walker inferred that he was part of the control group making the decisions, but did not mention if MJ-12 was involved in the decision-making process. If it were not for Fred Darwin surmising his involvement—and Sarbacher confirming it—we might never have known that Dr. Walker attended Top Secret meetings with other Research & Development Board scientists at Wright-Patterson Air Force Base.

As for the letter itself, Steinman, Cameron and Crain all found its contents both contradictory to Sarbacher's testimony as well as inconsistent with how the American military would most likely handle aliens on Earth.

First, Walker described human-looking aliens, whereas Sarbacher had indicated they were insect-like. Sarbacher told Smith that they had no idea how the recovered saucer worked; Walker, on the other hand, said that it had no unusual features and that "we" had been familiar with its propulsion system. The still-prominent athlete after forty years was rather unlikely, too, and forgetting what happened to the fourth alien was not much better.

Walker must have been well aware of the debunking and disinformation policies established in the early years; yet he admitted to having attended those meetings and volunteered the fact that he knew of MJ-12.

It was our general opinion that Dr. Walker was deliberately proffering disinformation to confuse the issue.

Why would Walker want to answer Steinman's letter? Why not throw it away and forget about it? One obvious possibility is that he wrote it simply as a joke. However, this idea remains problematic. After all, Steinman could well have gone to the newspapers with the story, or at least bothered Walker for yet more information.

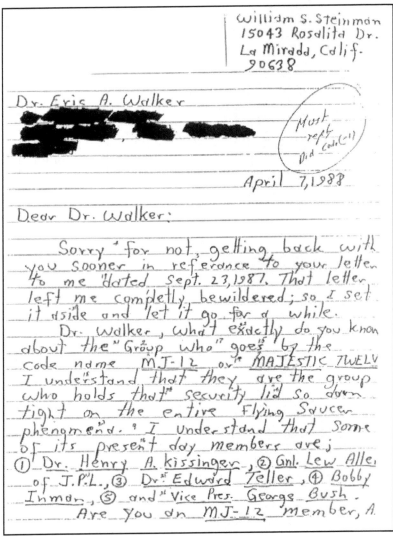

Eric Walker "Code Letter," page one.

In Dr. Walker's biography (written for him in 1960 when he was President of the American Society for Engineering Education), it states, "Walker must surely be one of the busiest men in the United States." This certainly rings true in light of the fact that his secretary did not permit a face-to-face meeting with Louis Winkler, Ph.D., of the Department of Astronomy at the Pennsylvania State University, allegedly because Dr.

②

If so, please have a talk with the
others to end this dangerous alliance
that was set up with the other world
beings (Project Aquarius).
    Dr. Kissinger is very aware of my
"feelings towards this entire issue, via
correspondence.
      Please get back with me as soon
as you possibly can.

          Very Sincerely

          Wm Stunman

Eric Walker "Code Letter," page two.

Walker was too busy flying back and forth to Washington, D.C. Winkler and Crain planned to confront Walker with his "Alien Letter" for comment.

In the 1988 presidential debate between Michael Dukakis and George Bush, Dukakis stated that Star Wars was a fantasy and that he would spend only one billion dollars for research on President Reagan's Strategic Defense Initiative.

Bush and the American Press both immediately jumped on Dukakis, asking him about the contradiction of spending one billion dollars on a fantasy. The same principal applies here.

Why would this very busy man take time out of his schedule to joke around with researchers about something that supposedly did not exist?

It seemed to Steinman, Cameron, and Crain that Walker thought that Sarbacher had talked much more than he actually had, and that Sarbacher had revealed Walker's actual role in the crashed-saucer hierarchy.

It must be remembered that at no time was Walker told exactly what Sarbacher had said. Dr. Walker was (unintentionally) left to figure that out for himself.

Walker Contacted Again

Steinman was confused by the "Alien Letter" and filed it away. Meanwhile, Cameron wanted to move forward with what he had already learned from Steinman. He forwarded several letters to Crain, who lived less than ten miles from Walker's State College residence. Obviously, contact could more easily be initiated from that vantage point. Crain and Cameron continued to dig deep into Walker's background. During the early part of 1988, Walker was at his winter residence in Hilton Head, South Carolina, and could not be reached at his home in State College. Crain finally spoke to Walker by telephone on April 20, 1988.

Little did Crain and Cameron know at the time, but Steinman had written another letter to Walker only two weeks previously. Steinman got another reply, which surely was a bizarre reply. Written inside a circle of Steinman's original letter were the words "Must Reply Did Code (-1)."

In the body of the letter, Walker had apparently written random numbers above Steinman's words.

Analysis of the "Code Letter"

At first, the "Code Letter" made no sense to any of the three researchers. Then Cameron came across a link that may explain why Walker answered in code.

One of the research arms of the National Security Agency is the Communications Research Division (CRD) of the Institute for Defense Analyses (IDA) at Princeton University. In his classic work on the NSA, *The Puzzle Palace*, James Bamford mentioned that the CRD of the IDA holds summer sessions in a well-secured building at UCLA. These are known as as SCAMP (Summer Campus, Advanced Mathematics Program) and ALP (Advanced Language Program). This secret fraternity consisted of several dozen individuals who excel mathematics and languages, and who are cleared and indoctrinated to review Top Secret code, cipher, and intelligence materials.

As we shall see shortly, Dr. Walker happened to be Chairman of the Board of the IDA for many years. Considering the extent of the secrecy IDA employed to hide the fact that it was on the forefront of the breaking and making of codes and ciphers for the National Security Agency, perhaps Walker sent Steinman a code letter to advertise his expertise in that field. With what purpose is unknown: the handwritten numbers (1 through 26) surely do not readily indicate a meaningful sequence of words from the letter.

Of course, it could be said that the "Code Letter" was a joke. If it had been, however, Walker went a long way to play it. Steinman sent his letter on April 7, 1988, to Walker's South Carolina address. Walker, rather than throwing the letter away, carried the letter back with him to Penn State, answered it, and mailed it from there. Quite a bit of thought and effort in relation to something that officially did not exist.

Walker arrived back in Pennsylvania on April 19th or 20th, 1988. On the 20th, Crain phoned and finally talked to Dr. Walker. During the four months that Crain and Cameron had waited for Walker, they had planned the interview based on useful advice given to Cameron years before by Bob Pratt, a well-known newspaper UFO-investigator. When interviewing people who did not want to talk, Pratt told Cameron, "just keep asking questions. Eventually, everyone talks."

Unfortunately, Crain did not know that Walker had just received Steinman's letter. Walker was now dealing with two UFO researchers at the same time and evidently decided to change his tune.

> Walker: Hello.
> Crain: Hello, is Dr. Eric Walker there please?
> Walker: This is he.
> Crain: I'm calling you from Julian which is about 8 miles from where you are.
> Walker: Yes.
> Crain: And the reason I'm calling, I've been doing some rather intensive research into some meetings that occurred in the late 40s and early 50s at Wright-Patterson Air Force Base involving crashed UFOs and alien occupants. And I understand that when you were executive secretary of the Research and Development Board that you had attended these meetings. Do you recall that?
> Walker: What meeting?
> Crain: It was some meetings at Wright-Patterson Air Force Base, and they were talking about alien occupants that were recovered. Can you recall that?
> Walker: You're talking about UFOs?
> Crain: UFOs, right.
> Walker: This is a subject that I don't talk about.
> Crain: OK. I understand from Robert Sarbacher that you were . . . that you attended those meetings.
> Walker: I say this is not a subject that I talk about.
> Crain: OK, so you're saying you don't want to talk about it because of what, national security?
> Walker: No, I'm saying I just don't want to talk about it.
> Crain: OK, can you tell me anything about it?
> Walker: Nope, not a thing.
> Crain: OK, it must be a national security reason then. It's the only thing I can think of.
> Walker: Well, there's nothing I can say, so there's no good talking about it. I'm sorry. Thank you.
> Crain: Thank you.

Analysis

As Walker had done in every communication up to this point, he denied nothing. Crain asked and rephrased questions, but Walker again replied that he did not want to discuss it.

It was not as if crashed saucers didn't exist and there was nothing to talk about. Nor was it that Walker was prohibited from talking about it. He simply did not want to.

Five times Crain asked him, and five times Dr. Walker gave the same answer. Crain left it at that, and he and Cameron contemplated their next move.

At this point, from all the data they collected, Cameron and Crain were convinced that Dr. Eric Walker knew a great deal about the government's handling of UFO-type material. Our investigation continued.

Since Steinman was having success with Dr. Walker through letters, the authors decided to write also. The worst thing that would happen is that Walker would not respond.

On April 24, 1988, Crain wrote to Walker, following up on their conversation. In this letter, he made reference to one of Walker's many previous editorials ("Now It's My Turn") he had written for the local newspaper in State College, Pennsylvania. The title of this one seemed especially appropriate: "The Need to be Right–Essential."

However, Walker returned Crain's letter with just a one-line response handwritten at the bottom of the page: "Why say anything?"

Walker had done a similar thing with Steinman's letter from earlier that month, returning the original with comments. The "Why say anything?" statement seemed to imply that, from Walker's viewpoint, saying nothing would be the best course of action. Once again, when faced with the findings of a UFO investigator, Walker denied nothing.

Crain made a second attempt to contact Walker by mail on June 7, 1988. In that letter, Crain told Walker that "several civilians have been shown a massive government document detailing our government's UFO retrieval efforts since the 1940s." He asked Walker, "Why do you want to keep what you know about UFOs and heard at those meetings at Wright-Patterson AFB a secret?"

Finally Crain told Walker, "To answer your question, why say anything, I say WHY NOT? Taxpayers financed these secret operations, yet you've decided we have no right to know anything about how these funds were utilized to advance science in determining the origin and function of UFOs."

Walker never responded to this letter.

New Information Revealed

From December 1987 to August 1988, Crain and Cameron worked together in this investigation, with only Cameron communicating with Steinman.

In late August, Crain wrote a letter to Steinman asking to exchange information that had been collected on Walker to see if anything new had been uncovered. Steinman telephoned Crain on September 8, and the two discussed the Walker investigation. Shortly thereafter, Steinman forwarded his file on Walker to Crain, and Cameron and Crain sent theirs to Steinman. Included with the transcript of the August 30, 1987 telephone interview were the three letters that Steinman had received from Walker.

Crain now had the "Alien Letter" and the interview during which Walker had stated that he had known of MJ-12 for 40 years.

Armed with some new information, Crain decided to contact Walker again. The following telephone interview between Crain and Walker—written down by Crain right after the conversation as accurately as he could recall it—took place on October 9, 1988:

Walker: Hello?
Crain: Hello, Dr. Walker. How are you today?
Walker: Good.

Crain: I'm doing some research now on something called Majestic-12. I understand you are familiar with that group.
Walker: Say it again.
Crain: Majestic-12.
Walker: I'm not familiar with that.
Crain: A friend of mine in California sent you a briefing document called Operation Majestic-12 dated November 18, 1952, to President Elect Eisenhower. Are you familiar with that document he sent you?
Walker: I'll have to check with my secretary. But no, I don't recall that.
Crain: Then let me ask you this: he claims he got a letter back from you with comments of what your opinion is on the document. It had to do with a crashed object back in the 1950s [the document, not the crash] with a flying saucer. Your letter indicated the beings were not found dead, but alive, and that they were integrated back into society.
Walker: I don't know what you're talking about.
Crain: Then I guess someone else sent the letter and signed your name to it.
Walker: That's happened before.
Crain: OK. I guess you can't help me on this.
Walker: O.K., good-bye.

The next day Cameron phoned Crain on another issue and was told that Walker had been interviewed again with little success, or so it appeared.

Crain read the interview to Cameron on the phone and Cameron's first reaction was, "Walker said 'my secretary.' Why does a 78-year-old man have a secretary?"

The authors guessed that Walker might still have had an office at Penn State, which turned out to be correct. Three more phone calls took place in the next 30 hours, during which Cameron and Crain discussed what Walker had said and what could be done next.

Since Walker maintained ties at Penn State with an office on campus, the authors decided to recruit someone else into the investigation: Dr. Louis Winkler, a long-time friend of Crain's who worked in the Department of Astronomy at Penn State. Winkler was a former Astronomy consultant for MUFON and wrote several technical papers on UFOs for various journals.

It was hoped that by introducing Winkler into the investigation, he could not only provide important assistance in finding out what Walker was really up to, but he could also serve as an excellent witness to anything that may happen when the authors would call on Walker again. Cameron and Crain hoped Walker would respond to Winkler, since Winkler also worked at the University. Crain showed Winkler the Walker file, and asked if he and Cameron should write Walker another letter, only this time using Winkler's official university letterhead.

Winkler said it could take weeks to get to the bottom of what was going on, and suggested phoning Walker, after which he and Crain could go over to meet in Walker's office.

Winkler phoned and set up a meeting with Walker's secretary for October 19, 1988, at 11:00 a.m.. Unfortunately, however, the night before the meeting Dr. Winkler took sick and was taken to the hospital, where he remained for a week. The meeting had to be canceled.

In a telephone call shortly after the cancellation, Crain asked Cameron whether another meeting should be set up; Cameron replied that if one were not, the investigation would be over. Cameron also referred to another one of Walker's articles where Walker plainly stated:

> I cherish the right to know. But I also cherish the right to know who makes false allegations and the right to defend myself against untruths.

Walker had received numerous letters from Crain and Steinman outlining what these researchers believed was going on. Walker had declined to respond to many of them. A face-to-face interview, with Dr. Winkler as witness, would definitely give Dr. Walker his "right to defend" himself.

Dr. Winkler phoned Walker's secretary for another meeting, but this time the tone had changed. Suddenly, Dr. Walker was too busy to meet with Dr. Winkler, so Winkler hung up. The next time Winkler phoned, the secretary told him that Walker was flying back and forth to Washington, D.C., and was still too busy to meet with. "Isn't this something we could do over the phone?" the secretary asked.

"No," replied Winkler. "I need to authenticate a signature." It is not known whether this message about authenticating a signature reached Walker. Walker had stated in an article that astronomy was a science he "knew little about." Whether it was a question of why someone in the Department of Astronomy would want to authenticate a signature or some other reason, the next call to Walker's secretary would be the last. Dr. Winkler called again to check with the secretary about a meeting and was again told that Dr. Walker was too busy, but this time she got off the hook; she suggested that Dr. Walker phone Dr. Winkler when Walker found some time.

Dr. Winkler relayed this to Crain, stating that in his opinion, Walker had no intention of having a meeting take place. He suggested to Crain that Crain simply use the material that he currently had. Cameron and Crain agreed that Dr. Winkler's phone would never ring.

"We played the game by Walker's rules," Cameron said. "We gave him a chance to defend himself. He's choosing not to do it." Walker never did call back.

This would not be the last contact with Walker, however. Steinman decided that he wanted to phone Walker again to ask him what he meant by the "Alien" and "Code" letters. What happened is best described by Steinman in a letter to Cameron dated December 8, 1988. Steinman wrote:

> I called Walker on the evening of November 25. 1988. He acted as though he didn't even know who I was. I tried to jog his memory by bringing up the previous telecon [i.e. telephone conversation] that I had with him on August 30, 1987, and the letter that he sent to me on September 23, 1987. He simply stated, "I don't know what you're talking about." That voice is the same voice that I talked to on August 30, 1987, plus his wife answered the phone both times, same woman's voice.

In a telephone call to Cameron, Steinman expressed some surprise at Walker, stating that he knew neither what Steinman was talking about nor who Steinman was. Cameron said that was exactly what he had told Crain in his last interview with him. "He's finally learned how to answer the UFO question," Cameron said. "If he had done that from the start, he wouldn't be in the mess he's in now."

Analysis & Conclusions

It is no wonder that Walker was skittish about more than one researcher finding him and wanting him to comment on a Top Secret government operation. We also assumed that his security clearances would be in jeopardy if it became known that he told what he knew about UFOs.

However, it was our opinion that the U.S. Government had no right to declare this discovery a secret in the first place—a secret they continue to try to conceal.

Had we learned anything from this investigation? Had Walker really written the "Alien Letter" to Steinman? One way we checked was to find Walker's signature on other documents. After spending several hours sifting through papers at the Penn State Archives, Crain could not find a single document or letter signed by Walker. However, we did locate a Christmas card that appeared to have been signed by him.

In March 1989, Cameron uncovered a Walker signature in an engineering bulletin released in 1948; Walker had signed his name at the bottom of the page.

In late 1989, Tom Mickus of Canada found another Walker signature in a report on Penn State. By comparing the three signatures, it seemed fairly obvious that Walker initialed the "Alien Letter."

We decided to go one step farther with the handwriting analysis and enlarged the comments on Steinman's "Code Letter" to see if they matched Walker's handwriting. Again, we ran into formidable difficulty in finding examples of Walker's penmanship, but Crain did uncover a speech that Walker was to give before a special meeting of the Faculty Senate at Penn State. On a memorandum attached to the speech (found in the Penn State Archives) Louis H. Bell had written, "Dr. Walker changed the opening statement in his remarks." Those changes are handwritten on the speech.

We looked carefully at the writing from the "Code Letter," superimposing Walker's known handwriting. Everything matched extremely well, making it clear that Eric A. Walker was in fact the author of the various letters to Steinman, Crain, and Cameron.

The signature above was uncovered by researcher Tom Mickus of Canada, who obtained it from a late 1960s Penn State report. As the reader can see, the "E" and the "W" are similar in all three signatures. There is little question that Walker signed the "Alien Letter."

The signature appearing above was the one signed at the bottom of Steinman's letter dated September 23, 1987. It has been enlarged to facilitate comparison. Notice how the swirl on the top part of the "E" comes back, similarly as with the signature below. The open "A" at the top also matches closely. It appears Walker completes his signature by giving the last letter a long tail to close. He does the same in all three signatures. He also puts a period after his name in the top illustration and the middle one.

Eric A. Walker's signature above is reproduced from the "Proceedings of the Conference on Administration of Research" (October 6-7, 1947), State College, Pennsylvania. It came from the *School of Engineering Technical Bulletin No. 29*. Notice how the shapes of the "E" and the "A" look remarkably similar to the center illustration. The signature above is dated January 1948; the center one is dated September 1987.

The aforementioned conference was the first of a series, and it was founded by Walker. Interestingly, one of the twelve speakers at the 1947 conference was Dr. Edward U. Condon, who later directed the U.S. Air Force UFO Study at the University of Colorado.

Incidentally, regarding the archives, it became clear that Walker's professional activities were not especially available for public review. Although there is a good deal of public relations-type material in the Walker file at the Penn State Archives, there is little detail on the kinds of things Walker worked on in his career. For instance, we could find nothing on what Walker did as Executive Secretary of the critically important Research and Development Board.

In an effort to secure additional detailed information on Walker, Cameron wrote to the Penn State University Libraries in December 1988. In a response dated December 12, it was explained to Cameron that many of Walker's files were on microfilm and not generally available to the public.

According to the University Archivist Leon J. Stout, Walker still personally possessed a "good deal" of his own material. If Walker was being truthful to Steinman during their early communication, it was possible that the notes taken at those meetings at Wright Field to which Dr. Walker referred were still in his possession.

Was Walker really familiar with the government's UFO-retrieval operation? Before we answer that question, let us review the facts that could make such an inference possible.

According to the MJ-12 Document, Operation Majestic-12 was a Top Secret Research & Development Board intelligence operation. Walker served as Executive Secretary of the Board from 1950-52. The previous Executive Secretary of the Joint R&D Board was Lloyd V. Berkner. It so happened that, on the MJ-12 Document, Berkner was listed as a member of Majestic-12.

According to Sarbacher, the Joint R&D Board was the group to which findings about UFO recoveries were ultimately reported. Steinman wrote that Sarbacher had positively identified Walker as the one person who attended *all* the meetings involving the original UFO recoveries.

For whatever reason, members of the Missile Committee (i.e., the Guidance and Control Panel) were invited to attend those meetings at Wright-Patterson Air Force Base, according to Sarbacher. It so happened that Eric Walker had an interest in missiles. According to the May 1968 issue of *Engineering Education*, Walker "has made significant contributions in acoustic guidance of missiles."

Sarbacher's 1983 letter to Steinman also stated that Dr.

Vannevar Bush was "definitely involved." Dr. Bush was described in the MJ-12 document as one of two persons who had recommended to President Truman that Operation Majestic-12 be initiated. Bush was the first Director of the Joint R&D Board established in 1946, of which Walker later became Executive Secretary. Bush and Walker were very good friends. Walker wrote in his book, *Now It's My Turn*, that "My closest relations with Van Bush, were from 1939 to 1955, when he was President of the Carnegie Institution of Washington and also, from 1940 onward, the key figure in national defense research."[38]

It is our opinion that the facts demonstrate that Walker was indeed involved in some capacity in government UFO-retrieval operations.

During their investigation, the authors discovered some interesting connections between Walker, Eisenhower, and the Pennsylvania State University.

For instance:

(1) According to the MJ-12 Document, the Majestic-12 group briefed President-Elect Dwight D. Eisenhower. At that time, Dwight's brother, Milton Eisenhower, was the President of Penn State. In 1956, Milton Eisenhower was succeeded as President by Dr. Eric Walker. And Walker had connections with the upper levels of the U.S. Government.

(2) In the television documentary, *UFO Cover-Up? Live!*, broadcast on October 14, 1988, an intelligence officer working inside the government implicated the U.S. Navy as being in charge of operations related to activities involving MJ-12. According to this agent, data collected involving UFOs was to be transmitted to the Navy for analysis. The Ordnance Research Laboratory at Penn State, of which Walker once served as director, received million-dollar contracts from the Navy to conduct research for the Department of Defense.

(3) Central Intelligence Agency memos dated between April and July 1976 indicate that the Agency's R&D unit was

receiving "UFO-related material from many of our science and technology sources who are presently conducting related research" and was discussing "propulsion systems" that were based on this work. In April 1988, Penn State was selected by NASA from among 115 candidates to receive a five-year grant worth up to $4.5 million to create the Center for Space Propulsion Engineering. The Center's Director, Dr. Charles Merkle, a Penn State professor of mechanical engineering, announced the new center would conduct basic research on rocket propulsion systems.

As we finished the Walker investigation and pursued other areas of our research, we continued to keep an eye on Walker and what happened when word got out that he was being investigated. Startling new evidence of Walker's involvement was uncovered. Thus we continued our study.

Continuing The Walker Investigation

In early June 1989, Stanton Friedman phoned Dr. Walker to see if perhaps he was talking now. Walker told Friedman that he had not been involved with UFOs since 1965.[*] Walker then told Friedman that people who study UFOs should research something else. What do you mean by this, Friedman wanted to know? Walker replied, "I can't tell you. That's all there is to it."[39]

Then, during the summer of 1989, the authors released their preliminary paper to a handful of selected UFO researchers. Cameron and Crain wanted to see how the UFO community would react to their report and to find out if their input could help open new doors for getting Walker to respond more positively.

This turned out to be a wise move. One of the first researchers to receive the paper was Thomas A. Mickus, a student at

---

[*] Interestingly, that date coincides with a UFO crash in Kecksburg, Pennsylvania, only 100 miles from Walker's home. Details of the Kecksburg crash are discussed in Chapter 8.

the University of Toronto and Moderator of the UFO-oriented computerized Bulletin Board Service (BBS) Network in Canada. Upon reading of Walker's apparent involvement, Mickus phoned Walker at his office at Penn State on August 11, 1989. Although cordial with Mickus, Walker lived up to his reputation as being evasive to direct questions.

Bill Moore and his contacts inside the intelligence agencies, generally referred to as the Aviary, also did some research on Walker. Conversations with six university presidents who knew Dr. Walker resulted in the following summary characterization of Dr. Walker:

Although approaching 80, Dr. Walker was still in excellent physical and mental condition. He was still "very sharp" and "very productive." Walker was described by all as essentially a "straight shooter" who did not lie but was very good at "talking around things" he did not want to—or could not—discuss.

Tom Mickus had reviewed all previous correspondence with Walker and was anxious to ask again about crashed saucer meetings at Wright-Patterson AFB. Had Walker attended? Mickus began by asking about Joint Research & Development Board meetings:

> Walker: Well I, uh [slight laugh], the early 50s, you know, is many years ago, and I attended a lot of meetings. Which one was this supposed to be?
> Mickus: I believe this [one] was centered at the Wright-Patterson [Air Force Base]. Apparently it was to deal with, sensational as it is, crashed flying vehicles of some sort, UFOs if you want to say that. And, like I say, I know it's many years ago, but apparently in a phone conversation with William Steinman, he has it down that you admitted attending some of those meetings. Indeed, it was the late Robert Sarbacher [who] actually pointed you out as the person who attended all of those meetings. Now I know that's some 40 years ago now. Did you have any comment on that?

```
                        Tom Mickus
                     UFONET BBS Network
                    Box 388, Station W
                     Toronto, Ontario
                      M6M 5C1 CANADA

                                            October 17, 1989

Dr. Eric Walker
222A Hammond Building
University Park, Pennsylvannia
16802                                    COPY

Dear Dr. Walker,

          Thank you for your most recent response on September 11th, of
"No Comment". It is encouraging to see that progress is being made
towards getting to the truth of the matter.

          In addition, I am happy to learn that the elderly gentleman
has a sense of humour. That is one of the secrets of long life, and
I am confident that you will be gracing us with your presence for some
time yet to come.

          Now as to the content of your response, I have pondered long
and hard over it. When people say "no comment", it usually indicates
one of several things:

          A) They are engaged with legal proceedings on the subject in   ✓
             question, and don't wish to jeopardize themselves.

          B) The subject is an embarrassing one for them, thus they     ✓
             don't wish to speak about it.

          C) The subject is a sensitve one, and thus are not privy      ✓
             to speaking openly about it.

          or

          D) For reasons not expressed above, they simply don't want   ✓
             to talk about it.

          If I may be so bold, which do you feel applies to your
particular situation? Would you likewise give the same response
of "no comment" to a NYT reporter? ✓ Surely you must know that such
a reply instead of diffusing the situation, only serves to fuel the
fires of speculation. ✓

          Again sir, if there is substance to these allegations, I would
appeal to you to come forward and at least inform the public in a
general way about what the government really knows on this subject of
UFOs. If not the government, then at least tell us your own story.
As a character in a just published novel on the subject says, "People
have a right to know. They had a right to know forty years ago."   why ?

          What have you got to lose?
```

Letter from Tom Mickus to Eric Walker, with Walker's checkmarks and comment.

> Walker: [garbled] Well, I did attend a lot of meetings, but I can't remember any substantive conclusions or anything like that.

Had Walker confirmed being there? Mickus continued by asking the nature of the meetings. Suddenly Walker experienced "complete memory loss."

> Mickus: Right, and as far as what was discussed there?
> Walker: As far as the what?
> Mickus: What was discussed, the topic, the subject matter of those meetings?

Walker: No, I couldn't remember that at all.
Mickus: But, you're saying that it had nothing to do with UFOs or alien bodies, or anything like this?
Walker: Well, I don't have any alien bodies in my office, I can tell you that.

As the conversation continued, Walker carefully avoided direct answers to any of the questions. Tom Mickus decided to get an on-the record yes-or-no answer to the question of a Walker/UFO connection.

Mickus: So, therefore you deny ever having any relationship whatsoever in your earlier government dealings with the discussion of UFOs or alien bodies, anything like that, you deny that was part of the Research & Development Board meetings and subsequent activities that you may have been involved with?
Walker: [slight laugh] You know, you're just wasting your time and money, and I'm sorry but I've got other things to do.
Mickus: Okay, but if I could just get an on-the-record comment, response from you on that, because I don't know, I think you may be hearing more about this because if this thing gets in wide circulation, you may have other people knocking on your door trying to get a reaction.
Walker: I don't have any reaction, I'm sorry.

Mickus tried to reiterate the question, but Walker said "thank you" and hung up.

As the reader can see, Dr. Walker refused either to confirm or deny his involvement in UFO crash recoveries to Mickus. Mickus followed his phone conversation by writing Walker a letter. He also included a dozen-and-a-half pages from the Cameron/Crain report for Walker's comments. Walker had refused to give a face-to-face interview about the report and suggested instead that the report be sent to him for possible comment. Only a few pages were sent, in order to prevent him from knowing the full extent of the report before making an on-the-record comment.

A little over two weeks passed. Then, Crain received in the mail a photocopy of Steinman's "Code Letter" from Richmond,

```
                                          Port Royal Plantation
                                          4 Stuart Place
                                          Hilton Head, SC 29928
                                          December 21, 1989


Dr. Henry Victorian
'Yerevan',
24 Prestwood Dv.,
Aspley Park,
Nottingham NG8 3LY,
England

Dear Dr. Victorian:

I have your very kind letter of November 16, 1989, and find it very interesting.  It is too bad
you were not able to take a photograph of the object or speak to some of the inhabitants
which might have given you a better understanding of their circumstances.  I would suggest
that you correspond with Mr. William Steinman who undoubtedly knows all the public
knowledge of such phenomena.  I am sure that he can bring you up to date if you can supply
him with the code.

His mailing address is:

                          15043 Rosalita Drive
                          LaMirada, CA 90638

Very truly yours,



Eric A. Walker


EAW/djs
```

Letter from Eric Walker to "Dr. Henry Victorian," a.k.a. Henry Azadehdel.

Virginia, postmarked August 26, 1989. It arrived in a stamped, self-addressed envelope that Crain had sent to Walker over a year before, in June 1988.

Walker had kept that envelope for over a year before using it.[*]

Thus, in a matter of fifteen days, Dr. Walker had sent to one researcher a photocopy of a letter he had received from another researcher. This action showed that he was keeping track of

---

[*] It is interesting to note that during the August 11 interview with Tom Mickus, Walker denied knowing who Bill Steinman or T. Scott Crain were.

material being sent to him. And he also was going a long way to keep the game interesting.

Walker never answered Mickus's first letter, so Mickus mailed a second one with essentially the same content. This second letter (dated September 5, 1989) finally evoked a response from Walker, who photocopied it and returned it to Mickus with the words "No comment. The elderly gentleman."

Walker's reply was postmarked September 11, 1989, and was mailed from Penn State's University Park Campus.

On either the 9th or 10th of September, Dr. Walker was contacted by a military contractor who did business at Penn State. This individual had actually been sent by William Moore, who had offered to help Cameron and Crain get to the bottom of the Walker affair. After some discussion, the contractor asked Walker if he had ever heard of MJ-12 or if he had ever been involved in the military recovery of a UFO. "No" and "no," replied Walker. This, even though Mickus's letter had to be nearby (Walker's reply to him was postmarked only a day or two later). And even though Walker had just received excerpts from Cameron and Crain's paper "UFOs, MJ-12, and the Government," in which he was linked to meetings involving crashed flying saucers. Walker mentioned nothing of this.

Mickus mailed a third letter to Walker on October 17, 1989, and Walker responded immediately. The check-marks appearing in the letter could be interpreted a number of ways, but it is our opinion that Walker checked off those statements to indicate an "affirmative" or "yes" answer.

Walker continued to maintain that civilians had no business knowing what the U.S. Government got itself into over forty years before. He continued to question why they had any right to know. Whatever it was, Walker checked off that "the justification for secrecy [is] still there after 40 years." The Walker reply is a fascinating reply from a man who we believed knew the basic working of the UFO cover up. Like times in the past Walker tried to give us answers without directly violating security or being openly involved. He could have simply thrown the letter in the garbage but instead spent time to directly reply to all the questions that Mickus had put to him.

Enter Henry Azadehdel

While doing research on a purported UFO crash in South Africa, Cameron corresponded frequently with a key investigator in the case, Dr. Henry Azadehdel, also known as Armen Victorian, an alleged British-Armenian physicist, and certainly one of the more fascinating individuals to have entered UFO research. During the time Azadehel or Victorian was active in the field, his credentials were challenged by several other researchers, including Timothy Good and William Moore. To this day, there remains an air of mystery about him.

Azadehdel had been helpful to Cameron in supplying material on the South African incident. Now, in late 1989, he learned about Cameron and Crain's investigation of Walker. Azadehdel took an interest in the case and wrote to Walker on November 16, 1989, from his home in Nottingham, England. In that letter, Azadehdel told Walker about a UFO crash in Bolivia (believed to have occurred in 1978), which Azadehdel and a German friend had investigated. According to Azadehdel, they came across the crashed, saucer-shaped object along a riverbank, in which three bodies were found inside and two outside the craft. Azadehdel also told Cameron about the purported incident and said that he had taken five pictures and "gotten out of there." (Azadehdel apparently didn't tell Walker in his letter that he had photographed the crash site.) Walker responded on December 21, 1989, and a somewhat cordial scientist-to-scientist relationship developed between the two parties.

Azadehdel phoned Walker on January 26, 1990, and they discussed a number of topics. Regarding UFOs, Walker assented to nothing but generalities. Majestic-12 and the associated documents were never brought up.

All that changed with a March 8, 1990 call to Walker. Azadehdel opened up with all sorts of questions about captured saucers and MJ-12. Walker admitted to having had a past association with MJ-12 and described MJ-12 as a "handful of elite." What follows are transcripts of Azadehdel's own notes of three phone conversations with Walker.

First, the phone conversation of January 26, 1990:

Mrs. Walker: Hello?
Azadehdel: Hello, good morning ma'am, is Dr. Walker in?
Mrs. Walker: No, he is not. He is out.
Azadehdel: That is fine. I am calling long distance. Do you know when he will be back?
Mrs. Walker: Well, I am pretty sure he is playing tennis. Oh, here he comes now. He is driving in. Just hold on. He'll be here. (I held the line for [a] few minutes.)
Dr. Walker: Hello?
Azadehdel: Dr. Walker?
Dr. Walker: Yeah?
Azadehdel: Very good morning to you. This is Dr. Victorian from Nottingham, Dr.
Walker: Well, how are you?
Azadehdel: Not bad, thank you, Doctor, and you?
Dr. Walker: Pretty good.
Azadehdel: Doctor, I was in the Long Eaton Library, I was talking to the librarian there, and I mentioned that there is a gentleman who was born here. Doctor, have you written anything that I can ask you to send us in order to leave in the library in Long Eaton?
Dr. Walker: I have written an autobiography, and it was published around three months ago, and I had a friend who took several copies over to England he wanted to leave in various places. It is called "Now It Is My Turn." [sic].
Azadehdel: Doctor, would it be possible if I ask you to send a copy autographed by you specifically for the Long Eaton Library?
Dr. Walker: Yes, I think so. Give me the address.
Azadehdel: You have my address.
Dr. Walker: Not here, no.
Azadehdel: I'll give it to you. (I started giving my address again to him spelling the name of the street I live in. Then when I wanted to spell the name of the area I live in, he

interrupted and said, "I know where Aspley Park is." Then after giving my address, I asked, "Doctor, did you get my second letter?"

Dr. Walker: No, I have not. See, I am not in Pennsylvania, so my mail piles up until I get back.

Azadehdel: Yes. I have replied to your first letter. I don't know the gentleman you have mentioned (referring to Bill Steinman). As a matter of fact, I have no contact with anybody else at all. I have been working alone on this subject.

Dr. Walker: Well, the man has a network with all the people interested in this, and he tries to keep all the information in one place.

Azadehdel: To be honest with you, I rather not to contact these people at all. I rather work alone and keep myself to myself.

Dr. Walker: Yep.

Azadehdel: There are five photographs available about the case I mentioned to you.

Dr. Walker: Yep.

Azadehdel: But, the entities photographed are all insect-like.

Dr. Walker: Aha.

Azadehdel: They were very light.

Dr. Walker: Do they have antennae?

Azadehdel: No. The skin was pale. Extremely large eyes. Three on the riverside, two inside. I had a German friend with me. Do you have any interest in botany?

Dr. Walker: No, not that I can get at.

Azadehdel: (I explained the circumstances [whereby we had been] led to taking the photographs to him.)

Dr. Walker: No ears. How many eyes?

Azadehdel: Two eyes.

Dr. Walker: Big eyes?

Azadehdel: Yes, big eyes. Extremely large eyes. Especially their forehead was very large. Their arms and hands were very thin. The same thickness of my five-year-old son's.

Dr. Walker: I say, I have no resources at all, no friends for these things where I am now.

Azadehdel: But, Doctor, have we ever captured anything at all? We must have.

Dr. Walker: SURE.

Azadehdel: Anything, did we learn anything?

Dr. Walker: Yeah, I think so.

Azadehdel: Doctor would it be possible if you can help me

with this? Dr. Walker: You know, you can contact Crain.
Azadehdel: Who is Crain?
Dr. Walker: The guy I wrote you [about]. The man I told
you about (He had not mentioned Crain's name in his only
letter to me. My guess is that he was throwing the name to
see whether I knew him or whether I would give the game
away. Or maybe there is a letter in the post to me in which
he has mentioned Crain's name. However, I told him the
truth that according to our correspondence to date I do not
know Crain.)
Azadehdel: In the letter you had written, there was
something about a Mr. Sti . . . Steenman?
Dr. Walker: Steinman. Him and Crain work together. (He
gave [the name of] Steinman's home town to me.)
Azadehdel: Well, I really try to keep out of them. With due
respect, you are a scientist, a well-known one, and you
know. I am a physicist and rather keep myself to myself.
My interest is purely scientific more than anything else. Is
it determined from which star system they come from?
Dr. Walker: I didn't get that.
Azadehdel: (I repeated the question.)
Dr. Walker: Ah, I do not think so.
Azadehdel: Is it still unknown?
Dr. Walker: I think that is the picture, I am not sure.
Azadehdel: But what amazes me, Doctor, is the frequent
appearance of these objects. Does this suggest that they
might have a base in one of our solar system planets?
Dr. Walker: Well, we can make a point of all these, but they
did not tell us.
Azadehdel: Have we ever been able to make contact with
them on the communication basis?
Dr. Walker: We promised not to tell.
Azadehdel: I can understand it. Does it mean that the
official communication has been made, and it has been
promised not to tell? Orders are that outside this circle
there are private [bits of] information they should not
know (the public?).
Dr. Walker: I do not think it is official. If three, four
individuals have got together on this, it can't be official.
Azadehdel: Do they constitute any threat to the national
security of any country?
Dr. Walker: Everybody decides on this on his own.
Azadehdel: I am told by the Ministry of Defense (in England) they don't constitute a national threat to this country.

Dr. Walker: Well, maybe they know.

Azadehdel: Do you know whether there is any cooperation between them (EBEs) and us, as an advanced civilization?

Dr. Walker: I think so. There have been occasions, but then I can speak only for myself.

Azadehdel: But, Doctor, would you consider them to be intruders as a scientist?

Dr. Walker: I don't think so. But, if they went into England as intruders, then I think yes, you could.

Azadehdel: Is anyone of them alive?

Dr. Walker: I cannot answer that.

Azadehdel: Forgive me, Doctor, I am not trying to be nosy. Believe me, please. It is just scientific curiosity that I have had for many years, I swear.

Dr. Walker: All right. If you swear it is private, you want to talk about it, then we talk about it.

Azadehdel: I swear that this is something which is private, and I am eager to learn.

Dr. Walker: I'll send you the copies of the book. You read it, see what you learn from it. Of course, I don't have them here. It would take a little while.

Azadehdel: Doctor, thank you. I am grateful for your time, bye.

Dr. Walker: Bye.

Next, the telephone conversation of March 8, 1990:

Mrs. Walker: Hello?

Azadehdel: Hello. Is Dr. Walker in, please?

Mrs. Walker: Yes. (I waited for a short while.)

Dr. Walker: Hello?

Azadehdel: Hello. Dr. Walker, this is Henry from Nottingham.

Dr. Walker: Hello, how are you?

Azadehdel: I am fine, thank you. Doctor, I have sent you a book earlier on this week. I hope you would enjoy reading it. It is called The Open Verdict. It is about 25 scientists who worked in MoD (Ministry of Defense), and all died in mysterious circumstances.

Dr. Walker: Well, I have not received it yet. Have you received my book?

Azadehdel: No, Doctor. I sent this book on Tuesday by airmail. You should receive it in 10 days or so. But, Doctor, I was reading a book titled Above Top Secret. There were some documents there referring to a group better known as

MJ-12. Have you heard of them?

Dr. Walker: For [a] long time now, I have nothing to do with them. Azadehdel: Are the documents authentic?

Dr. Walker: (Smiles) [sic] I don't think so.

Azadehdel: Doctor, but is there any such group still active?

Dr. Walker: (Silence) How good is your mathematics?

Azadehdel: As good as it could be for a doctor in physics, but why? Dr. Walker: Because only a very few are capable of handling this issue. Unless your mind ability is like Einstein's or likewise, I do not think how you can achieve anything.

Azadehdel: Well, Doctor, for many years now I have been trying. But, are there government scientists?

Dr. Walker: Everybody mistakes about this issue. I gather by that you mean whether they work for the Defense establishments of the military.

Azadehdel: Yes, Doctor, that is what I meant.

Dr. Walker: Well, that is where you are wrong. They are A HANDFUL OF ELITE. When you are invited into that group, I would know.

Azadehdel: Is it a group like Bilderbergs, Pugwash, or anything like that?

Dr. Walker: I didn't get that.

Azadehdel: Is this group like the Bilderbergs, Pugwash or the Trilaterals?

Dr. Walker: (Silence for a long while.) Something like that.

Azadehdel: Are there any members of the ordinary public in this group?

Dr. Walker: What do you mean?

Azadehdel: I mean ordinary people who have dedicated years of their lives studying UFOs.

Dr. Walker: No.

Azadehdel: Are you a member of that group?

Dr. Walker: I cannot answer that. How good is your seventh sense? How much [do] you know about ESP?

Azadehdel: I know to some degree about ESP and EVP. But what has this got to do with it?

Dr. Walker: Unless you know about it, and know how to use it, you would not be taken in. Only a few know about it.

Azadehdel: Doctor, are there any military people in that group?

Dr. Walker: No.

Azadehdel: Have we used any derivative of the learnt technology in the military?

Dr. Walker: I cannot answer that question. You are trying to squeeze the answers out of me. If you are invited into this group, I would know.

Azadehdel: Are the members 10, 12, 14, are they all Americans?

Dr. Walker: I cannot give you the numbers, and no, not necessarily, they are not all Americans.

Azadehdel: Doctor, have we master[ed] the knowledge, are we working together with the entities?

Dr. Walker: No, we have learnt so much, and we are not working with them, only contact.

Azadehdel: Have we captured any saucers, any material from the discs to study?

Dr. Walker: The technology is far behind what is known in ordinary terms of physics that you take the measure and obtain measurements. You are pushing for answers, aren't you? (smiles.) [sic]

Azadehdel: Doctor, I have obtained a report called Project Magnet. Have you ever met Wilbert Smith, who worked on this project in Canada?

Dr. Walker: No, I don't believe having met this person.

Azadehdel: Is the concept on the Electromagnetic or Gravity?

Dr. Walker: As I said, it is far behind the known level of physics that is known. A very few have knowledge of it.

Azadehdel: OK., Doctor, let us change the subject. What do you usually read?

Dr. Walker: Well, at the moment, I am reading The Spy Catcher [sic]. Azadehdel: You are a little bit behind, Doctor, in that department, aren't you?

Dr. Walker: (He laughs.) Well, I have not had the time. But it is interesting. I like books like this.

Azadehdel: Well, Doctor, in that case you would enjoy my book. I would send you hereafter some books.

Dr. Walker: Are you familiar with the Theory of Relativity? Do you know whether we have used it or not?

Azadehdel: Yes, I am in fact familiar with it. But, whether we have used it, I guess my answer would be Yes and no.

Dr. Walker: That is correct, yes and no.

Azadehdel: Doctor, I guess this subject is like chasing the whirlwind.

Dr. Walker: Well, yes. But if you capture that whirlwind, what do you want to do with it?

Azadehdel: It is a very good and valid question, one which. . . that sort of analogy from my point of view does not apply to it. I am not going to pass on a judgment on it, to whether it is good or bad, and hence I should not follow it up for those reasons. I am a scientist, looking for the answers and solutions. I guess like any other scientific problems, which I might encounter.

Dr. Walker: As I said, very few who are not officials have been able to work [with them], and if you are invited into their circle, I would know.

Azadehdel: Doctor, thank you very much for your time. We should chat again.

Dr. Walker: Thank you, yes, we should. Bye.

Azadehdel: Bye, Doctor.

Finally, "extracts and highlights," as Azadehdel put it, of the phone conversation of August 18, 1990. This phone call was not recorded because of a strange scrambling of the tape. Just after the call took place and Azadehdel was about to transcribe it he found that it had been overrun by a loud squealing noise. He phoned up Cameron and played the tape for him. The tape started off fine. Dr. Walker's wife answered the phone, as was the pattern. As soon as Dr. Walker came on the squealing noise began and absolutely nothing could be made out.

> I called at 6:15 local time. His wife answered the phone. I asked to speak to Dr. Walker. He picked up the receiver after a while. He told me that he has just arrived back from a trip to England where he spent some time in East Anglia. According to his comment he had a bit of [a] bumpy trip back. The plane had developed problem[s] and had to go back again. He called it "my bicycle trip to England."
>
> He told me that all the mail addressed to his home address would [be] automatically directed to his office. He also added that he has not been able to answer his mail for over three months and has not been to his office for almost six weeks.
>
> I recommended him to read Howard Blum's book Out There. He said he will. Then I started my questions.
>
> I asked him if he could give me the name of the group who actually presided to deal with this subject (UFOs).
>
> After a long silence he replied. "I do not know it by memory, and I do not have it here at home."
>
> I asked him whether he could give it to me in later date. He replied: "Well. I don't know whether I can or cannot.

I have to look it up."

I asked "Or the name of the person or persons who did the autopsies." He replied: "I have to. . . you know [I] have not been thinking about this for three months, so since I have just walked in I cannot say whether I can give you or I cannot."

I asked: "Does the name Dr. Strughold ring a bell with you?"

He replied: "As I told you it might [sic]."

I asked whether he knows of a Dr. Jeffrey Johnson.

He asked me instead what the first one's name was, which I repeated, and [I] gave him a very brief information about him and added that he worked with Dr. Stapp and then repeated Dr. Jeffrey Johnson's name again.

He replied: "There were several Johnsons at that time."

Then I moved on by saying that after having read one of Dr. Bush's books and reflecting on what you had told me about the seventh sense and ESP and then the Navy's tests and approach on Remote Viewing (RV). Bush seems to have a negative view on this approach and yet you have highly praised him in your book. I also added "He definitely knew about the whole thing and yet seems to brush the whole thing aside, who would that be?" He replied: "Well, you know, if the person's view of what is important differs with people. Vannevar Bush had a great many important things [he was] trying to pursue; that and anything like this was not of great importance. You think it is important, other people don't."

I said: "It definitely was important to you at one time, was it not, Doctor?" He answered: "Who, me? Oh, for two or three days, yes. But I had work to do. I had to do other things."

"What did the classification to do with MAJIC or MAJESTIC grade of classification [sic]?" He asked me after a long silence to repeat, which I did.

Then he replied: "Well, you know those names came to different compartments, and just using a word like those might mean this for one period of time and might be something different in another period of time."

"But at that particular time on the UFO subject, was it the designated classification?" He replied: "I do not recall what the code was, how long before the code changed, or what compartment it was."

"But the MAJESTIC TWELVE did exist, did it not?"

"I don't know."

Then I referred to Kadena and documents there with MAJESTIC TWELVE destined to be shredded in 1979.

He laughed very loudly and said: "You know, it is [a] ridiculous situation what the hell difference it makes whether it is shredded or not. After all, forty years have gone by and nobody has blown up the world."

"But, the bodies which were recovered, they are kept on, they must have been." He replied: "How do you know there were bodies? Maybe they walked away. You just assume too many things. Most of the things are wrong. (Then he again laughed.)"

"So, in other words, there were never any bodies involved?"

He answered: "I did not say that."

I then referred to what he had just said—that maybe they walked away.

He answered: "You jump to the hasty conclusion. Maybe some walked away; maybe some did not walk away. As I say, it is none of your business. Just to satisfy your curiosity, it is not going to do any damn good except making you happy. Is it not true? Are we to change all the plans and regulations just to make you happy? If you say that you are looking for the truth, you will never get it anyway, so forget it."

"But, why I could not get it, Doctor?"

He answered: "Why should you?"

"What is [it] about that particular truth that I should not get it?" He answered: "Why should we bother to spend time and money just to make you happy? Answer me that." I answered on the grounds of human respect. He said: "What respect?" I answered: "I surely have taken the time and paid the money to call you, to look up to you as a top scientist from whom I could learn something. Is there anything wrong in this?" He replied: "Right now I am tired. I want to go and take a shower and have something to eat. Call me later maybe." Then we said good-bye to each other.

ASSESSMENT: From the tone of his replies I could clearly sense that he felt cornered and was seeking for an excuse to escape my questions. I also sensed that he has done some homework about my research work and my curiosity in finding out about the facts, which clearly had not made him happy. Or, it [is] just maybe a false assumption on my part.

The conversations between Azadehdel and Walker certainly

seem to indicate that Walker participated in government UFO research.

As time went by, UFO enthusiasts continued to contact Walker—with embarrassing results. It got to the point where he began to poke fun at people trying to get him to talk.

In a letter dated April 5, 1994, Tobias D. Wabbel (of Germany) wrote to Walker about his interest in the search for extraterrestrial intelligence (SETI). Near the end of his letter, he asked Walker if he knew the date the truth was coming out about Roswell, was there a Majestic-12 committee in existence, and was President Clinton "in the know" about the Roswell crash.

Wabbel got the following response, dated April 29, 1994:

> Dear Mr. Wabbel:
> I am sorry that the person to whom you addressed your letter cannot answer you just now. He is not here. We do not know where he is.
> Every once in a while he announces that he is off to Ursula or Gambit or such a place, and then he disappears for a couple of months. His leavings are always at full moon.
> After a while he reappears with much baggage and announces he must hole up to transcribe or translate. Then he goes out west for a few weeks. Each time he comes back he looks five years younger. He will see your letter when he returns.

The Kit Green Investigation

Throughout 1989, there were discussions with Bill Moore about the developing Walker story. Moore offered to help as well as to find out for himself exactly what Walker's role might have been. "I find myself essentially in agreement with what you have to say," Moore wrote Grant Cameron in September of 1989. "I do not know what is going on with Walker either, but I am convinced something is. That is why I offered to help."

This effort to help by Moore led to one of the most dramatic and high level conversations on UFOs ever to become public.

"My source is also very interested in this matter and will do anything that he can to help," Moore stated. "Not only do I trust him implicitly, but I feel certain that he can get some straight answers out of Dr. Walker as soon as he knows just what questions to ask."

"My source, whom I shall refer to as B.J. for the sake of convenience, is equally impressed with Dr. Walker's background—indeed so much so that he agrees the man is (or has been) in all the right places to have been involved with such a thing. B.J. is also very good at approaching high-level people about such things and has been of considerable help to us in the past on similar matters."

The man that Moore was referring to turned out to be Dr. Christopher C. "Kit" Green, given the Aviary name Blue Jay or B.J. by Moore and Shandera. Green had headed up the "weird desk" at the CIA during his years there as Senior Division Analyst with the Office of Scientific and Weapons Intelligence (1969-1983). According to Moore, Dr. Green was, "a person close to the President of the United States, capable of checking on information to determine its reliability."

Years later, Green himself would confirm his presidential UFO connection when he spoke to Pulitzer-prize nominated reporter, Gus Russo. Green told Russo, "I have spoken to three former presidents and the subject always comes up, not as a briefing, but they also want to know the truth. But apparently they aren't cleared for it."[40]

Green was a man who knew something about the "core" UFO story that the government was trying to keep secret. He stated that in 1986 he, physicist Hal Puthoff, and researcher Jacques Vallee had distilled down "what they knew about the subject into the Core Story."

Green detailed some of what he knew and believed in an interview with Mark Pilkington and John Lundberg. "Simply put," Green told Pilkington, "the Core Story is this: The ETs came here, maybe once, maybe a few times. Either through accident or by design, the U.S. government acquired one of their craft. The only problem was that the physics that powered the craft were so advanced that for decades we humans have struggled to understand it or replicate it."[41]

In early 1990, after many months, the meeting between Green and Walker finally took place in Walker's Penn State office. During the first part of the meeting, the two talked about the old days. In particular, they discussed the CIA's role in the Glomar Explorer project—this was a secret program to recover a sunken Russian nuclear submarine in the Pacific. Both men had been involved with it. This conversation went well for quite a few minutes.

Then Green brought up the subject of UFOs. With that, the atmosphere changed. Walker suddenly became upset and agitated. He began to speak loudly, directing his voice to a pile of books in the corner of the office. He appeared to be giving Green an indirect signal that the room was bugged. In a loud voice he challenged Green that the President of the United States had not told him he had to talk to Green. Green was shocked at the sudden turn of events. Essentially, he ended up being thrown out of the office.

Moore later told Cameron that he now thought he knew what Walker's role had been related to UFOs, and it was not quite what Cameron was claiming. He promised "possibly" to tell him in the future, but never did.

The Death of Eric Walker

Unfortunately for the UFO community, Dr. Eric Walker died of a heart ailment on February 17, 1995.

For eight years, Walker had dodged questions about his participation in UFO meetings at Wright-Patterson Air Force Base in the early 1950s. During the early part of this investigation, however, when he was less defensive and more forthcoming, he "let the cat out of the bag."

This was especially so during his August 30, 1987 telephone

interview with William Steinman. Walker admitted attending meetings at Wright-Patterson involving retrieved flying saucers and their occupants. When Steinman asked for details, Walker gave another lead when he replied, "I am sure that I have notes concerning those meetings. . . . I would have to dig them out and read them over in order to jog my memory."

Shortly after Walker died, Crain wrote about him in the *MUFON UFO Journal*:

> Several years ago, a series of articles about Walker appeared in *State College: The Magazine*. I met with the author of the series, and filled him in on Dr. Walker's involvement in UFO research. During one of the last interviews with Walker, he asked if they could have a follow-up discussion about UFOs. Walker initially agreed, but on the day before the interview, declined, stating that he had changed his mind.
>
> At various times over the past few years I have written Walker, asking at this point in time, would he be willing to talk about his involvement in government UFO research. Walker never answered any of my letters after our book was published. It's hard to say how many people called or wrote Walker upon publication of our report.

In light of the fact we made some serious allegations about Dr. Walker's UFO involvement as a government employee, (not only in our book, but on University Public TV and a local CBS affiliate), one would think that a man of his reputation, would want to set the record straight, and quench any rumors about what was true or not true. To my knowledge, Walker had no public comment about what we reported.[42]

What's left now are the alleged notebooks, which could be a key piece of evidence to support a government cover-up. But where are they? It would be reasonable to assume that they either ended up in his wife's possession, were passed on to the children, or were handed over to the Penn State University archives.

Crain made various trips to the archives up to October 20, 1995. He sifted through box after box of private material. In

36B

T. Scott Crain, Jr.
P.O. Box 11
Port Matilda, PA 16870

October 31, 1995

Brian K. Walker
949 Oak Ridge Avenue
State College, PA 16801

Dear Dr. Brian Walker:

I'm writing you in reference to your late father, Dr. Eric Walker. He was a great man, who made many outstanding contributions not only in science and engineering, but also as a leader and innovator at Penn State University.

I have a strong interest in some of Dr. Walker's early contributions while working for the government (specifically, in the early 1950s, while working for the military Research and Development Board.) Dr Walker had indicated to a friend of mine (William Steinman), he had in his possession his notes/diaries of meetings he attended as Executive Secretary of the R & D Board, held at Wright-Patterson Air Force Base. I have made several visits to the Penn State Archives hoping to review those notes that Dr. Walker said he had, but found nothing. I did find his meeting notes while he served as a member of the Institute of Defense Analysis, but none from the R & D Board. Is it possible some of his records are still at home or went to another location? If some papers are still at home, would it be possible to review these records?

On the evening of December 9, 1965, an unusual object, possibly debris from a satellite, crashed in a wooded area near Kecksburg, Pennsylvania. In a conversation with Dr. Armen Victorian, Dr. Walker said he was called out that night and went to Kecksburg to examine the clean-up operation. Do you recall your father ever discussing what happened that night, or have any information regarding the incident?

I realize these are unusual questions, but your father appears to have had some interest in unusual phenomena. A prompt reply would be appreciated, even if you can't help me with these questions.

Thank you for your time,

T. Scott Crain, Jr.

36B

Letter from T. Scott Crain to Brian Walker.

one box, labeled "Report of Activities 1947-49" he expected to find notes regarding Walker's time at the R&D Board. He uncovered not a single document, diary, or notebook on the R&D Board or UFOs. However, Walker was also a member of the Institute for Defense Analyses (see next chapter), in which Crain found detailed notes of various meetings in thick notebooks.

But nothing related to UFOs. It appears that Walker did not

turn over any such material to the Penn State Archives.

Since Dr. Walker's wife was getting on in years, Crain contacted Dr. Walker's son, Brian Walker. Crain wanted to know if he had files, especially those relating to "unusual phenomena," and whether he could examine them. The younger Walker replied that "we have received several request similar to yours," and that after reviewing "approximately 10,000 pages of unofficial papers," he "found no mention of these issues."

Three years later, in 1998, noted UFO researcher and author Palmiro Campagna said that he had contacted Brian Walker by phone. In his January 1, 2004, email to Crain, he wrote:

> Yes, I contacted Walker in 1998. I tracked him down through the University but when I called the number I had, his wife answered and told me they were recently separated/divorced., I forget exactly which. In any event she gave me his number. I spoke with him and followed up with a letter. He then wrote back to me. He said that prior to his father's death, he had an opportunity to review his father's files. He says he definitely saw a large folder devoted entirely to one or more UFO events. He says the file was never found after his father's death. He said he recalls it contained drawings but not actual photos of alien craft. (he had initially said photos so I quizzed him on that specifically in my letter.) He remembers some official government documents in the files but not their contents. He then indicated there were two events in particular, one in Pennsylvania and one in Southwestern US. He did not recall the names of any associates and said Dr. Sarbacher was never mentioned by his father. (I had asked him about Sarbacher and whether his dad knew him.)

In 1995, when Crain had asked Brian Walker about his father's UFO file, Walker denied having anything relevant. Yet, according to Campagna, in this 1998 telephone interview, Brian Walker stated that prior to his father's death he did indeed see a large folder devoted to several UFO events. The file, however, has been missing since Eric Walker's death.

Next, we looked into the background of the Institute for Defense Analyses (IDA). Dr. Walker had become a Trustee of

BRIAN K. WALKER, M.D.
949 OAK RIDGE AVENUE
STATE COLLEGE, PENNSYLVANIA 16801
TELEPHONE (814) 234-7741

11/15/95

Dear Mr. Crain,

I have reviewed your letter dated 10/31/95. We have received several requests similar to yours.

Unfortunately, we have not located any material relevant to these issues. All of my father's official papers were given to Penn State University.

I have reviewed approximately 10,000 pages of unofficial papers and found no mention of these issues.

My father never mentioned anything to me about any event in December, 1965.

Sincerely,

Brian K. Walker

Letter from Brian Walker to Scott Crain.

the IDA in 1958, Chairman of the Board of the IDA in 1981, and Chairman Emeritus upon his retirement in 1986.

The IDA is a kind of think tank that brings together experts in science, economics, technology, and the military—as well as other fields—to work for the government. Most of the research done by the Institute is initiated by the Defense Department on a contractual basis. The Institute's findings are for the most part a secret. Somehow, this seemed like the ideal job for Dr. Walker.

Chapter 3:
The Institute for Defense Analyses (IDA)

The Institute for Defense Analyses constitutes graphic evidence of how faceless men with a general disdain for Congress and without publicly scrutinized opinion have moved into the policy-making apparatus of government.
– Paul Dickson

In brief, it can be said of IDA that it is an ingeniously devised mechanism for getting talented and much sought after people to work on problems of importance to their government.
– *Science,* May 17, 1968

Defense industry contractors and government sponsors alike know that they can entrust IDA with sensitive or proprietary data in full confidence that the privacy of the data will be preserved
– IDA in *Profile,* an IDA brochure

In the hierarchy of military [think] tanks," wrote Paul Dickson in his classic book on think tanks, "none ranks higher than the Institute for Defense Analyses (IDA)."[43] The IDA, according to Bruce Smith in his book on the RAND Corporation, pays the highest salaries of any of the hundreds of think tanks, and therefore attracts the best consultants.

The Institute for Defense Analyses has basically one customer for which, by 1990, over 90% of its $60 million annual consulting was done—the Pentagon. It is for this reason, as well as the level of security involved, that the IDA has become known as "the think tank to the highest echelons at the Pentagon."[44]

What goes on inside this building with no sign outside is very secret. Seventy-five percent of IDA work is Top Secret and the other twenty-five percent is "For Official Eyes Only." Some of the work done at the IDA is so secret that not even IDA trustees are cleared to see it.[45] The IDA is not an organization affected by the Freedom of Information Act (FOIA), nor does it seem to be affected even by Congressional requests for information.

To give an idea of the status and independence of the IDA, consider this story. Back in 1964, shortly after the Gulf of Tonkin incident, the IDA produced a study on it. When the U.S. Senate Committee on Foreign Relations requested the report, the IDA simply refused. Committee Chairman Fullbright then led the resulting charge to get a copy. In short, he didn't get it.[46]

If someone wanted a confidential, objective analysis of the UFO problem, certainly the IDA would seem to be the ideal place to get it done.

The IDA was established in 1956, when Charles E. Wilson, then Secretary of Defense, approached Dr. James R. Killian, then President of MIT and Chairman of the President's Board of Consultants on Foreign Intelligence Activities, to use MIT as a source of civilians to assist the Joint Chiefs Weapons Systems Evaluation Group (WSEG). Dr. Killian rejected the idea, but agreed to help if other universities assisted as "this would help recruit talent."[47]

On April 5, 1956, five of the major military research and development universities—Massachusetts Institute of Technology, California Institute of Technology, the Case Institute of Technology, Stanford University, and Tulane University—formed a non-profit corporation, with Killian as Chairman of the Board. Retired Air Force General James McCormick, Jr., served as the first President of the corporation.

Shortly thereafter, seven more universities—University of California, University of Chicago, Columbia University, University of Illinois, University of Michigan, Princeton University, and Pennsylvania State University—joined, bringing "the number of participating universities to twelve."

Each university was represented either by its President or

by another high official of the university. Dr. Eric Walker—who represented Penn State on the aforementioned corporation's Board of Trustees—joined in 1958 and never left. In 1981, Dr. Walker was elected Chairman of the Board of the IDA, where he remained until 1986, when he became Chairman Emeritus.

According to the IDA's own literature, "The initial purpose in creating [the] IDA was to increase interaction between scientists and engineers in the universities and a small group of analysts in the Office of the Joint Chiefs of Staff known as the Weapons Systems Evaluation Group (WSEG)."[48]

Not only is everything produced at the IDA Top Secret, but, according to Dickson, there is an air of military security surrounding the place. "Inside," he wrote, "two uniformed guards stand at an elevator to make sure that all visitors have an escort. Even the lady who brings around the coffee wagon rates an armed guard."

The IDA has almost no contact with the outside/public world. It releases to the public as little as it can about the work it does. A spokesman for the IDA told Dickson that "the IDA 1969 report was only half as thick as the previous edition because "we've determined that we're giving out too much unclassified information, which could lead to conclusions about the classified work we're doing."[49]

At the IDA, especially during the Walker years, there was a pressured existence. Located in Washington, D.C., it was near the seat of power. By contrast, at the RAND Corporation thousands of miles away in California, there always existed a relaxed, short-sleeve attitude.

The IDA started out with offices on Connecticut Avenue, with over one hundred members of its staff "inside" the Pentagon itself. The organization then moved to a new, ten-story building "across the parking lot from the Pentagon." It became known as "the paper-clip building," and those who wrote of the IDA's presence so close to the Pentagon, said that its location was no accident. (The IDA has since moved to Alexandria, Virginia, just outside of Washington, D.C.)

When Stanton Friedman and William Steinman first contacted Dr. Walker about his alleged role in the UFO cover-up, they had no idea they were talking to the Chairman of the Board of the most powerful and secretive think tank in the country. This is because, for one thing, Dr. Walker's IDA membership did not appear in the *Who's Who in America* at that time (1983).

Walker, therefore, sat overlooking this most secretive place and its 750 professionals, support people, and consultants. The names of those associated with the IDA might best be described as the "Who's Who of What's What."

Consultants of IDA studies that have been published or leaked include Gordon Gray and Henry Kissinger. Both of these men worked on the 1968 study entitled "The President and the Management of National Security," and both have been rumored to be members of MJ-12. Another rumored MJ-12 member, Dr. Edward Teller, (inventor of the H-bomb) helped IDA with a Top Secret Project called "Strat-X" in 1967, which examined new missile-delivery systems.

Men who have sat on the Board of Trustees with Dr. Walker include some of the most influential and powerful people ever to walk the corridors of power in Washington. Included are:

Richard M. Bissel, who headed up the V-2 and SR-71 programs and was deputy director of the CIA.

Andrew Goodpaster, who was a Staff Secretary and Defense Liaison Officer in the White House under President Eisenhower and Assistant to the Chairman of the Joint Chiefs of Staff under President Johnson.

Zbigniew Brzezinski, who was an Assistant for National Security Affairs to President Carter.

Maxwell Taylor, who was President Kennedy's Chief Military Advisor and was elevated to Chairman of the Joint Chiefs of Staff.

Dr. Herbert York, who was Chief Scientist for the Defense Advanced Research Projects Agency (DARPA), Director of DARPA, Director of the Defense Research and Engineering Office, and a member and Vice Chairman of the President's Science Advisory Committee.

Louis V. Tordella, who was Deputy Director of the National Security Agency (NSA) for thirteen years and was described by James Bamford in his book *The Puzzle Palace* as "the golden boy of the Puzzle Palace" and about whom it was said: "never before or since has anyone person held so much power for so long a time within the American Intelligence Community." And, "if the NSA was the darkest part of the government, Tordella was the darkest part of the NSA."[50]

Howard P. Robertson, who chaired the 1953 CIA-sponsored panel to examine UFO reports, who was Director of the Weapons Systems Evaluation Group, (WSEG) and who served as a "classified employee" for the CIA.

Many non-profit corporations have lawyers who sit as trustees to help with legal advice. The IDA is no exception. In keeping with the quality of its other trustees, the IDA does not have just any lawyer. The IDA has had lawyers like Marx Leva, who was Special Assistant and General Counsel to the Secretary of Defense from 1947-49 and Assistant Secretary of Defense for Legal Matters from 1949-51. Leva was editor of the *Harvard Law Journal* in 1939, and overseer of the Journal from 1950-55.

Although the IDA started out as a support group for WSEG, according to Bruce Smith in his RAND book, within six years of its beginnings, "the IDA was the principal advisory organization serving the Office of the Secretary of Defense as a whole."[51]

Most of the contracts to the IDA are from the Director of Research and Engineering, the Defense Advanced Research Projects Agency (see Chapter 4), the Director of Defense Test and Evaluation, and the Joint Chiefs of Staff.

The IDA has played a major part in weapons on the leading edge of technology. These include the most secretive items covered by the Pentagon's black budget. The contributions to weapons of the past that IDA admits to having worked on include "significant roles in a broad spectrum of developments central to U.S. national security today: over-the-horizon radar, ballistic missiles of defense, multiple independently targetable re-entry vehicles (MIRVs), Trident-type submarines, forward looking infrared systems, the advanced Sidewinder AIM-9L missile, concepts of electronic sensing and battle management and many others."[52]

Chapter 4

Defense Advanced Research Projects Agency

The Advanced Research Projects Agency (ARPA), established in 1958 as an operating agency under the Director of Defense Research and Engineering, was redesignated as the Defense Advanced Research Projects Agency (DARPA) on March 23, 1972 and made a separate agency of the Department of Defense under the direction, authority, and control of the Secretary of Defense.

– United States Government Manual 1975/1976, U.S. Government Printing Office (revised May I, 1975)

DARPA is entrusted with the central research function of DOD [Department of Defense]. Its function resembles that of a corporate research division in private industry, which is responsive to the highest levels of corporate authority. Its programs focus on proof-of-concept demonstrations of revolutionary approaches for improved strategic, conventional, rapid deployment, and sea-power forces, and on the scientific investigation into advanced basic technologies of the future.

– *Defense Advanced Research Projects Agency*, a DARPA brochure.

From 1956 until his death in late 1962, Wilbert Smith and his inner circle worked on experiments designed to crack the secret of anti-gravity propulsion. In the United States, many government efforts were being made along the same lines of research. Major Donald Keyhoe, USMC, wrote in his book *Aliens From Space* that:

> When AF [i.e. Air Force] researchers fully realized the astounding possibilities, headquarters persuaded scientists, aerospace companies and technical laboratories to set up anti-gravity projects, many of them under secret contracts. Every year, the number of projects increased. In 1965, forty-six unclassified G-projects were confirmed to me by the Scientific Information Exchange of the Smithsonian Institution. Of the forty-six, thirty-three were AF-controlled. The Navy had three; Army, one; the Atomic Energy Commission, one; NASA, two, and the National Science Foundation, six. In addition, there were at least

twenty-five secret contracts that could not be listed.

At the start, some researchers warned the AF not to expect an early breakthrough—getting the answers might lake years. To reduce the odds, the AF increased its attempts to capture UFOs.[53]

UFO investigators Lawrence Fawcett and Barry Greenwood had heard of these and other rumored anti-gravity programs. They filed a Freedom of Information Act Request with the U.S. Army Research and Development Group for documents related to one rumored project known as Project Bluebolt. Colonel Benedict Freund, Group Commander, responded to the FOIA request on March 18, 1975, (in part) as follows:

> It is our consensus here that if the Dept. of Defense is supporting such research it is funded by ARPA (Advanced Research Projects Agency). ARPA's mission is to support those research efforts that are of high risk and appear beyond the purview of any one service.[54]

On the two-hour television special *UFO Cover-Up? Live!*, shown on October 14, 1988, just three weeks before the Presidential election, researchers William Moore and Jaime Shandera related their experiences with ten government informants, all claiming to have government UFO connections. Over a number of years, these ten described to Moore and Shandera how the government was able to cover up the UFO situation.

During the program, Moore and Shandera produced a flow chart based on what they said they were told.

Most of the groups on the chart were concerned with administration or intelligence. Of the more than one dozen organizations listed, only one Research and Development organization was mentioned, that group being DARPA.

The Department of Defense Directive 5105.41 created DARPA in February 1958. According to a DARPA brochure, "Its creation was, in part, a reaction to the [Soviet] launching of Sputnik." The Sputnik satellite was the first artificial Earth satellite, and its appearance resulted in a "national emergency"

Shandera (l) and Moore on the set of *UFO Cover-up? Live!*, October 1988.

in U.S. military and government circles, because it meant that the Soviets, despite their backward economy, might possibly win the military technology race that had been going on since World War Two.

The Americans had been caught off guard before. In 1941, the Japanese surprise attack on Pearl Harbor caused great physical and psychological damage. In 1949, the Soviets detonated their first atomic bomb, which had not been expected for many years to come. The Air Force began to sponsor Special Studies Projects at MIT to develop a defense against the new Soviet threat.

By 1958, Washington had endured enough technological surprises, and DARPA resulted. "Technology is characterized by rapid change," wrote Dr. John S. Foster, "with new opportunities arising from widely expanding knowledge. In this situation, it is important to invest part of our R&D resources to the leading edge of technology, to explore areas of high risk with a potentially high payoff. We find that a small, highly capable, flexible and independent organization is needed to

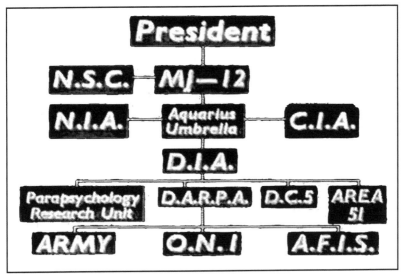

MJ-12 flowchart, according to Moore and Shandera.

conduct this type of activity, and we look to DARPA to fulfill this requirement, its function is to act as a leader and catalyst, demonstrating military potential as fast as possible."[55]

According to the brochure, however, "DARPA's creation was also, in part, a realization of the long-recognized need for a high-level organization within [the Defense Department] . . . to formulate and execute research and development" projects that "expand the frontiers of technology."

Flying saucers exhibit a remarkable technology, which, if understood, would surely yield a huge military benefit. Stephen Possony, a military strategist, analyzed UFO sightings for the USAF in 1951 and 1952. He also appeared on the CIA Robertson Panel on UFOs in 1953.

"We must be certain," wrote Possony,

> . . . that we have missed no decisive bits in the Technological War, that we have abandoned no leads [that] . . . the enemy could exploit for a decisive advantage over us. For every weapons system he has, we must have a counter, either through defending against the weapon or through riposte against him if he uses it. More importantly, we must keep a sufficiently technological base to allow us to

generate the counter systems to any new weapons he constructs or may suddenly invent."[56]

"Technological surprise in particular can bring about near disasters," wrote Possony, "not the least of which is brought about by psychological effects on the population."[57]

It should therefore come as no surprise that in a Secret CIA memorandum about UFOs, dated June 14, 1954, a request was made for "all intelligence measures required to identify, to assess and to report the use by any foreign power or nation of non-conventional types of air vehicles, such as, or similar to, the 'saucer-like' planes presently under development by Anglo/British/Canadian efforts."[58]

More definitively speaking, the CIA worried about a flying saucer-related technological surprise from the Soviets. In a September 24, 1952 memo to the Director of the CIA, from H. Marshall Chadwell, Assistant Director for Scientific Intelligence, Chadwell outlined the Intelligence requirements associated with flying saucers:

> 1. The present level of Soviet knowledge regarding these phenomena.
> 2. Possible Soviet intentions and capabilities to utilize these phenomena to the detriment of the United States security interest.
> 3. The reasons for silence in the Soviet press regarding flying saucers.[59]

The fear over the "silence of the Soviet press" was legitimate, as the Americans had done a similar thing a decade previously in World War Two; the Americans had pulled all references on atomic research from *The Physical Review* and other journals where such things were discussed. One high-ranking physicist in Russia had interpreted this as a clear sign. He went to Stalin and told him "the Americans are building a bomb."

Other agencies can rule out flying saucers as fantasy, but DARPA must consider: "What if the UFOs are real, and if so, will the Soviets be able to crack the mystery first?" The strategic and psychological implications would be staggering.

DARPA is, by its role, forced to consider the possibilities. If the Soviets recovered a crashed UFO and were able to duplicate its technology, would they use it as a weapon?

Even Wilbert Smith, in a 1951 discussion with Major Keyhoe, identified the Russian flying saucer threat, and Smith was not known for strident Cold War rhetoric:

> "When we do get the answers," Smith said soberly, "it will be a tremendous thing—and we better get them before the Russians do. Magnetically powered discs would be terrible weapons. Their range would be unlimited, and their speeds would be beyond anything we've even dared hope for. They'd make perfect guided missiles, and they could easily carry A-bomb warheads—perhaps even the H-bomb, when we get it.[60]

A primary concern for DARPA is "lead times," which have been a key to military strategy ever since Vannevar Bush first brought scientists and military men together. In fact, the concept of lead times can explain much of the importance of the problem, the extreme security clearances surrounding UFOs, and the (rumored) massive efforts by both sides to solve the mystery.

Stephen Possony, the technological military strategist, outlined the problem:

> The United States has devoted a great deal of effort to reducing the time required to translate a scientific theory, discovery, or invention into a practical weapons system, In spite of much study, we have not reduced the time interval to less than five years. To develop and produce a weapon in even this fairly long time costs billions of dollars.
>
> The ultimate goal is to gain a strategic advantage by acquiring a major new family of weapons while concealing from the enemy the fact that it is being developed. The appearance of a brand new weapon often is termed a breakthrough. When a nation makes a breakthrough of this type, as we did with the atomic bomb, the British with radar, the Soviets in space, an entirely new arena for military operations is opened up. If a breakthrough leads to a military advantage that the enemy cannot counter in time, such as a domination of air, space, or deep water, the

breakthrough may be decisive.[61]

Because of the high percentage of "unknowns" in the studies, as well as compelling evidence that the military has possessed "some rather peculiar hardware" since the late 1940s, we have come to suspect that American scientists would have used every resource at their disposal to unravel the saucer technology because of the lead-time problem.

As outlined by Possony, a lead-time in a weapons system of only a few years could be a crucial element in a war. With flying saucers in their possession, scientists would have an opportunity to look at "technology of the future." Flying saucer technology may be a hundred, a thousand, or even a million years more advanced than what we have today. To have this knowledge and gain such a lead over the enemy would be worth almost any investment. For an enemy trying to catch up, the cost and economic strain would be great.

Disregarding UFOs, as U.S. authorities have claimed to have done, would be utter foolishness and the gravest threat to national security.

Possony also remarked that in any technological race, to secure and protect gains, competitors must use various tactics. A key one is "to misinform and disinform the opponent." Scientific papers are purposely released that are false or use false formulas, and scientific documents are leaked that are half true and half false.[*] "Disinformation," stated Possony, "makes the enemy doubt the accuracy of his findings."

There has been speculation among some researchers that the MJ-12 document received in the mail by Jaime Shandera from an anonymous source was really a disinformation effort on the part of the Defense Department to deceive foreign powers into thinking that the U.S. had access to a technology inaccessible to them.

In an article from 1986 on U.S. disinformation efforts, David

---

[*] Half-true and half-false documents are used because it is nearly impossible to determine which part is true and which is false. If the documents were totally false or totally true, the opponent would be able, with analysis, "to separate the wheat from the chaff."

M. North wrote:

> The CIA is a chief coordinator for the release through various channels of deliberately false, incomplete, and misleading information. The disinformation effort covers 15-20 programs, six or seven of which are Defense Department projects.
>
> Programs likely to be covered by the Defense Department's disinformation policy include the Air Force's special mission aircraft flying in Nevada. . . .[62*]

Victor Marchetti, the former Executive Assistant to the Deputy Director of the CIA and co-author of *The CIA and the Cult of Intelligence*, expressed an interesting viewpoint on UFOs. In his 1979 article, "How the CIA Views the UFO Phenomenon," Marchetti wrote:

> My theory is that we have, indeed, been contacted—perhaps even visited—by extraterrestrial beings, and that the U.S. Government, in collusion with the other national powers of the Earth, is determined to keep this information from the general public.[63]

Marchetti went on to say that the overarching reason for such secrecy was "to keep the public uninformed, misinformed, and, therefore, malleable." The uninformed public—and sometimes the U.S. Congress—is often left in the dark on black budget weapons projects funded by the Department of Defense. The stealth aircraft were a good example. For years, the U.S. Government denied that these super-secret aircraft even existed. But the project had been researched and tested by a major think tank and then offered to the military for practical military applications.

According to an article by William J. Cook in *U.S. News and World Report*, DARPA alone moved forward to prove the technology of the Stealth aircraft. William J. Perry, who supervised DARPA during the Carter administration, said that after a prototype was successfully flown, the Air Force initiated

---

[Note from the authors: More details about unusual aircraft test-flown at Nellis Air Force Base in Nevada are discussed in Chapter 8.]

its own program that led to the development of the F-117A Stealth Fighter and B-2 Stealth Bomber.[64]

A similar strategy could have been implemented in the case of a recovered alien UFO. The hardware could have been delivered to a facility where an organization like DARPA could take it apart and develop a prototype American craft using the duplicated alien technology.

The idea is not as farfetched as it sounds. UFO researcher Tony Gonsalves suggested an interesting UFO/B-2 link. According to Gonsalves:

> In the late '0s, aviation pioneer Jack Northrop—the founder of the company responsible for the B-2—designed a flying-wing bomber, the YB-49, which in many ways closely resembles the B-2. The YB-49 was a radical departure in aircraft design that closely followed a radical event, the Roswell UFO recovery. That aircraft development and the Roswell crash were also close together geographically.[65]

The YB-49 (perhaps originally designated XB-49) was an experimental design for the ill-fated B-49 flying-wing bomber that had been developed to the point that it could be allocated for service test and evaluation. It had not originally been very successful; whereas the Air Force built around two thousand B-47s, it built only about thirteen YB49s.

Curiously, the Air Force ordered all the YB-49 planes destroyed in 1952. Gonsalves believed he could explain the Air Force's unusual behavior in this regard. He pointed out that the YB-49 and the B-2 Stealth bomber are both flying wings with identical wingspans. Suppose, he continued, that the YB-49 was a test vehicle which was produced as a result of the UFO technology recovered at Roswell. Indeed, during the life span of the YB-49 (1948-52) there a number of boomerang-shaped UFOs reported along the West Coast. Gonsalves speculated:

> . . . that we acquired the "gross" UFO technology back then, but lacked the computer technology to literally fly the system. Our computers at the time were far too big to be fit

into a plane. Back then, the Air Force probably had to fly their plane by the seat of their pants, with no computers. Thus, they found the YB-49 to be not just unusable, but unsafe. Might that justify its complete destruction?

But by the 1970s, our technology had caught up with the UFO technology. Computer technology had not only become very sophisticated, but could be compacted into small enough sizes to be placed inside planes. This, I hypothesized, caused the Air Force to reactivate the flying wing, but this time with the benefit of refined computer technology.

Thus, the UFO/B-2 was born—probably in the mid-'70s.[66]

On October 9, 1957, less than a week after Sputnik, Neil McElroy was sworn in as Secretary of Defense. To get America "back on track" and "in the game," the U.S. Government formed the Office of Defense Research and Engineering and the Advanced Research Projects Agency (ARPA).* Among the three men called in by McElroy to consult on the future of military research and development was Dr. James Killian, then Chairman of the Board of the IDA and Chairman of the President's Science Advisory Committee.

The creation of DARPA was announced in President Dwight D. Eisenhower's January 9, 1958 State of the Union address, and it was up and moving by March 1958. McElroy chose Roy W. Johnson, then Vice President of General Electric Company, as the first Director. John Clark, commander of the Navy's Missile Test Range at Point Mugu, California, was appointed Deputy Director.

DARPA's share of the military R&D future would include "advanced research projects including all of those involving satellites, space flight, and missile defense."[67]

Killian recommended Dr. Herbert York as the first Chief Scientist at DARPA. York also headed the newly created DARPA division within the IDA itself. In 1958, the new organization had only a small skeleton staff, but even in 2011

---

* Later redesignated as DARPA

there were only 240 employees—with a budget of $3.2 billion.

In the creation of ARPA, according to Dr. York, the IDA provided a portion of the engineers and technicians who worked for the small staff of administrators and directors. It is for this reason that IDA became known as the "brain-trust" of ARPA. The IDA, acting as the hiring hall, approached various aerospace, chemical, and electrical companies; it gleaned the U.S. government as well as non-profit institutions for people. IDA and ARPA officials "negotiated with a number of corporations, all doing business with the Pentagon." Each was asked to nominate "rising members" to come to work for ARPA. The IDA paid the salaries because of the obvious conflicts of interest.

Two years later, due to Congressional investigations, ARPA changed the system to one of study contracts, which would have been more consistent not only with the law but also with the way IDA had been structured to run.

Four years after ARPA got off the ground, Dr. York was instrumental in initiating a "Top-Secret study and work group" for ARPA. This group of the brightest up-and-coming scientists evolved into what the *New York Times* later called "the cream of the scholarly community in technical fields." The group was originally called "Project Sunrise," but the name finally adopted was "the Jason Group."

Chapter 5
Jason

Jason had extremely high levels of clearance to government information. Top-Secret is a low level of clearance.
– Jason Member and Nobel Laureate Donald Glaser, as quoted by Dr. Charles Schwartz.

The year was 1969, and a person we will call "Colonel Reme" was working just off the Princeton campus. There he was in charge of security for a document vault. One day, a document dealing with UFOs, marked "Secret," was processed by Colonel Reme. The document stated that one of the priorities was "not to shoot at them." Colonel Reme suddenly developed an interest in the subject of UFOs.

One evening, Dr. Freeman Dyson—then head of the Princeton Institute for Advanced Study—was scheduled to speak on the Princeton campus. The subject of his lecture was "extraterrestrial life and the SETI program." Colonel Reme, a new convert to the subject, went over to hear what Dr. Dyson would say.

To Colonel Reme's amazement, the subject of UFOs did not come up even once during the whole lecture. There were no references—either pro or con—to UFOs. When the lecture was over, Colonel Reme approached Dr. Dyson to find out about the omission. In a lecture on extraterrestrial life, Colonel Reme asked, why had you omitted UFOs?

Dyson was immediately interested. He stepped forward and

said, "Why, have you seen one?"

"No," Colonel Reme replied.

Dyson's interest vanished instantly, and he quickly stepped back. "I don't deal in the occult," he stated. Colonel Reme left the lecture convinced, by this short encounter and Dyson's strange reaction, that Dyson knew more than he was admitting.

Dr. Dyson was a member of an elite group of scientists known as *Jason*. "The scientists think about the unthinkable behind locked and guarded doors," wrote *New York Times* reporter Tom Buckley. "They are in rooms that are swept electronically for bugs every day. They wear special identity cards, use scrambled telephones and secure computers, and keep their documents in armored, double-locked filing cabinets." The idea for Jason came from a six- to seven-week conference in 1958 known as "Project 137," initiated by economist Oskar Morganstein and physicists Dr. Eugene P. Wigner and Dr. John A. Wheeler.

Through the intervention of Dr. Herbert York and Dr. Charles Townes, some of the physicists who attended Project 137 were regrouped the next year to deal with critical defense problems. Thus, the Jason group was born, and it has flourished ever since.[*]

Dr. Herbert York invited thirty of the most up-and-coming academic physicists in the country to the first Top Secret Jason meeting. Twenty showed up. York and IDA Vice President Dr. Albert G. Hill arranged a program of briefings by senior Defense Department officials on critical problems.

All the participants arranged to dedicate their consulting time to ARPA and the Department of Defense in exchange for "uninhibited access to information and high officials."[68] ARPA provided funds for the Jason operation, and in 1965 was dispensing around $520,000 yearly to Jason.[69]

One of the most important functions of the Jason group was

---

[*] The name "Jason" comes from the legendary Greek seeker of the Golden Fleece.

to become, in effect, a second "Manhattan Project group." By the late 1950s, much of the high level scientific input was still coming from the original Manhattan Group: I. I. Rabi, Jerrold Zacharias, G. Kistiakowsky, E. D. Lawrence, Edward Teller, and other "old boys." With the problem of Sputnik and the apparent missile gap, Jason became an attempt to replace the World War Two era scientists with a well-picked, younger group. Thus the group's original name, *Sunrise*.

Many of the Jasons were nominated by the "old boys," and most were their protégés. Freeman Dyson was once J. R. Oppenheimer's demesne. John Wheeler was a close friend and protégé of Albert Einstein. Marvin L. Goldberger, the first team leader of Jason, completed his Ph.D. in Chicago under Enrico Fermi. At the University of Chicago, Goldberger had helped recruit Murray Gell-Mann and Harold Lewis, who later became Jason members. Another Jason member who had worked under Fermi was Richard Garwin, whom Fermi described as "the only true genius I have ever met."[70] Garwin, too, went on to become a leading member of the Jason consultant group.

Getting control of the consulting time of these brilliant young physicists was, it was hoped, the solution to a longstanding Defense Department problem. Since the best candidates for advice were comfortable academicians on American college campuses, buying all their consulting time was a way to use their knowledge and yet allow them to remain in the academic world.

During World War Two, many scientists had volunteered their time as "Dollar-a-Year" men, but by the late 1950s, there was no great attraction for skilled scientists from American campuses to accept low paying government jobs.

In his book *Making Weapons, Talking Peace*, Dr. Herbert York outlined some of the technical problems that were displayed before the Jasons at their first summer session (held in 1959). One of them—that of electromagnetically implemented anti-gravity propulsion—was one that had long interested Wilbert Smith and many other UFO researchers.

This point was discussed between researchers Grant Cameron and William Steinman. The subject of flying saucers had been rumored (more than once) to be the most highly classified secret in the United States—and Jason dealt with the most critical defense issues. Had Jason discussed UFOs? If it had, it would clearly show that the subject was of critical interest, rather than of passing disinterest—as long maintained by Defense Department spokesmen.

Dr. York was in San Diego, just down the road from William Steinman, so Steinman gave him a call. The two discussed Jason for a while, and then Steinman brought up the subject of UFOs—had the subject been discussed? Dr. York stated that it hadn't been discussed during the time he was involved with Jason (up to the late 1960s) but that he didn't rule out the possibility of there having been discussion of UFOs after he left. "They may have been discussed," he told Steinman. "I don't know."[71]

The Jason summer sessions were surrounded by extreme security. In one example, "the meeting was so secret that the school's janitor had to receive a high security clearance in order to clean the building."[72]

Those who worked for Jason were first-rate researchers. "Of the some 100 people who have seriously participated in Jason in the first 25 years," wrote Dr. York, "eight have been Nobel Laureates (these would include Donald A. Glaser 1960, Eugene P. Wigner 1963, Charles H. Townes 1964, Luis W. Alvarez 1968, Murray Gell-Mann 1969, Burton Richter 1976, Steven Weinberg 1979, Kenneth G. Wilson 1982), all of whom received that honor after they became associated with Jason."[73]

If Wilbert Smith's information from Canadian Embassy sources had been correct—that flying saucers were the most highly classified secret—then, logically, Jason would have been involved at some point. The reasons for this conclusion are as follows:

(1) The most highly classified secret would be a weapons secret, and the Jasons were weapons experts with high security clearances. As Stephen Possony, who did weapons analysis for the Pentagon in the 1950s, stated, "the more silly the (weapons) proposal—the higher the classification." The Jasons analyzed all major new weapons programs, including MIRVs in 1969. This Jason Group, chaired by Harvard Professor Dr. Paul Doty, worked directly with and for Dr. Henry Kissinger. The group was described as "high level consultants or officials," and "all held high security clearances."[74]

(2) Most of the Jasons were physicists, and a recovered flying saucer would be a physics problem. The presence of a saucer might defy the present understanding of "the laws of time and space." The Jasons would have a "need to know" and would be the best, most capable people available to re-write "the laws of the universe" in order to account for the saucer's presence and modus operandi.

(3) Flying saucers have always been a rumored "Black Budget" item, an item protected from Congressional criticism and leaks. Many of the Black Budget items are run out of DARPA, and Jason was created by and for DARPA. Richard Garwin, a long time Jason member and consultant, told Tim Weiner of the *Philadelphia Inquirer*, "I know quite a lot of black programs."

(4) Jason has a history of confidentiality as well as expert opinions, which would be two excellent requisites for working on the UFO problem.

(5) In a technological race between the Soviets and the United States, the subject of UFOs and their propulsion systems would be an item of national security. As an IDA spokesman once said, "You can figure that any matter of great concern to the Department of Defense will be the concern of the Jasons."[75]

Cooper Connects Jason to UFOs

The authors of this book could find no official documents linking a Jason meeting to a flying saucer recovery operation. But this does not mean that meetings did not occur or that Jason members were not involved in UFO retrievals. A man by the name of William Cooper made one connection to Jason in 1988. He said that he once worked with the Commander in Chief of the Pacific Fleet (CINCPAC) Staff OPSTAT (Operational Statistics) Reporting and Naval Intelligence Briefing Team. Cooper claimed that he had read of the Jason involvement in a 1972 document prepared for a briefing of CINCPAC. Cooper stated that, at the time, he was a petty officer on the briefing team.

Jason, according to Cooper, had received a commission from President Eisenhower to "sift through all the facts, evidence, technology, lies and deception and find the truth of the alien question."

According to Cooper, Jason is MJ-12. This MJ-12 group, he states, "is an advisory team of scientists whose only purpose is to evaluate information and make recommendations."

Unfortunately, Cooper never documented any of his statements, and even openly admitted releasing some false information about UFOs and MJ-12. Some of this supposedly was promulgated in order to test Bill Moore, and some to confuse the U.S. Government until someone could verify his information as being truthful. The authors of this report attempted to verify Cooper's claims but were unsuccessful.

In a January 23, 1989 interview with Grant Cameron, Cooper stated that the Jason information had been retrieved by hypnosis from the briefing papers he had seen in 1972. Although Cooper seemed to have recalled a number of UFO Project names (e.g., Maji, Sigma, Plato, Aquarius, Garnet, Pluto, Pounce, Redlight, Snowbird, Joshua, etc.) as well as details of the cover-up, Cooper, when Cameron asked him for the names of the Jason members involved, stated that none had been recalled but that some might in a future hypnosis session.

Cameron asked Cooper which universities the Jasons came from. Cooper mentioned Yale and a number of other universities. In connection with Yale, he mentioned "Skull and Bones," thereby implying, we suppose, the involvement of then-President George H. W. Bush. As Yale was not one of the homes of Jason members, Cameron had his doubts about what Cooper was saying.

Cameron also asked Cooper if "MAGIC" had anything to do with the cover-up or if any of the same people had been involved. He did this because Cooper was making all sorts of claims about MAJIC and the higher MAJI (Majority Agency for Joint Intelligence). Strangely, Cooper had no idea what Cameron was talking about, even though "MAGIC" was one of the most highly classified items during World War Two and was controlled mainly by the Navy. Since Cooper claimed to have a Navy background, this fact seemed strange if not a total giveaway.

As to Cooper's claim that Jason and MJ-12 were one and the same, it should be noted that Jason and MJ-12 are not even the same type of organization.

Jason is simply a group of top physicists who allot their consulting time to working on technical problems for the Department of Defense. They have no administrative or decision-making function. They simply provide their objective opinion on any problem that they are asked to work on.

MJ-12, as explained in the documents, was a distinguished group of scientists, military officials, and intelligence officials established by President Truman to control the recovery of UFOs. They appeared to have administrative and decision-making capabilities.

We discovered other inconsistencies in Cooper's statements about the Jasons. One example is illustrated in Linda Moulton Howe's book, *An Alien Harvest*, where we read:[76]

Howe: Was there anything in the papers about what the government is trying to do about it?
Cooper: It said the President, which President I don't recall, had commissioned a group to sift...

In Cooper's December 18, 1988 release (reproduced on p. 183 of Howe's book), neither was the President named nor the group identified.

However, shortly after Cameron, looking for a UFO-related connection, released his list of 32 Jason names, Cooper included Jason material in his January 10, 1989 "Final Release."

Cooper wrote in his "Final Release" (dated the day after that on which he had talked to Howe), "President Eisenhower commissioned a secret society known as the Jason Society (Jason Scholars) to sift...."

Since Linda Moulton Howe had been given a copy of the Jason list before Cooper released his January statement, we couldn't help but wonder if Cooper had amended his story after having seen Cameron's list. Although Linda Moulton Howe denied having told Cooper about Cameron's list, Cooper's sudden recollection, and later errors on the topic of Jason, led us to believe that Cooper had not seen any of this in a government document. Until evidence can be offered to the contrary, we must continue to regard Cooper's remarks connecting Jason to MJ-12 as very questionable and unsubstantiated.

Jason Member Investigates Saucer Crash

An unusual claim linking a saucer recovery to a Jason member made headlines in November 1949, when Sam Petok of the *Los Angeles Free Press* reported details behind a purported UFO crash in the mountains of Sierra Madre, Mexico. Petok got his facts from Alma Lawson, a Los Angeles businesswoman, who had gotten the story from a "sober and conservative" scientist friend, whose name she refused to divulge.

Analysis

The story of the Sierra Madre turtle-disk affair is of little value without knowing who the scientist was who allegedly visited the crash site. When William Steinman read the account in the May 1950 issue of *Fate* magazine, he followed up by contacting Alma Lawson (now deceased) and asked her if, after all these years, she would identify the scientist in question. In response, according to Steinman, she named Dr. Luis Walter Alvarez, a Professor of Physics at the University of California, Berkeley, and a Jason member. Alvarez worked on the Los Alamos atomic-bomb development project (1944-45) and was awarded the Nobel Prize in Physics in 1968.

It is also interesting to note that Alvarez served as a member of the Robertson Panel (1953), a CIA-sponsored group whose mission it was to determine public policy regarding flying saucers. The conclusion of the panel was for the Air Force to adopt, as a means of controlling public opinion on UFOs, a policy of "debunk, discredit, and conceal." Serving with Alvarez on the Robertson Panel was Dr. Lloyd V. Berkner, an expert in geophysics and a designated member of Majestic-12.

If Dr. Alvarez had been involved in a saucer recovery operation, would he talk about it? Steinman attempted to answer that question by contacting Alvarez by letter on May 3, 1984.

Although Alvarez did not respond, Steinman did not give up. In a letter to Grant Cameron, dated December 8, 1988, Steinman stated that he had confronted Dr. Alvarez in 1986 about his alleged involvement. In that letter, Steinman wrote:

> I contacted Dr. Alvarez in private, when he admitted that he did take part in the recovery of a [flying] saucer in Mexico. He would not go into detail concerning the events and who else was involved.
>
> I wrote him a formal letter, trying to get him to answer me in writing concerning his experience concerning the Mexican recovery. He would not answer.

Obviously, stories like this are difficult to verify, especially when the participant refuses to make a written statement of his experiences. Yet, on the other hand, if Alvarez had been on the expedition as a government investigator, he would not have been likely to make written, public statements about visiting flying saucer crash sites.

Since, Alma Lawson had claimed, "among the men were several physicists from the University of California" who visited the crash site, Cameron contacted the University Archivist at the University of California, Berkeley, for a list of physicists from the 1949-50 calendar. Alvarez was on the staff at the time in question. (As we mentioned, Dr. Alvarez went on to become a Jason member and advisor.) Other members of the 1949-50 physics staff who went on to become Jason members included Dr. Harold W. Lewis, listed as an Assistant Professor of Physics, and Dr. Wolfgang Panofsky, listed as an Associate Professor of Physics.

Although this does not prove that these Jason members were a part of this recovery (if there ever was a recovery), it does suggest that, if physicists were being used, it would be very hard to avoid Jason members, who pervade physics faculties at major U.S. universities.

In the May 1950 issue of *Fate* (Volume 3, Number 3), the Sierra Madre crash is discussed. In the article, "Spaceships, Flying Saucers and Clean Noses," the unnamed author stated:

> If it is true, and it might be, we'll certainly get no information out of Army Intelligence, and if said scientist were to come out and back Miss Lawson up, he'd be left high and dry with his "fantasy," simply because he couldn't show a "fried corpse" of a little man, or even a fragment of a *plato volador* [Spanish for flying saucer].

Since Dr. Alvarez died in September 1988, we may never know the full extent of his involvement in this affair.

Is Jason Involved with UFOs?

Dr. Robert Sarbacher isolated a number of people whom he believed to be involved in the putative government UFO-recovery program. Sarbacher named Bush, von Neumann, and Oppenheimer, all of whom had been involved in the development of the atomic bomb and were collectively referred to as "the Manhattan Group."

Jason has been referred to as "the second Manhattan group" it was set up to continue the work of the original group and has now by the 21st century built third and fourth generation. Consider also that Oppenheimer was the Director of the Princeton Institute for Advanced Study when he was supposedly involved in crashed-saucer analysis. If the same policy had been perpetuated, then it would come as no surprise that the two Jason members, Freeman Dyson and Marvin Goldberger, had also been involved in crashed-saucer analysis. Both of them, after all, had at one time also held the position of Director of the Institute for Advanced Studies. Furthermore, both von Neumann and Sarbacher had been in the company of the Institute. Many Jasons have done time at the Institute, and it seems not unlikely that the services of some of them would have been used.

The Jasons "wear many hats," and it is possible that they may have been involved with UFOs through one of their other positions. The reason why the Jason connection was first postulated was because of the characterization of the Jasons as "the top group around" for tackling technical defense problems. Some members of Jason, however, have held top positions elsewhere in the defense structure.

The flow chart presented on the television documentary *UFO CoverUp? Live!* showed DARPA as being part of the infrastructure. Not only is Jason considered to be the think-tank support-group for DARPA, but Jasons also have held top positions in DARPA.

If the U.S. Government does have a crashed-saucer program, the Jasons would be one component of the government that the Defense Department would likely put to use. One unknown in the scenario is just how elaborate and extensive the infrastructure is for such a program. If the program is at the testing stage, numerous physicists and technicians would be needed. It seems unlikely to us that all of these people could be recruited without the knowledge or help of the Jasons, who control most of the major physics faculties at key universities. It would also seem that Defense Department officials would be prone to seek out the best advice obtainable for a crashed-saucer program, since such a program would not at first glance seem to be one that concerned itself with problems that were going to be easy to solve.

The Jasons are considered to be "the best" in basic physics, and it is our opinion that surely some members of this elite group would be consulted for a project of this magnitude. One instance of such consultation may well be connected with the Sierra Madre crash, in which Dr. Luis Alvarez might have been involved. Another scientist who might have been aware of the degree of involvement of the Jasons was Dr. Eric A. Walker, who, as previous mentioned, was a Trustee of the Institute for Defense Analyses for fourteen years, during which time the Jasons comprised a division of the IDA.

Political Changes for Jason

The Jason Group involved itself not only in scientific issues but also in political ones. In 1973, the Jasons and the IDA were singled out for their prominent roles in American involvement in the Vietnam War.

Dr. Walker and other university presidents making up the Board of Trustees were forced to sit on the trustee board as public individuals, when, at the same time, universities no longer wanted such direct involvement of their leaders with the Pentagon's chief think tank.

Jason was forced to leave the IDA in 1973, because its members' lectures were being boycotted all over the world due to the group's position within the military/industrial complex. Jason moved to the Stanford Research Institute (SRI) in Menlo

Park, California—considered by some to be a demotion, because of its distance from the center of power (in Washington, D.C.). Also, the SRI was considered to be a think-tank for the corporate world, rather than the military.

However, just like which university presidents sat as public members on the IDA's Board of Trustees, not much changed except the paperwork.

The Jasons still worked for DARPA, whose brain-trust was the IDA. The Jasons' work remained centered on military matters.

And the Jasons' work at the SRI was still sponsored by DARPA (under contract No. DAHCI5- 73-C-O370)—in accordance with the following injunction:[77]

> The contractor shall establish and support a special study group to continue the work of the IDA Jason group. Under ARPA sponsorship, this group, which will number approximately 40 part-time consultants drawn primarily from the academic community, will work on technical problems as deemed appropriate by ARPA and the group [itself]. In general, the group will study basic defense research problems, identify basic research problems of potential value to the national defense that are not now receiving adequate attention in the scientific community, develop conceptual contributions toward [the] solution of technical problems of the Department of Defense, and investigate other areas of study as may contribute to the mission of ARPA. Technical work will include a two- or three-day briefing session normally [to be] held in the fall and spring; defense-related laboratory visits; and time continued work throughout the year.

Later Jason moved to MITRE, an Air Force think tank created in 1958 by MIT and noted for its advanced work on weapons, communications, and computer systems.

2013 Update

In the past few years, a small but possibly related story has been developing which involved both the Jasons and a key player in the UFO mystery at the highest levels of government.

The story, when viewed with other historic events, may actually illustrate the main reason the UFO mystery is being covered up.

The person involved in the latest Jason story is Dr. Ron Pandolfi, who since 1983 has been the man that the White House goes to for UFO information. He is also rumored to be in charge of all the phenomenology files (UFOs, psychic phenomena, remote viewing) at the CIA.

In October 2008, the MITRE Corporation, a non-profit organization which manages Federally Funded Research and Development Centers (FFRDCs) supporting the Department of Defense, released a Jason study on high frequency gravity waves. Pandolfi was named as having provided "continued help in arranging briefers and documentation." At the time Pandolfi was on the National MASINT Committee in Office of the Director of National Intelligence ODNI (which is the office that provides intelligence briefing to the President and other senior White House executives) which requested the study by the Jasons.

Researcher Gary Bekkum, who had blogged about the Jason study a year before it was made public described the study and its possible link to UFOs.

The Jason study initiated by Pandolfi debunked a Chinese-American research collaboration into the theory and application of "high frequency gravity waves" (HFGW) for communication and surveillance.

Some theories of HFGW are loosely related to the esoteric research of UFO propulsion systems, including the so-called Podkletnov effect, named after the Russian experimentalist who briefly dazzled the aerospace industry, including NASA, with claims of antigravity effects and gravity-like force beams.[78]

The conclusions of the Jason study concluded that HFGW was a waste of time, specifically:

> No foreign threat in HFGW is credible, including:

(a) Communication by means of HFGW
(b) Object detection or imaging (by HFGW radar or tomography)
(c) Vehicle propulsion by HFGW
(d)—or any other practical use of HFGW.

Because the study failed to reference the work of a renowned expert in the field Raymond Chiao, it was felt by some that the Jason study had been used by Pandolfi to discredit research on HFGW so that it could be moved into the military black world for research.

If true, the incident was reminiscent of the actions taken by the U.S. government in the fall of 1941 when they banned all mention of things related to atomic energy. Army intelligence at the time went as far as to block access to back issues of magazines like the *Saturday Evening Post* that had done articles on atomic energy so as to "wipe the whole subject from memory."

The ban on atomic references extended to science fiction writers and newspaper cartoon strips. One science fiction writer, Philip Wylie, was apprehended in 1944 by Army intelligence and reportedly told by a major that "he was personally prepared to kill him, if necessary, to keep the (atomic) weapon secret."[79]

If this use of the Jasons was an effort to trade scientific openness for security, the plan was not the first time that Pandolfi was accused of having moved innovative scientific research into the black world where it could be researched without the foreign intelligence services or the American public watching.

In 1994 Pandolfi struggled to wrestle away the remote viewing RV program back to the CIA from the DIA which controlled it. He was prevented from moving the program until 1995 because RV administrators such as Dale Graff and Jack Verona kept him off the distribution list as they feared he would shut the program down.[80]

Remote viewing was a protocol-based system where the mind

was used to view distant or unseen targets across time and space through paranormal means. The CIA was the first to develop for spying it but by 1995, when it was finally shut down, many government agencies had become involved.

RV was developed in 1974 through work done at the Stanford Research Institute by Dr. Russell Targ and Dr. Harold Puthoff. The RV phenomena also may have ties to UFOs, as most researchers now agree that there is a strong consciousness connection to UFOs. The importance of this was first described by Wilbert Smith, who stated in his memo in 1950 to the Canadian government that American officials told him that they were working on "mental phenomena" associated with the saucers. Many who have worked in the RV field have also been involved with UFOs.

During the five White House administrations that backed the RV program it was used with success to deal with a lot of intelligence problems where SIGINT and HUMINT could not reach. President Jimmy Carter got to see some of the results of remote viewing and said: "The results are unbelievable. Proven results of these exchanges between our intelligence services and the parapsychologists raise some of the most intriguing and unanswerable questions of my Presidency."[81]

Finally, Pandolfi got control of the RV program and moved it back to the CIA in 1995. He initiated a study carried out by the American Institutes for Research (AIR). They were to perform a retrospective evaluation of the results generated by the remote viewing program which was code named in 1995 as Stargate. The conclusion of the report is that there was insufficient evidence of the utility of the intelligence data produced. "There's no documented evidence it had any value to the intelligence community," stated the President and CEO of AIR David Goslin.[82]

The program was immediately shut down and just in time. Although Stargate was classified, many different agencies were using psychics and the leaks of what was going on with the classified research increased. The biggest threat was writer and researcher Jim Marrs, who had discovered the program, interviewed most of the remote viewers being used, and was about to publish a book called "The Enigma Files" on the entire secret paranormal program.

Pandolfi had to race to close the program before the book came out. The publication of Marrs book was mysteriously blocked. The book editors left the country and the new editor asked Marrs to write the book as fiction. Marrs flatly refused. The book was cancelled and did not get published for five more years. National radio talk show host Jeff Rense reported on the book:[83]

> Marrs was informed that the decision had been taken at the suggestion of a lawyer. Not only was Marrs not allowed to speak to the lawyer responsible, but the publisher told him that nothing could be done as the injunction had been ordered from a higher corporate level.

The CIA had to say remote viewing didn't work, and kill the effectiveness of Marrs disclosure. If the book came out before the program could be shut down, it would be impossible to then say it didn't work because it had been running for two decades and was still operational.

The Marrs book was blocked, the RV program was cancelled, and the media reported that the program had been a $20 million dollar waste of money. The CIA plan had worked.

In the years since the RV program was shut down there has been increasing evidence that the program had been moved to the NSA to fight the terrorist threat after 9/11. Reporters such as Gus Russo reported that the remote viewing program was alive and well hidden under black budget cover in the NSA. Now according to Russo, "the NSA considers the use of 'psychic information' as a legitimate form of signals intelligence, suggesting a transmission medium may have been confirmed by NSA scientists." Russo reported that the psychic spy research was being directed by NSA's SIGINT division from

Fort Meade, Maryland.

Future support for the rumored RV program at NSA came when Uri Geller, a key psychic in the initial remote viewing program told author Jon Ronson that he had been reactivated as a psychic spy by a man by the name of "Ron." Ronson related the story in his book *The Men Who Stare at Goats*.[84] Questioned by Gary Bekkum, Pandolfi denied that he was the Ron that Geller was referring to.

After Geller, Chris Robinson came forward to say that he had been recruited as a consultant for a new RV program within U.S. intelligence. Robinson was a British psychic who had visions of planes hitting large buildings, just prior to the 9/11 attacks. One of the people Robinson identified as an intelligence official working with him for years was former senior NSA official Tom Drake, who was outed as an NSA employee when the NSA put him on trial for treason for talking to a Baltimore newspaper reporter. The Drake case fell apart and never went to trial.

The prime example of this effort to move scientific research out of the public arena and into the black world is the shutdown of the USAF UFO Project Blue Book which took place in 1969. Like the Jason and AIR stories, the USAF used what at first glance appeared to be an independent group to evaluate the UFO evidence they had been collecting since 1947: The University of Colorado.

Just like the Jason and AIR conclusions, the university study concluded that future UFO investigation was a waste of time, and recommended that the program of collection be stopped. According to the final report, there was no "indication of threat to our national security," "no evidence submitted that represented technological developments or principles beyond the range of modern scientific knowledge," and "no evidence indicating that sightings categorized as 'unidentified' were extraterrestrial vehicles."

Like the HFGW and RV research, the Air Force was able to

move the research to contractors in the deep black classified world, where research could continue without the questions and scorn of the media and the public, and without foreign enemies of the United States taking notes.

In all three cases it was much simpler to do research in total secrecy while secretly monitoring related research going on in the white world.

As with atomic energy research prior to WWII, it appears that the U.S. military has a system to review research in the white world looking for ideas that can be applied to military technology.

Pandolfi, at the CIA, appears to be the UFO gatekeeper, as part of his job to review new and exotic technologies. Pandolfi, however, has denied this notion, telling people UFOs are just a personal interest. Despite the fact the CIA may not be the key agency behind the UFO cover up, part of Pandolfi's job (like that of his predecessors at the CIA, Kit Green and Arthur Lundahl) appears to involve four aspects.

The first of these would be to monitor developments in the UFO research field, and the state of development in the government. A close friend of Pandolfi's told Cameron, "Pandolfi would know all the politics behind the scenes. He would be the first point of contact for all this (UFOs), you know what I mean. He would be the front man, the visible guy. But he would also know the invisible. He would know where to point you but he wouldn't tell you."

Another friend of Pandolfi, John Alexander described Pandolfi on his website with these few but telling words, "Those who should know—do."

Because the UFO phenomena is so far ahead of the present state of military technology, Pandolfi has told friends such as UFO researcher Dan Smith (who claims to have had over 1,000 conversations with Pandolfi) that researchers are tracked rather than the sightings.

The second aspect of Pandolfi's job appears to be to capture

PROPOSED OFFICIAL U.S. GOVERNMENT UFO/ET
DISCLOSURE PROGRAM

Prepared for the

CENTRAL INTELLIGENCE AGENCY
and
STEVEN SPIELBERG

POTUS
BRIEFING

EYES ONLY

CLASSIFICATION – UMBRA RED

U.S. Government Liaison Control Officer: **Dr. Ronald Pandolfi**
Production Control Executive: **Gordon Novel**

Cover of the "POTUS Briefing," developed by Gordon Novel with backing from the CIA's Ronald Pandolfi, promoting an alien technology group known as RAM Gravionix, as well as a film script on the alien cover-up.

leading edge technologies that are viewed to have applicable military benefits.

The third is to monitor those working on leading edge technologies in the white world to make sure no classified information is being leaked. Many of those working on these technologies have security clearances related to work they may have done in the past related to other programs they were on. Cameron was told by at least one source associated with the

Aviary (a group of people who have been associated with UFOs), that Pandolfi is not well liked. He is at times a trouble-maker who has on occasion accused people of security violations where none existed.

The fourth and possibly most bizarre part of Pandolfi's job seems to bring some sort of effort to disclosure the UFO "Core Story," and a promotion of UFO technologies. This seems to run contrary to his first three jobs. Pandolfi has regular contact with a number of UFO researchers. He has also made many statements pointing to a reality behind the UFO phenomena including telling Smith that, "that he had tracked 200 individuals that had been briefed on UFO/ET."

More bizarre is the story that Pandolfi appears to have been cleared by the CIA to do what he is doing. Shortly after Pandolfi met Smith, Smith reported him for some of the things he was saying. Pandolfi reported that it led to a $100,000 investigation by the CIA Inspector General and that he was cleared of any wrong doing. He reportedly told the Inspector General he did not have any need to know about the aliens.

Pandolfi had, at least for a period of time, an association with Gordon Novel who was promoting an alien technology group known as RAM Gravitronix and a film script on the alien cover-up called "POTUS Briefing."[85]

In conversations Cameron has had with UFO researchers who are friends of Pandolfi, all held him in high esteem and none had a bad thing to say about him.

Chapter 6:

Wilbert B. Smith and the Majestic 12 Connection

In 1950 I was attending a rather slow-moving broadcasting conference in Washington D.C. and having some free time on my hands, I circulated around asking a few questions about flying saucers, which stirred up a hornet's nest. I found that the U.S. government had a highly classified project set up to study them, so I reasoned that with so much smoke maybe I should look for the fire.
–Wilbert B. Smith, Official Director of the Canadian Government's UFO Investigation, 1950-1954

Any nation that could figure out how the discs operated and could duplicate their maneuverability would have a missile defense and delivery system inestimably in advance of the systems presently developed or even logically contemplated and would therefore be in a position to control the planet Earth.
–Charles Berlitz & William L. Moore, *The Roswell Incident*

"No question, but they exist," he insists, "their reality is known and recognized by those in authority, but deliberately nothing is said about it because the problem of what to do about them remains unsolved."
–Donald Keyhoe quoting Wilbert Smith

Wilbert B. Smith was a Canadian radio engineer and UFO researcher. He graduated from the University of British Columbia in 1933 with a B.Sc. in Electrical Engineering and, one year later, obtained his M.Sc. at the same university. Smith joined the (Canadian Federal) Department of Transport (DOT) in 1939 and later became involved in implementing Canada's wartime monitoring service. In 1947, Smith was put in charge of setting up a network of ionospheric measurement stations, many in Canada's remote North.

In the late 1940s, Smith became curious about flying saucers after reading a magazine article on the subject. In September 1950, Smith interviewed American scientist Dr. Robert Sarbacher in Washington, D.C., and discovered that the Americans had recovered a flying saucer. (Ref. Chapter 2.)

Smith's investigation into the subject led him to believe that flying saucers might be operating on magnetic principles, a related subject the DOT was already working on. At the time, the DOT was investigating the collapse of the Earth's magnetic field as a potential source of energy. Smith believed that the work being done at the DOT might be able to explain how flying saucers operated as well as lead even to the discovery of a new technology.

On November 21, 1950, Smith proposed that a "special project" be set up within the Department to study this relationship; Smith's proposal was approved, and the project came to be named "Project Magnet." Using facilities at the DOT, with assistance from government departments such as the Defense Research Board (DRB) and the National Research Council (NRC), Smith's project went into high gear in order to (A) collect high quality data, analyze it, and draw useful conclusions from it, and (B) question our basic concepts in hopes of turning up a discrepancy that may prove to be a key to a new technology.

Three days later, on November 24, 1950, Smith wrote to the DRB Chairman, Dr. Omand M. Solandt, concerning an article Major Donald Keyhoe, USMC, was proposing to write for *True* magazine dealing with the Canadian government's work on flying saucers.

While in Washington in September 1950, Smith had picked up not only Frank Scully's book, *Behind the Flying Saucers*, but also Keyhoe's book, *The Flying Saucers Are Real*, which also had just been published. Smith met with Keyhoe and related to him details of the technical scientific work being done in Canada on the propulsion of flying saucers. (This was before the Canadians classified the subject.) It was this material that Keyhoe wanted to publish.

Along with the memo Smith forwarded to Solandt, was a copy of Keyhoe's article together with the suggestion that "others in the group" should make other changes they felt necessary. The publication of the article, after the Canadian DRB had made the necessary changes, would, in Smith's words, rest with the U.S. Research and Development Board (RDB). If the U.S. Research and Development Board "permitted" it, Keyhoe would publish the article.

Another set of documents that Smith left in his files is correspondence from January 1951 with Gordon Cox at the Canadian Embassy. Smith reported to Cox that both Dr. Solandt (who had just been to Washington) and Mr. A. Wright (a military attaché in Washington) were seeking more information related to what the Americans were doing. This search aimed at gathering more information to add to Dr. Sarbacher's claim that the Americans had recovered a downed flying saucer.

Most significantly in this January 3, 1951 letter is that Smith fingers Vannevar Bush as the person in the Research and Development Board who would approve or reject Keyhoe's attempt to publish the aforementioned article on the propulsion of flying saucers. The article, after redrafting and approval by "the group" in Canada, was to be sent first to the Canadian Embassy, from where Major Keyhoe was to take it to Dr. Bush at the Pentagon.

Finally, Wilbert Smith announced, "Doctor Solandt has requested we respect fully the United States classification on these matters." (We assume that he was referring to the crashed-saucer material that Dr. Sarbacher had told Smith about.)

Dr. Omand Solandt elaborated upon his letter in two letters he exchanged with researcher William Steinman in 1983. Dr. Solandt answered Steinman's first letter of April 19, 1983, on May 11, 1983.

Steinman had asked Solandt to elaborate on the information that Wilbert Smith had placed before him on November 20, 1950 (ref. "GeoMagnetics Memo" in Chapter 2) and on what Dr. Solandt knew about the whole flying saucer program.

In his reply, Dr. Solandt stated that Dr. Frank T. Davies—and not himself—was Smith's main contact in the

DRB on flying saucers. This was a revelation to Steinman, because Dr. Davies, Superintendent of the Telecommunications Establishment at the Defense Research Board, had never before been named in connection with UFOs.

Cameron approached by telephone a member of Smith's "inner circle," Art Bridge, who had worked for Dr. Davies, and asked him why Davies's name had not come up before.

"Frank T. Davies?" Bridge asked.

"Yes, Frank T. Davies," Cameron replied.

"No way," Bridge said. "Working with Wilbert on flying saucers? No chance. Davies was too high level for that. He never would have been involved."

"I've got a letter signed by Solandt that says he was," Cameron responded.

"Well, that letter I would like to see!" Bridge rejoined.

In Solandt's response to Steinman's second letter, Solandt identified another high-ranking person involved with Wilbert Smith, namely, Solandt's friend in the United States—Dr. Vannevar Bush.

There were other revelations in Dr. Solandt's letter.

First, even though Solandt had been briefed on November 20, 1950, by Smith on the flying saucer research and development program in the United States and had also been involved in the case of Major Keyhoe taking the propulsion article to Vannevar Bush at the Pentagon, Dr. Solandt told Steinman that he "did not recall" Bush heading up the flying saucer study program. He did, however, admit that they and Vannevar Bush had discussed the subject on a number of occasions. In a June 8, 1991 interview with ufologist Henry Victorian, Solandt said, "Not that they (U.S.) were doing any work on it. They were watching it very closely as far as I knew, I got my information from Van Bush. At that time I used to see him a couple times during the year, and that was a subject that we sometimes discussed, but we never did any joint work on it."

Second, Dr. Solandt stated that Wilbert Smith had had "frequent" discussions with DRB members, including himself, on the subject of flying saucers. He denied knowing of any contact between Smith and Bush.

Third, Solandt stated that the Canadians were not allowed access to material in the United States higher than Top Secret (in response to the statement Wilbert Smith had quoted in the January 3, 1951 letter about "respecting U.S. classification on these matters." In his 1991 interview with Victorian, however, he contradicted this when asked if the Americans would have shared such "very secretive or above top secret" material. "They certainly would have," replied Solandt. "If we would have shown interest in it and the need to know. We have shared some above top secret information. This is not exactly what we regarded as being very important.

On January 6, 1951, Gordon Cox at the Canadian Embassy answered Smith's January 3, 1951 letter with yet more revelations.

Cox told Smith that he was only one of three people at the Embassy cleared to talk about "the matter" (crashed flying saucers). The Embassy, according to Cox, was "all eyes and ears" trying to obtain further details. Cox was actually waiting for the Americans to make an official statement. Cox confirmed Vannevar Bush's involvement, stating that they at the Embassy were waiting to see what Bush had to say about the article on flying saucer propulsion that Smith had provided for review.

By 1952, plans had been made by Arnauld Wright, DRB Liaison Officer at the Canadian Embassy in Washington, to discuss the Canadian program with "the American scientists" working with the flying saucer program. Smith, however, discouraged this and said that the results should be fully discussed with "an entirely Canadian group" before talking to the American scientists.

There is evidence to indicate that meetings did take place in

1952. Later that year, Smith allegedly received a piece of a two-foot "disc." It was this piece that Smith said had been shot off by the U.S. Navy, supplied to him by the U.S. Air Force, and returned not to the USAF, but to "the hands of a highly classified group." When questioned about it in 1961 by Ohio researcher C. W. Fitch, Smith refused to identify the group.

As has been established already, Smith must have had at least indirect contact with Vannevar Bush. In the first place, Smith had sent Bush the flying saucer propulsion paper; secondly, he affirmed in the Top Secret GeoMagnetics Memo that Bush was the head of a "small group" working on the modus operandi of the saucers. If this small group was MJ-12 (which was most likely), then either Smith (in mid 1952) did not yet know the names of the members, or else Dr. Donald Menzel was not a member (as claimed by the Presidential Briefing Paper on MJ-12 supplied to Jaime Shandera in 1984).

This is because, in 1953, Menzel and Smith came together at a scientific gathering in Ottawa, Canada. Menzel had explained the 1952 UFO sightings over Washington, D.C., as simply a temperature inversion. Smith challenged Menzel to explain some actual sightings by this theory used to explain UFOs over Washington. Weather reports at the time of the sightings showed temperature inversions of one or two degrees. For sightings to be optical illusions, Smith figured the inversions would have to be 1000 or 2000 degrees. "Menzel refused to discuss any sightings in detail," Smith said. "I insisted to the point of rudeness and finally he admitted he couldn't explain any."

If Smith had known that Menzel was a member of Bush's "small group," he wouldn't have bothered to argue.

Other evidence to support the fact that Smith had some kind of access to at least some members of the group is Dr. Solandt's statement to William Steinman that "I am sure that these [Smith's ideas] were discussed informally with Dr. Bush."

Not only ideas, but also hardware was exchanged. In an

interview with reporter Richard Jackson of the *Ottawa Journal*, Smith said:

> I personally have handled a lot of 'hardware,'the bits and pieces of wrecked UFOs. The chemical structure of the metal we know, but its hardness, its tensile strength is something we never have seen before.

Later that same year, in a November 1961 telephone interview with researcher C. W. Fitch, Smith told him that he had "handled several pieces of hardware."

In a 1961 letter to Fitch, Smith went even farther and reiterated the fact that "government officials" –and not the U.S. Air Force—were in charge. "You seem most interested in 'UFO' hardware," Smith wrote. "There is a great deal of this around, most of it in U.S. official (NOT USAF!) hands."

Researcher Grant Cameron questioned Bridge, the "inner-circle" member, who had done metal analysis reports for Smith after 1956. Asked how many pieces he had handled, Bridge responded with one word: "Lots."

James Smith, Wilbert's son, also stated that:[86]

> Many times I remember blue military cars pulling up to the house leaving packages for him for him to do metallur-gical analysis on. We asked him what they were and he said that they were chunks of identified things that the military had either shot down or found . . . on a couple of incidents I remember a couple of packages about the size of a loaf of bread coming in. The box would contain metal that he had been told that the Air Force had shot a chunk of a flying saucer. They had already done some analysis on it and they wanted him to have a go at it . . . it came from the states.

Researcher Scott Crain contacted Carol Halford-Watkins, who later became the Editor of Smith's *Topside* magazine following Smith's death, to find out what she knew of Smith's involvement in handling UFO "hardware." Halford-Watkins stated in a June 14, 1977 letter to Crain that:

> In his day, Wilbert B. Smith made several trips to Wash-ington to consult with N.A.S.A. officials & others interested

in the UFO phenomena and I recall that he once told me that there was a Top Secret room in the Pentagon, which housed UFO data, and a collection of UFO fragments which he personally handled.

In an interview with researcher Robert Grove on July 8, 1962, less than six months before Smith's death, Grove told interviewer Earl Neff about a trip he had just made to see the dying Wilbert Smith. Once again, Smith talked openly about "hardware." Grove stated:

> Smith was constantly visited by Canadian government officials, as well as American government officials, who were upper echelon officials. They had attaché cases that were chained and locked to their wrists . . . He had a number of these visits. They had samples that they wanted him to analyze—hardware or metal that they had found. According to Smith, the United States military intelligence has tons of hardware. They readily admitted to this upon interview by Mr. Smith during the period of time that he was director of the research project [i.e. "Project Magnet," 1950-54]. Smith also stated that they had much film.

Finally, there is the story of the crashed flying saucer itself. In a January 13, 1977 letter to Grant Cameron, John Musgrave, a researcher in Edmonton, Alberta, Canada, stated that, according to a reliable source, "while Smith was in Washington he 'happened' to wander around an air base and got a peek at a captured UFO." This story is significant in that it was related to Cameron when crashed-saucer stories were discounted by a vast majority of ufologists, and because Musgrave's letter was written before the Top Secret "Geo-Magnetics Memo" had been declassified. (See Chapter 2.) Only after (inadvertent) declassification of the memo did it become apparent that Smith might have had access to top levels in Washington. In fact, Musgrave told Cameron that he didn't believe the story himself.

"Since this was in the '50s," Musgrave wrote, "I rather suspect Smith actually thought he had seen crashed UFOs under wraps. It was planned that he get a peek, and that it was a model just for that purpose—but that's my bias."

This would seem to be a lot of work just to fool Smith, and to what end?

The fact that the putative "flying saucer" may have been real comes from a completely independent source, again, long before the crashed saucer or alien body stories became popular.

Berthold E. Schwarz, MD, in his book *UFO Dynamics—Book II* tells of a story related to him in confidence years before by Harold Sherman, a noted researcher and writer.[87]

According to Sherman, Silas Newton, "who had been the key figure" in Frank Scully's original 1950 book about crashed flying saucers stated that "through the intervention of Wilbert Smith he had actually seen the humanoids himself."

This is a significant disclosure because Newton, a key person in Scully's 1950 crashed flying saucer book, has long been accosted by many researchers as an untrustworthy con man. Through this humanoid story told to Sherman, he tells a story that now fits with what we know about Smith.

The story gives Newton credibility because he told it long before it became public that Smith had been given access to the bodies. Moreover, if Newton made up the story about seeing the bodies, it makes no sense that he would claim to have been given this ultimate Top Secret access through a foreigner, not known to be connected to the U.S. government. He would surely have claimed access through some high level U.S. official, or through his mysterious group of eight scientists known collectively as 'Dr. Gee."

The Newton story is also significant because it was not known in 1972 (when Sherman related the Newton claim) that Smith was very interested in the Aztec crash. This fact did not become apparent until 1983, when the Sarbacher-Smith transcript was released, in which Smith asks about the validity of Scully's book. Sarbacher then provides further support for Newton when he tells Smith "the facts in the book are substantially correct."

According to James Smith, his father told him that he saw alien bodies. In 1998, researcher and author Palmiro Campagna wrote the following in the Postscript section of his 1998 soft-cover edition of *The UFO Files*:

> According to James Smith, on one of his many trips to the U.S., Wilbert Smith told his son that he was shown recovered bodies from a recovered craft. Wilbert Smith described the bodies as small and humanoid in appearance.

In July 2000, Grant Cameron interviewed James Smith by telephone and asked about the story told by inner circle member Buck Buchanan, about Wilbert Smith having seen a crashed saucer near Washington, D.C. James Smith confirmed that the story was true. When asked if he had heard it from his father or someone else, James stated his father had told him. James said he was also told about the bodies directly from his father, just before he died.

On April 6, 2002, James Smith appeared on the Toronto radio show *Strange Days...Indeed.* He recounted both the fact that he had seen a lot of the hardware that had been rumored concerning his father. In the same interview James confirmed the fact that United States officials had indeed showed his father alien bodies. James said:

> He was in the States a lot...and on several occasions he was invited off to be shown things along this line. It was pretty well under the Official Secrets Act, he told us. However, before he passed away in 1962, when he felt that the Act could no longer get him, I did ask him and he did say "Yes, I saw the bodies."

As to what the aliens had looked like:

> The descriptions that were out and about were fairly accurate... I think there was descriptions of smallish types... I don't remember a lot of those details. It just satisfied my curiosity that he had seen them and that they

were real.*

Smith wrote several reports relating to the subject of UFOs for the Canadian government. By 1952, his work on Project Magnet (initiated in 1950) had led to a report which he submitted to the Canadian Government. In it, he declared that flying saucers appeared to come from other civilizations and to operate on magnetic principles. A year later, in 1953, Smith concluded in another report that there was a high probability that flying saucers were extraterrestrial vehicles utilizing a technology more advanced than ours.

Smith's research continued as he attempted to obtain instruments that would detect an approaching UFO. Researcher Arthur Bray wrote in Ronald D. Story's book, *The Encyclopedia of UFOs,* that:

> Smith established the world's first "flying saucer sighting station" at Shirley Bay, outside Ottawa, in November 1953. This station consisted of a small wooden DRB building, containing some highly sophisticated instrumentation specially adapted to detect flying saucers. These instruments were: a gamma-ray counter, a magnetometer, a radio receiver, and a recording gravimeter. These four instruments produced traces on a multiple-ink graphical recorder which was checked periodically to note any disturbances.

On Sunday August 8, 1954, Smith and his colleagues were in the station when the now famous fly-by occurred. What happened next is best described by Smith himself:

> For months I and my like-minded associates had watched the sensitive gravimeter in vain. On occasions, when large commercial airliners would pass by, our hearts

---

* James reference to "descriptions that were out and about" referred to the descriptions of the 1950s, which described small humans or aliens that could pass as humans. The notion of greys was never discussed by Smith and his research group. An example of this was the reaction by Bridge, when Cameron provided him a copy of the Sarbacher letter to Steinman for comment which described the alien bodies as "insect like." Bridge phoned days later absolutely shocked at the insect description. He told Cameron that the Smith group had discussed the aliens many times and that this type of alien was never brought up.

The flying saucer observatory as it sat on Defense Research Board property outside of Ottawa. Note the receiving antenna, which monitored all signals in Canada.

would skip a beat as the instruments would register "aerial activities" But on August 8, at 3:01 p.m. the gravimeter began acting strangely. First it wavered slightly, drawing a thin line on the graph paper being used to measure the movements of the instruments.

Without further notice or warning, the gravimeter went wild. All evidence indicated that a real UFO had flown within feet of the station. . . . After watching the instrument for a few seconds, we ran outside to see what was causing the odd reaction. Unfortunately, our area was completely fogged in and whatever was up there could not by seen visibly.

Whatever it was, the instruments had recorded evidence that something very strange had flown near the station.

At this point, Wilbert Smith made the fatal error of his career. He told the press about the incident, stating that if there was nothing wrong with the instruments, then they had just recorded the overflight of the Canadian capitol by a flying saucer. When the instruments were found to be in working order, the Canadian government found itself in the situation of having confirmed the reality of UFOs.

The public relations problem was handled quickly. Two days later, on August 10, the DOT officially closed down Project Magnet, and Smith's power to make official statements on behalf of the Canadian government was summarily revoked.

The official government press release read,

> For the past three and a half years the Department of Transport has carried on an investigation of Unidentified Flying Objects. Considerable data was collected and analysed and many attempts were made to fit these data into some sort of pattern. However, it has not been possible to reach any definite conclusion, and since new data appear to be similar to data already studied, there seems to be little point in carrying the investigation say further on an official level.
>
> It has therefore been decided that the Department of Transport will discontinue any further study of Unidentified Flying Objects and Project Magnet, which was set up for this purpose, will be dropped.[88]

Strangely the press release went on to say that Smith would continue to gather UFO reports,

> Mr. W.B. Smith, P.O. Box 51, City View, Ontario will continue to receive and catalogue any future data on a purely unofficial basis.

Every member of Smith's inner circle was questioned about the closing of the station and the end of Project Magnet. Without exception, they replied that the ostensible absence of evidence of UFOs (which was what the government claimed was the reason for the end of Smith's government work) had absolutely nothing to do with it. Even Wilbert Smith himself blamed "well-meaning but misguided journalists looking for spectacular copy" to be the cause of his undoing.

Smith had become a public relations problem with his openness on the subject of flying saucers and his public disclosures on behalf of the Canadian government regarding their presence.

As a goodwill gesture, the DOT permitted Smith to continue using its facilities for his private research—but with no government financing. Smith continued his research up until his death in December 1962. He was secretly joined by a group of other government employees who devoted their space and time to help Smith.

During his life, Smith had spoken up forcefully about what was going on, even though he did not give specifics about what he had obtained through classified channels. He claimed that he had handled "hardware" from discs—not UFOs. He said openly that the Washington officials had a highly classified group working on flying saucers.

Probably the most blatant statement made by Smith on the subject of flying saucers occurred in a letter he wrote to Ronald Caswell. In the Smith files, this is the only letter found written to Caswell. Yet, in the letter, Smith describes plainly what he regards to be "not his opinion" but rather what is actually going on.

Smith and the UFO Landing Base

After Smith died, new stories emerged about other secret flying saucer projects he had been involved with. There were also stories that Smith had discussed privately, including one he told his wife and some close associates: that the Pentagon had a room where they had a collection of small UFO pieces and items associated with UFOs.

Probably the most dramatic of these stories concerned a Top Secret Canadian government effort to land a flying saucer in 1954 at the Department of Defense Research station at Suffield, Alberta—sometimes referred to as Canada's Area 51.

The army base is a 2,690 km square stretch of land with heavy security and no flyovers.[*]

The story of an attempt to land aliens there was first told in 1967. It was the 100th anniversary of Canadian independence. Many cities and towns across the country built special buildings and tourist attraction to celebrate the centennial.

In St. Paul, Alberta, their idea was to build a UFO landing base. When the day came for it to be opened, none other than the Minister of Defense, Paul Hellyer, showed up to cut the ribbon.

Hellyer then told a very interesting UFO story, which he said he got from the Canadian Defense Department's "expert" on UFOs. The story would turn out to be fairly accurate, based on information that would later be found inside the UFO community.

In his speech Hellyer stated that a Top Secret committee had been set up, and it had approved the UFO landing base. This was a major revelation, as the two UFO projects previously made public (Magnet and Second Storey) were both official UFO government programs, but neither was classified at the Top Secret level.

Thus, the UFO landing attempt at Suffield became a third Canadian government UFO program, and Top Secret, at that.

---

[*]The 1954 attempt by the Canadian government to talk to an alien was the same year that other high level alien contact claims were being made in other countries. In the United States, there is the famous story about President Eisenhower leaving a holiday in February while in Palm Springs to go 100 miles northwest to Muroc AFB to meet with aliens. In the United Kingdom, contact with aliens was said to be made that year by Air Marshall Sir Peter Horsley. Horsley had been Deputy Commander-in-Chief, RAF Strike Command. In this key position, he would have had a key control role related to the nuclear weapons held by the British. At the time of the alien contact, he was in the employ of Her Majesty the Queen and His Royal Highness Prince Philip, Duke of Edinburgh, as equerry. Horsley recounted the experience in his autobiography, *Sounds from Another Room*. He claimed to have met with an alien by the name of Janus, and reported that Janus wanted to meet with the Queen's husband—the Duke of Edinburgh." Janus warned Horsley of the "dreadful specter of (mankind) blowing up his world" which was the other thing that really disturbed Horsley. In conversations with researcher Tim Good, Horsley recalled that this extraordinary man "knew all Britain's top-secret nuclear secrets," and "by the end of the meeting, I was quit disturbed, really."

NEVER USED

UFO Landing Site Was 13-Year Secret

By VICTOR J. MACKIE
Special Journal Correspondence

The Canadian government 13 years ago made available the defence research board experimental station at Suffield, Alberta, as a landing site for Unidentified Flying Objects, Defence Minister Paul Hellyer has now disclosed.

Nothing ever materialized from that top secret project.

saucer in the early evening hours. He was relaxing with neighbors on his back patio. His description of the UFO— substantiated by his friends —was similar to descriptions reported by Manitoba people in the same week

Mr. Hellyer has refused to commit himself one way or the other on the reports. He said he was keeping an open mind on the subject.

Ottawa Journal, July 20, 1967.

The actual identity of the committee will probably always remain a mystery. In the first place, the Canadian government claimed the committee records were destroyed in 1957. Then, in 1979, despite Hellyer's confirmation of the story, Yurko Bondarchuk, a Canadian researcher, was told: "we have no record of any such project and... from the information I have, we never had one."[89]

Still, Hellyer gave much detail in his 1967 speech:

> Several groups became convinced that some unknown beings were trying to make contact with the Earth. One group made a strong representation to the committee . . . because there had been attempts made by Canadian and U.S. Air Forces planes to shoot down the UFOs the flying saucers were reluctant to land.
>
> It was argued if there was ever to be any contact, the hazards had to be removed. The UFOs had to be provided with a safe place. Accordingly, in an effort to give the 'believers' a chance to demonstrate the existence of the flying saucers trying to make contact with the Earth, the defense Research Board was designated as a landing area. The step brought no results . . . insofar as the committee was concerned no evidence had been produced to prove

their existence.

Implicit in the Hellyer announcement was the idea that the aliens knew where to land because someone was talking to them. Knowing later that Wilbert Smith had claimed such contact, this made him the most plausible source of contact with the aliens. Most likely, the "group [which] made a strong representation to the committee" was connected to Smith.

In 1973, Major Donald Keyhoe USMC (Ret) wrote about the attempt to land extraterrestrials in Canada from what the USAF had discovered. According to Keyhoe, Canadian defense officials decided to abandon the attempts that had been made to shoot down a UFO and move to entice the extraterrestrials through what became Project Lure.

> Hoping to lure aliens into landing, the Defence Research Board established a restricted landing field near its experimental station at Suffield, Alberta. All RCAF and commercial pilots were banned from the area.
> At first, some Defense Research officials expected to use radio and searchlight signals to attract the aliens. But high military officers warned that this would expose the capture purpose and alarm the public, so (that part of) the plan was abandoned...the top secret project was continued for several years.[90]

That was all researchers knew until a 1978 interview in Ottawa by Cameron with Wilbert Smith's widow, Murl. She was presented with a front page copy of the *Winnipeg Free Press,* which reported Hellyer's 1967 opening of the St. Paul UFO landing base.

When asked if her late husband had been involved, Mrs. Smith quietly read the article and then replied, "Yes he was."

She told Cameron that Wilbert Smith had always wanted a chance to convince the government that the aliens existed. He believed strongly that the government should talk to the aliens face-to-face to learn all the elements beyond their simple reality, such as their place of origin and their current activities on Earth.

The Top Secret memo that Smith had sent in 1950 to the his superiors in the Canadian government mentioned that he had been told by U.S. officials that flying saucers were real, and that they were the most highly classified secret in the country.

The memo, however, went on to state that the U.S. authorities were investigating along other lines which might possibly related to the saucers, such as mental phenomena. Also, that they were willing to share information with the Canadians.

Smith had worked on the "mental" aspect of the phenomena mentioned by the American officials. Indeed, he believed that he and his inner circle group of government employees had made communication with an alien by the name of AFFA.

As far as we know, there were at least three separate sources for the messages coming from AFFA. Smith had a series of questions that were provided to each source to check for consistency. He believed that if the government would stop shooting at the objects, he might be able to get AFFA to land for a meeting. He approached what Mrs. Smith identified as the government. According to her, the three members of the government were the R.C.M.P., the Department of Defense, and the Prime Minister. It may be that these three groups were the unnamed members of the Top Secret committee referred to by Hellyer in his 1967 speech.

Mrs. Smith added that her husband had been in contact with the Prime Minister, who at the time was Louis St. Laurent. The preliminary copy of Smith's "Project Magnet Report" had been provided to St. Laurent. The report sat on his desk for three months, at which time Smith and St. Laurent both agreed that the time was not right to release it.

Continuing her story, Mrs. Smith added that in contacts made through Mrs. Frances Swan, a contactee in Elliot, Maine, (just down the street from abductee Betty Hill), Wilbert Smith was informed by AFFA that, in order to land at Suffield, he would need protection against being shot down. This part of the story is actually told in a declassified FBI document which detailed the FBI's investigation of Mrs. Swan. (A number of agencies had files on Frances Swan, including the Canadian government, U.S. Navy intelligence, FBI, USAF, U.S. Secret Service, and the CIA.)

According to Mrs. Smith, Wilbert Smith put this demand to the government or committee, and the committee agreed that no one would shoot down AFFA's craft. Up to this point, both sides were telling the same story, and there are documents to prove these events did occur.

Following this, AFFA (through Mrs. Swan) demanded that once he had landed and talked to whomever was there to meet him, he would be allowed to take off without any interference. The R.C.M.P. and Defense Department agreed to this, but when Smith approached what was described as the "government," a cabinet meeting was held to discuss the matter. When the meeting was over, the "government" could not give a 100% guarantee that AFFA would be allowed to take off once he had landed at Suffield. At that, Smith immediately called off the planned landing.

That is the story Mrs. Smith told.

Requests were placed to the R.C.M.P. and the Defense Department for information or documents on the Top Secret UFO committee. All respondents replied that they had no information. A request was put in through parliamentary representative Lloyd Axworthy for a ministerial inquiry. Axworthy's reply was, "I can't help you."

Further questions were put to Hellyer, who confirmed he had given the speech, but stated it would have been written for him. He did not even recall giving it, as it had happened many years before his interest in UFOs. He did recall that the man who had provided the story had reportedly been a R.C.M.P. officer in 1954, and by 1967 was a senior Defense Department official. This, incidentally, confirms Mrs. Smith's contention that the R.C.M.P. was involved, even though it is simply a federal police force, and should not have been involved on an army base.

Mr. Hellyer summed up the story this way, "I can assure you there is no UFO cover-up, at least on our side of the border."

What gives the story added weight is the fact that the U.S. Navy intelligence, CIA, and FBI also studied the case. Indeed, in 1959, the CIA actually made contact with the same alien at the CIA's top secret National Photographic Interpretation Center (NPIC) in Washington, D.C. This is where all the U-2 and SR-71 spy photos were developed and analyzed.

From the documents that have since been released, it is known that U.S. Navy Intelligence and the CIA had actually known about the alien, as they conducted an investigation of Mrs. Swan starting in 1954. Navy Intelligence sent two agents to Maine, Lt. Commander Robert Neasham and Commander Julius Larsen, to investigate Mrs. Swan in 1959.

Even more interesting was that, during their investigation of Swan, she taught Neasham how to make communication with AFFA, and Neasham appeared to be successful. After he raced back to Washington, Neasham and Larsen told NPIC's Director, Art Lundahl about what they had learned. Lundahl had a strong interest in UFOs, and part of his job was to manage the CIA's UFO files. He once wrote James McDonald, a prominent researcher at the time, that UFOs were "a most important subject." Some rumors went as far as to claim that Lundahl had briefed three U.S. Presidents on the subject of UFOs.

At NPIC, Lundahl asked Neasham sit down to make contact. The officer went into trance and Lundahl asked questions of the man. As the session went on, Lundahl asked AFFA for proof. Speaking through Neasham, AFFA replied, "What would you like?"

Lundahl asked AFFA to show his craft.

"Go to the window," came AFFA's reply.

According to a handwritten memo describing the event:

At this time, approximately 1400, 6 July, 1959, these three

men saw what they have indicated was a flying saucer. They described the object as round, with the perimeter brighter than the center. Lt. Commander Neasham checked with Washington Center (Radar) and was informed that for some unknown reason radar return from the direction in which the ship was supposedly seen had been blocked out at the time of the sighting.

Lundahl immediately made a phone call to the head of the USAF Blue Book investigation, Major Friend at Wright-Patterson AFB. Friend was told to fly to Washington for an emergency meeting.

This meeting, held two days later, first reviewed what had happened. Neasham was then asked to go back into trance. Once again, he was able to make the contact with AFFA, and once again, he was asked by those present to see the craft again. Now, however, AFFA stated that the time was not right.

Friend returned to Wright-Patterson and wrote up the event to his commanding General. He was very impressed by what he had witnessed, but was told to drop it because another agency (CIA) was already handling it.

"I was convinced that there was something there," said Friend.

> "It didn't make much difference whether they (the navy Commander and the woman in Maine) were in contact with people from outer space or with someone right here on Earth. There was something there that we should have found out more about."

During the early 1970s, Lundahl told the story of this encounter to documentary film producer Robert Emenegger. Emenegger, along with Lundahl and Robert Friend, went to the NPIC building where the contact had taken place, and the crew filmed through the window the location where the flying saucer had reportedly flown by the window in broad daylight.

Fascinated with the story being told by the high-ranking CIA agent, Emenegger asked Lundahl tell the story on camera. Lundahl replied that this would not be possible. "You have to understand," he said, "I'm still on duty." Robert Friend did go on camera, however. As they stood in the building, he told the story of how the CIA communicated with an alien—the same alien who had offered to land at a Top Secret Canadian military base.

Chapter 7:

Aliens . . . Or Hocus Pocus?

Part of our intelligence process is to be involved in counterintelligence, to lead the enemy in another direction by providing those misdirecting dots.
—From the book, Homeland Security and Intelligence

Something does not make much sense here. Why would someone in Washington mount a disinformation effort if the only result is to confuse members of the UFO research community, which is a very small group without much influence over the public at large?
—Researcher and author, Jacques Vallee

My gut feeling, but don't quote me, my gut feeling is that those [MJ12] documents were originated by a person within [the] DIA and that they were sent to Moore or whoever this other guy is, in order to discredit them. My personal feeling is that it was a government operation. I wasn't involved in it, but it was a government operation.
—Richard Doty to aviation writer Philip Klass, January 8, 1988

In the early 1980s, in the period of time just before and after the appearance of the MJ-12 document, a number of strange developments resembling disclosures occurred in the UFO field. This was probably exactly what was intended, as not much happens in life by accident.

These apparent disclosure events, however, are strictly an American phenomenon. The event of people coming forward to provide insights and documents on the UFO cover-up has occurred dozens of times in the United States. Right next door in Canada, on the other hand, there has not been a single UFO whistle blower.[91] The same applies to most countries in the world. What this means is unknown, but it is a factor that should be carefully weighed when considering what is actually going on in relation to United States UFO whistle blowers.

The other thing that should be kept in mind is that these "disclosure leaks" are only a few of a much longer list of such events. If the entire list were to be considered, it would require a book to detail them.

The events described in this chapter began at the end of the Carter administration, just as Ronald Reagan was about to take over the White House. Carter had experienced a UFO sighting and was a strong believer that sunshine is the best disinfectant when it comes to government. The first indication that the UFO story was about to start coming out was in a small news item that appeared in the prominent *U.S. News and World Report* magazine in 1977, just after Carter took the oath of office. The White House was rumored to have been behind the story,

> Before the year is out, the Government - perhaps the President - is expected to make what are described as 'unsettling disclosures' about UFOs—unidentified flying objects. Such revelations, based on information from the CIA, would be a reversal of official policy that in the past has downgraded UFO incidents.[92]

There were a few clearly defined UFO leaks earlier, such as the apparent green-lighting of the UFO documentary, *UFOs, Past, Present, and Future* in 1974 by the Nixon administration, but it appears that the floodgates opened on whistle blowers and government leaks just after Carter administration agencies released thousands of UFO documents through the Freedom of Information Act. Carter had fought for open government as exemplified by his June 28, 1978 Executive Order 12065—*National Security Information*, which introduced the "public interest balancing test." This became an important consideration in the way UFO (and any other subject) FOIAs were dealt with. The test introduced a new aspect to judicial reviews. Courts in reviewing UFO documents for release "were forced to consider the public's interest when deciding declassification requests under the Freedom of Information Act."[93]

Carter also ordered the Department of Justice to instruct agencies "to release information that could legally be withheld if the release could not be clearly harmful." The security system was revamped to "eliminate needless initial classification . . . reduce the time that documents remain classified."

Carter estimated that 250 million pages of documents would be released because of the changes.

When Reagan took the oath of office, the flow of UFO information continued. Ronald Reagan was known to be very interested in UFOs. He had at least two personal UFO sightings and made references in speeches to how the world would unite if faced with an invasion by aliens. Reagan actually went as far as to announce in June 1981 to a group of people who had gathered at the White House to watch Steven Spielberg screen the movie ET, "I wanted to thank you (Spielberg) for bringing E.T. to the White House. We really enjoyed your movie, and there are a number of people in this room who know that everything on that screen is absolutely true."

Project Aquarius

Moore was the researcher who provided the main documents during the 1980s to the effect that the U.S. Government had been involved in UFO crash retrieval operations. Besides being involved in the public release of the MJ-12 Document, Moore released other government papers associated with UFO phenomena.

Ostensibly through one of his government informants, Moore obtained documents that supported the idea that the U.S. Government had contact with alien life forms. The first set of documents is entitled "Executive Briefing—Project Aquarius."

In a May 21, 1989 letter to Scott Crain, Lee Graham explained how he obtained a copy of the Project Aquarius documents on May 2, 1987, from Moore. In that letter, Graham wrote:

> Mr. Moore has indicated to me that the "PROJECT AQUARIUS" document is the typed results of an oral briefing accorded President James Carter on June 3, 1977. Mr. Moore does have more pages of the "PROJECT AQUARIUS" document and has promised that I will be given a grace period in which to circulate the same before

the public release.

Researcher Lee Graham indicated that the "Project Aquarius" document had been retyped and that he had viewed the declassified original.

Crain asked Moore to elaborate on how he had acquired the "Project Aquarius Briefing Document" and why he was withholding the balance of the document. Moore answered these questions in a letter to Crain dated September 23, 1989. Moore wrote:

> I was told the original briefing to which it allegedly pertains was an oral briefing and that the briefing officer used hand written notes as an aide-memoir. The version I have is allegedly a typed transcript of those notes, which the briefing officer later composed as a memo to file. Naturally I have no way of proving this as I only have the source's word for it.

Regarding the Aquarius Telex and the Aquarius Briefing Document (see Appendix III), the authors have no way of proving their authenticity. Like the initial warning from Falcon that he would not break the law (thus not release classified information), the documents are probably a mixture of true and false material.

In this capacity, it serves as a control mechanism in case anyone else comes forward with a similar claim. In other words, should anyone supply any portion of the "missing text," we would be in a position to refute or verify. In this light, Bill Cooper claimed to have seen the same document as part of his experience. Cooper then [released] a typed version of what he said was the complete text of the document. His only mistake was that he assumed the version we had was precensored and that we would have no way of knowing what the allegedly missing text said. Unfortunately for Cooper, we were able to expose his version as being exactly identical to ours with respect to uncensored lines, and completely different from ours where Cooper had filled in what he assumed was missing from our document.

When Cooper was confronted with this, he changed his story and tried to claim that the reason the text of our document differed from his was that it was we who had been provided with an altered document. (Even more amazing here is that some people actually believe him!)

On December 15, 2003, Robert Collins, who had worked with Moore, made a statement about this transfer of the alleged Carter briefing document to Bill Moore. Researcher Bill Hamilton had asked Collins, "Wonder if he (Moore) knows the truth now." Collins said of Moore and the Carter briefing document:

> Not more than us right now. He (Moore) did meet our Mr. X back in 1979 and Mr. X gave him a copy of that reconstructed Carter Doc to take snap shots of in a Motel room. Like in the case of our Dan Burisch everything was always Cloak & Dagger & Mysteries. Secret meetings, cryptic messages you name it. Personally I got sick of it, all those games and no meat. Both Bill & Jamie (Shandera) hated me for that. Bill predicted I would have a nervous breakdown. Said when that happened we should meet and talk about it. Well, still kicking but just barely.

Collins had provided a 1976 President-elect Carter briefing document that he stated "is a reconstruction done by certain people who attended the briefing. Since note taking etc. was not allowed certain people were tasked to memorize certain sections of the briefing. Then they all got together afterward and reconstructed the briefing from memory." Collins named Dale Graff, a former physicist at the Foreign Technology Division and later Director of the Stargate remote viewing program as one of the people who attended the briefing.

"Ernie Kellerstrass in Dayton Ohio," wrote Collins, "maintained that Dale did attend the Carter briefing and was one of the ones who took mental notes with others for document reconstruction."[94]

When Dale Graff denied this claim, Collins responded, "Of course Dale denies any of that maintaining he doesn't have any

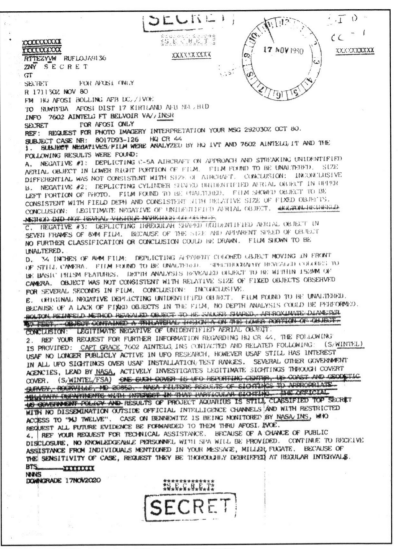

The Aquarius Teletype, dated November 17, 1980.

inside knowledge and lies even to his best friends."[95]

Another document released by Moore, often known as the "Aquarius Telex Document," also makes references to MJ-12 and was widely circulated in the UFO community. It was dated November 17, 1980. Although it looks like a Teletype message sent by AFOSI Headquarters to Kirtland AFB OSI, AFOSI

Headquarters claimed it never sent the message and called the document a forgery.

In a letter dated April 3, 1983, researcher Richard Hall of the Fund for UFO Research wrote to attorney Peter Gersten that:

> The AFOSI document is not authentic in the sense of not being an original; Moore has retyped it and done a cut and paste job, as he acknowledged in answer to my direct questioning when he attended our meeting three weeks ago.

In responding to a letter written by Crain to Hall on May 16, 1989, Hall clarified the meaning of his letter to Gersten. Hall wrote in his May 20, 1989 letter:

> The situation is described in the letter [of] Moore attending [a meeting] of the Fund for UFO Research Executive Committee and acknowledging to those present (including Maccabee) that he retyped (rewrote is not quite accurate) the Aquarius document and pasted the various markings onto the retyped copy. My understanding is that he did so only because the original was not sharp enough to reproduce clearly. I don't condone his doing this without saying so, but I did not then nor do I now think he faked or fabricated anything.

Robert Hastings wrote in his paper, "The MJ-12 Affair: Facts, Questions, Comments,"

> Why would Moore do such a thing? If a genuine message was sent to Kirtland AFB OSI, dealing with Bennewitz's photos, MJ-12, and the rest, why didn't Moore disseminate it in its original form? Wouldn't the "retyped" version of it, if discovered to be such, raise doubts about the credibility of the information contained in it?

Crain asked Moore to explain his side of the story. In a reply dated September 23, 1989, Moore said, "I did not retype the document, nor do I know who did."

Moore went on to say, "I know the version I was handed was a retype, because I had seen the original earlier on. The reconstructed version which appears in *Focus* is the combined

would be imprudent to make a copy of the "Hilltop" document public
at this time. Should anyone feel they have information which
pertains to this event or could assist us in investigating it, the
authors would be happy to hear from them and invite their
cooperation.

THE CARTER BRIEFING NOTES (MAR. '83)

In early March of 1983, Moore received a phone call telling him
that some information was going to be made available to him but
that he would have to go and pick it up. "You will be receiving
some instructions," the caller said. "You must follow them
carefully or the deal is off."

After making a cloak-and-dagger trip across the country, Moore
ended up in a motel on the edge of a mid-sized city in upstate New
York. At precisely 5:00 P.M., according to arrangement, an
individual came to the door of Moore's room bearing a sealed brown
manila envelope. "You have exactly nineteen minutes," the person
said. "You may do whatever you wish with this material during
that time, but at the end of that time, I must have it back.
After that, you are free to do what you wish."

Inside the envelope were eleven pages of what purported to be a
Top Secret/Orcon document entitled "Executive Briefing, Subject:
Project Aquarius" and bearing the date of June 14, 1977. "May I
photograph this?" Moore asked: "May I read it into a tape
recorder?" The courier, who stood quietly in the corner of the
room the entire time, replied, "Both are permitted. You have
seventeen minutes remaining."

Moore hastily adjusted the shade of the lamp on the night table
and, placing the pages in its light one-by-one, took the best
pictures he could. In order to assure scale later, he took a
quarter from his pocket and placed it on the lower left corner of
each page as he photographed them. Once that task was complete,
he quickly undertook to read the text into a pocket recorder,
taking care to read in the word "line" at the end of each line,
as well as verbally noting punctuation marks, etc. so that a
complete reconstruction of the text could be made in proper format
should the photos not turn out. (They did, but all were of low
contrast and, although legible, some were moderately out focus as
well.)

When the time was up, the courier collected the pages, carefully
counted them, replaced them in the original manila envelope, and
left. It had been an unusual experience, the entire significance
of which remains unclear to this day.

*****

The documents themselves seem to be a transcription of notes
either intended for use in preparing a briefing, or taken down
during one and typed later. Much of the information therein is

Part of Moore's notes on his acquisition of the Aquarius Briefing Document (see Appendix III).

product of both my and Rick Doty's memory."

Moore explained his involvement with the Aquarius Telex in his 1989 MUFON Symposium speech. He described it as a legitimate document that Falcon had showed him in February 1981. When he saw it the next time, it had been changed, making it the half true / half false material that Falcon had warned him he would be receiving in 1980. "The Aquarius

Document is an actual example of some of the disinformation produced in connection with the Bennewitz case," Moore stated. "The document is a retyped version of the real AFOSI message with a few spurious additions. It was apparently created by AFOSI, or at least I assumed it was, and it was handed to me in March 1981, with the intention that I would pass it to Bennewitz."

The document, like the other documents provided to Moore, would achieve two purposes. It would reinforce the Aquarius Project and MJ-12, but it would also serve to discredit Bennewitz. The plan was that when Bennewitz released the document as genuine, AFOSI would announce that it was a counterfeit and it would help discredit Bennewitz, who was causing problems with his observations about what was happening at Kirkland Air Force Base.

Evidently, the document had been retyped from a real AFOSI message with various spurious changes.

The New MJ-12 Documents

Skeptics of the original MJ-12 documents such as Phil Klass, Robert Hastings, Brad Sparks, and Kevin Randle all claimed the documents were a hoax. Many researchers pointed to Moore and Doty as the authors of the documents. Over a quarter century later, many still believe that.

The MJ-12, Aquarius, and Aquarius Telex documents, however, were only a few of the many MJ-12 documents that would flood the UFO community. During the 1990s, the purported leak of such documents went from a trickle to a flood. Despite such a large quantity, there has never been any serious discussion or research into why a handful of researchers should suddenly be inundated with documents.

As an example, in 1994 aviation writer Don Berliner received an undeveloped roll of film containing images of a "Special Operations Manual 1-01" (SOM 1-01). Berliner sent the document to many other researchers. Most concluded that it was probably a hoax like the MJ-12 and Aquarius documents. In 2006 New York based researchers, Clay and Shawn Pickering, received what appeared to be a revised or retyped copy of the same SOM 1-01 document from their secret contact, a Naval Officer named Richard Theilmann, who was anonymous at the time, and whom they referred to as Source A."[96]

The main flow of documents, which began appearing in 1992, came to be known as the "new" MJ-12 documents. The primary source of these documents was former U.S. Marine Timothy S. Cooper, who said he had obtained them from sources using names such as Thomas Cantwheel, S-1, and S-2. The documents were turned over to father and son UFO researchers, Robert and Ryan Wood, who spent years analyzing the veracity and origin of these documents. They have both strongly supported the authenticity of most of them.

Ryan Wood characterized the documents in the following way:

> . . . newly surfaced documents, many of which date years before the Roswell crash...telling the exciting story of the U.S. government's work on retrieval and analysis of extraterrestrial hardware and alien life forms from 1941 to present The Majestic documents tell a mind-boggling story of deception, intelligence and counterintelligence, revolutionary alien technology, missing nuclear weapons, and compartmentalized secrecy.

Ultimately, these new MJ-12 type documents totaled over 4,000 pages of documents and pictures of MJ-12 support teams. No one has been able to determine exactly where the documents originated, but before Moore left the research field, he seemed to predict that the government was capable of producing such a flurry of UFO documents. "One thing is sure," Moore told researcher Ann Druffel. "Government agents are faster at planting 'data' than civilians can check and verify it."

When these thousands of new pages of MJ-12 documents and photos started to flood the UFO community, Moore and Doty were gone from the UFO scene. Moore quit the field shortly after speaking at the 1989 MUFON UFO conference in Las Vegas. Doty became a police officer in New Mexico.

What are the chances therefore that Moore and Doty were behind the 4,000 new pages of documents leaked years after they quit the field? To put it bluntly, not good. It makes much more sense that some agency with great resources and expertise was behind the massive release of material. The question is, why? Why would some agency leak over 4,000 pages of documents and pictures into a small field of researchers who are generally ignored by the government, media, and the general public?

The new MJ-12 documents released were very sophisticated. This would be expected, as they would have to be in order to get researchers to believe their possible authenticity. The documents pointed to many personalities and organizations that might have been involved in the UFO cover-up. Ultimately, most of the UFO community concluded that they were all probably hoaxes. Any further discussion about the documents was unnecessary.

Yet the reason for the massive document release was generally ignored by most researchers. No one questioned why an organization would go through so much work to put this material into the UFO community. The UFO community, after all, and particularly the portion that studied UFO documents, was very small and had no influence over public or media reactions.

So why spend all the money on the document download, when at first sight it appeared that no one believed the documents, and they had gained no public acceptance?

One theory that came to be accepted by some in the UFO community is an idea Moore claimed was given to him by the Falcon. The whole operation, according to Falcon, was that the UFO documents were put out like fly paper to ensnare Soviet spies. On the surface this might seem plausible. After a closer look, however, it appears to be just another cover story, or a story given to Moore to make him do things that might otherwise seem wrong. If he believed he was saving the country from the godless Soviet communists, he would be more willing to spy on other researchers, or pass on phony documents to them.

There are several reasons the Soviet theory make no sense.

1. If 95% of the UFO community disbelieved the documents were legitimate, how would much more sophisticated Soviet spies fall for the same documents and get themselves caught?

2. Were the Soviet spies expected to phone up Moore and Shandera to find out where the saucer research was taking place?

3. According to Moore, Falcon was Soviet spymaster Harry Rositzke. However, it is important to note that Rositzke was reportedly brought out of retirement to run the operation. He was therefore hired by someone more senior in the CIA who had come up with the idea. Would such a high level person make a plan to catch Russians with the MJ-12 documents—which did not even deal with technology? Were they so short of spies to catch Russians that they needed Moore, Shandera, and an old Soviet spy catcher from the past to run the operation?

4. Moore maintained that he only passed one phony document, which was given to Bennewitz. Why would such an operation require the services of a Soviet spymaster?

5. Moore was given a great deal of material about organizations and names of people who had been part of the UFO cover-up. How did this fit into the plan to catch Soviet spies? Moore stayed with the operation, believing that he was getting an insight into the cover-up. Would he and Shandera have hung on till the early 90s (without pay) if they believed they were merely bait for Russian spies?

Another theory is that the new MJ-12 documents were a disclosure attempt by the government. However, this also received criticisms. Researchers such as long-time government insider John Alexander quickly pointed out certain fallacies about it. For instance, if a government agent such as Falcon wanted the UFO story out, why would he mail photos of the documents to Shandera's mailbox or mail them to Tim Cooper? Why would the government not go to the *New York Times* or *Washington Post*, where there was money, government contacts, and the best investigative reporters around to get to the bottom of the story? Going through a major paper would also give the story instant credibility when it was finally released. This disclosure explanation did not seem to explain the 4,000+ pages of UFO documents very well, either.

The theory that seems best to explain both the MJ-12 documents released by Moore in the 1980s and the new MJ-12 documents that were gathered and analyzed by the Woods in the 1990s is that it was done for two purposes. First, a gradual disclosure of UFO information while maintaining the overall cover-up, sometimes known as a "limited hangout." Second, an effort to keep researchers in the UFO community off balance by adding disinformation to the legitimate leads that research-ers were obtaining.

Dr. Christopher (Kit) Green, who was in charge of the UFO files for the CIA during the seventies, explained how such a gradual UFO disclosure might work this way.

> So, what do we do? There are studies on both sides of the problem. Some show that people will go crazy and jump off bridges when they are presented with this information. Others however, say that if you don't want them to go crazy, what you do is systematically desensitize their fears. . . . If you are a psychiatrist with a patient you can do that in a very systematic way. . . . But if you are a government working with a population it's a lot more complicated. . . . So we have to ask ourselves, how can we tell people what they deserve to know, and maybe, what they need to know? If you give them the Core Story right off the bat, they'd get sick, so you do it slowly over ten or twenty years. You put out a bunch of movies, a bunch of books, a bunch of stories, a bunch of Internet memes about reptilian aliens eating our children, about all the crazy stuff that we've seen

recently in Serpo. Then one day you say, "Hey, all that stuff is nonsense, relax, it's not that bad, you don't have to worry, the reality is this."—and then you give them the real story.[97]

This concept best explains the leaking of 4,000+ pages of UFO documents into the UFO community. Some secret group, say AFOSI, which Moore said is in charge of placing disinformation inside the UFO community, or the CIA, who Moore took directions from, is carefully releasing the key elements of the UFO story within a haze of disinformation.

According to this theory, none of the UFO documents that have been leaked over the years are legitimate, but the key elements of the true story are contained within them. Green, speaking of such leaked material, said it is hard to "reject the material out of hand, even if the story that it's telling is patently not true. . . it might have served a purpose to someone, somewhere, perhaps conveying information in a heavily codified form. One of the ways that you can access the value of the information is to see who is drawn to it."

This theory also takes into consideration that the UFO subject is the most highly classified subject in the United States and the real documents are therefore safely stored behind many levels of security. Because the government successfully shut down the public Blue Book UFO study in 1969, it put them in a position of being in the clear on ever having to publicly talk about UFOs ever again. The closing of Blue Book ended the public pressure to disclose the truth. It left most UFO groups without an adversary and just struggling to survive. The closing of Blue Book was the final piece of a debunking program that made the subject of UFOs completely toxic to scientists, politicians, and the media. The government had effectively won. The UFO game was over.

So why then would the government then spend piles of money, invest the time to hire Falcon, and produce scores of sophisticated UFO documents to be dropped into the UFO community? Doing this effectively revives the idea that the

UFO story is true and that the government is lying. Why then would officials choose to turn the glowing embers of a dying fire into a raging forest fire of new alien/government tales?

If Green is right, the government is desensitizing the UFO community so that when the time is right, they can tell the public what they deserve or need to know. They indirectly tell the UFO research community, which in turn spreads the word to the general public. No government admissions are necessary to get the truth out, and the cover-up remains under control.

The government needs to do it over a number of years, and maintain the UFO cover-up as they do it. The plan is to tell the story but provide nothing concrete (such as a traceable confirming document, piece of hardware, or alien body) that would bring down the cover-up. This continued cover-up is necessary because once it breaks, the government loses control over what happens next, and governments do not like to face situations they cannot control. Moreover, the government does not really know for sure what will happen when there is confirmation that the extraterrestrials are here, and the government is not in control.

The plan seems to be to leak documents and stories that are close to the real thing, but which are altered and therefore always prove to be hoaxes when examined carefully. Researchers latch onto the documents and stories. They debate the evidence, which makes it public. Eventually, the document or witnesses telling the story are discovered to be fakes. The researchers expose the situation and quickly move on, looking for the next big story. By then, however, the ideas of alien underground bases, government alien interactions, and an alien presence on Earth are out. The documents die, the story is out, and most importantly the cover-up continues while the government continues to determine what they are going to do about a phenomenon over which they have very little control.

This theory, that officials might actually be using hoaxed documents containing key elements of the UFO story that they wish to disclose, is supported by a statement made by Ron Pandolfi. In a discussion with his friend Dan Smith about the MJ-12 documents, Pandolfi indicated there were elements within the documents that were in fact classified information. Since part of Pandolfi's job is to protect classified information, he hinted that an investigation might be in order. "Ron [Pandolfi] is now stating that some of the faked MJ-12 documents contained actually declassified information unrelated to UFOs," Smith stated. "Ron wondered out loud if persons involved in the MJ-12 document affair would respond to an FBI warrant concerning the transfer of classified material to the KGB."[98]

Kit Green has also made statements indicating that the leaked UFO documents may contain some elements of truth and told investigative reporter Gus Russo that he had been the recipient of many such documents. Russo wrote,

> He (Green) also notes that over the years he has received thousands of UFO-related government documents in unmarked envelopes. Although some are obvious fakes, others, according to Green, contain information that correlates with known, but still classified, scientific studies.

A related theory that seems to support the rational for so many phony UFO documents being leaked into the UFO community by some government organization is to keep UFO researchers off balance. This is particularly true when it comes to looking at the MJ-12 documents released to Bill Moore.

In 1980, Moore published *The Roswell Incident*, which was the first major study to highlight the many witnesses at Roswell in 1947, and which gave credence to the idea that there was an extraterrestrial crash, complete with alien bodies. The book sold over a million copies and Moore attained overnight media credibility. But if the media suddenly sees credibility in the UFO story, the cover-up becomes at risk. Therefore, it was necessary to neutralize Moore's credibility. Thus, ten days before his Roswell book hit the stands, he received a call from the Falcon, who offered to help him in his UFO research. Moore accepted the offer, was given the MJ-12 documents, and within a decade became discredited among most UFO researchers. He then left the field.

This same pattern was repeated on many other occasions. When Linda Moulton Howe, for example, completed and aired her 1980 Emmy Award winning *A Strange Harvest*, detailing hundreds of mysterious cattle mutilations in the western United States, which she tied into UFOs, she too was contacted and offered help with her UFO research from AFOSI. Along with the offers of help came offers of UFO film for her next documentary, which she was doing for Home Box Office. Unlike Moore, she did not take the bait. She did, however, lose the documentary waiting for Doty's promise of a film of an alien/military encounter at Holloman Air Force Base.

But Moore did take the bait and eventually went public with the MJ-12 and Aquarius documents. When most researchers determined the documents to be hoaxes, Moore ended up being blamed for the situation. Many actually accused him of being the author of the documents. Moore went from being one of the most highly respected researchers to being so disrespected that he left the field. He sold or gave away his files and books, and disappeared.

Those who gave the documents to Moore and other research-ers achieved their goal. They were able to release the basic Core UFO story to the public without having to make any public admissions. At the same time, they were able to main-tain the secrecy surrounding the classified aspects of the UFO subject, such as the technology of the saucers, the mental aspects connected to the phenomena, and the more trouble-some aspects, such as abductions and cattle mutilations. They were able to do all this without releasing classified information and thereby breaking the law. At the same time, those in charge were able to discredit a top researcher—Bill

Moore—who might actually have been listened to by the mainstream media

Chapter 8:

The Falcon and the Birds
Behind the Curtain

If an individual, flashing credentials of an agency of your government, invited you to cooperate with him in studying UFOs, what would you do?
–Bill Moore

There are now 12 in the Aviary. They hold a variety of 'need to know' security clearances, and seem to know each other. Hawk is a person well-connected in areas of study in ESP since the 1960s, with impressive credentials. Blue Jay is a person close to the President of the United States, capable of checking on information to determine its reliability. Partridge is a scientist privy to UFO information collected by the government. Chickadee is well-placed in the Pentagon and versed in scientific data. Heron is enigmatic and puzzling; he seems to 'speak in riddles.' Sparrow is the code name for Richard Doty, a former agent for the Air Force's Office of Scientific Information (AFOSI), and was the original go-between between Falcon and myself, and so on.
–Bill Moore

CIA Asset: Bill Moore

In the early 1980s as the document disclosures began most UFO researchers believed these strange disclosures were being put out by two individuals: Air Force Special agent Richard C. Doty and Air Force scientist Robert Collins.

Years later, it is now apparent that Doty and Collins were only two of many high level information sources that were involved. The group became known as the Aviary.

The researchers who gathered all these sources together were Bill Moore and Jamie Shandera. Some were contacted by the two researchers, while others took the initiative and approached Moore and Shandera.

At the time no one knew how Moore and Shandera were able to gather together such a powerful group. Thirty years later the picture is a bit clearer. They could achieve this because neither were ordinary researchers. Both had done work for the CIA.

In a conversation with Bill Steinman, Moore confided that

while he was a university student, the CIA, which had been recruiting on many American campuses, had approached him. He told Steinman that he ended up doing some "footwork" for the CIA, and "wrote a couple of reports" for the agency. After Moore became a UFO researcher, he renewed his ties to the agency. He told Steinman that "he was using the CIA." He added that this was how he obtained access to his "deep throat sources."

Shandera also had worked for the CIA. After Moore left the UFO field he did an interview with his friend and radio host Greg Bishop. In that interview he discussed his discovery that Shandera had also worked for the CIA. The fact that both men were CIA assets might help to explain why, in 1982, when Moore was being overwhelmed with UFO information from Falcon, he chose Jamie Shandera (a film producer with no UFO research background) to help him instead of his friend Stanton Friedman. Friedman, one of the most respected researchers in the field had helped Moore break the Roswell case, and the book that came out of it that had been a bestseller. He however ended up on the outside about the birds, even though he was doing a lot of the background research on the MJ-12 document for Moore.

Of course, while Moore and Shandera found their connections useful in gathering information, no one knew about their CIA backgrounds.[99]

If one accepts that Moore was in fact a CIA asset helping to release the UFO story without causing a disastrous, full disclosure, then many of Lee Graham's statements make much more sense.

Graham, who knew Moore well and had met with him many times, reported that Moore claimed to have been on the "inside," although he never mentioned the CIA. Graham documented these comments and reported them regularly to the Defense Investigative Service (DIS) officials who were investigating his own security clearance related to his UFO activities. In an FOIA filed with the DIS, Graham clearly recalled how Moore claimed a government connection.

> On the 16th of October 1986, I had dinner with the individual (Bill Moore) who provided me with this document (see enclosure – MJ-12 document). He stated that he HAD NOT been contacted by ANYONE representing the Defense Investigative Service and that he WOULD NOT BE, because your computer system is flagged not to interview or investigate him!

The Identity of Falcon

No one knows for sure how many high-level informants Moore and Shandera had, but it was quite a few. In order to talk more freely about them without any monitoring groups being the wiser, Moore and Shandera gave each one a bird name, and their collection of sources became known as the Aviary.

Many researchers would publish articles about the Aviary, try to guess who each bird was. The birds themselves were of no help, since most never knew they had even been given a bird name.

The most important of Moore's birds had come from the man that whom he code-named Falcon.*

For years, people wondered who this Falcon was. Many assumed it had been Richard Doty, although Moore and Doty both denied this.

Finally, years later, Moore spoke to fellow researchers Brian Parks and Greg Bishop. Falcon, he said, was veteran super spy CIA Harry Rositzke.[100]

But long before Rositzke's identity was known, Moore had talked about how Falcon contacted him back in 1980, just days after beginning a publicity tour for his book, *The Roswell Incident*.

---

* Many believe Shandera's key informant within the Aviary to have been the Raven. Richard Doty identified Raven as former CIA Director Richard Helms, although some have written that there may have been two Ravens, and that the one Shandera dealt with might have been former CIA Director Robert Gates.

In what would be Moore's last UFO lecture given in 1989 to the MUFON annual convention in Las Vegas Nevada, he recounted how the Falcon encounter began:

> In early September 1980, I was approached by a well-placed individual within the intelligence community who claimed to be directly connected to a high-level project dealing with UFOs. This individual told me that he spoke for a small group of similar individuals who were uncomfortable with the government's continuing cover-up of the truth and indicated that he and his group would like to help me with my research into the subject in the hope and expectation that I might be able to help them find a way to change the prevailing policy and get the facts to the public without breaking any laws in the process.

In order to stay within the law and not disclose classified material Falcon told Moore that the material he would be given would be partly true and partly false. That, he was told, is how the government operated. At this point Moore would have realized that nothing he would receive (including the MJ-12 document) could be considered completely true.

It would be up to Moore to figure out what was wheat and what was chaff. Moore quickly accepted the challenge seeing the opportunity to get inside the cover-up to see how it worked. Years after he left the field Moore defended his decision to work with Falcon and the other birds. He told his friend Greg Bishop:

> You have a choice. You're in or you're not in. If you're not in you don't know anything. If you're in you see where it goes. So what do you do? I chose to go with it. I guess I am really glad I did. If I had it to do over I would probably do the same thing. I think most people would if they were approached the way I was, and given the choice, would have opted into it. Virtually any UFO researcher worth his salt would have...Once you are into it you don't make the rules. You either pretty much follow it, or you are out of it. I think I did as much in the way of shaking and shuffling and looking under rugs as I could possibly do in order to maximize what I was able to learn from it.[101]

If Moore were interested (which of course he was), future meetings between him and Falcon would be handled through a liaison, AFOSI agent Richard Doty. Moore was given jobs to do such as monitoring and providing information about the activities of the Aerial Phenomenon Research Organization (APRO) founded by Coral and Jim Lorenzen. Moore was APRO's Director of Research. According to Greg Bishop, Moore was also given other spying duties, such as locating and investigating non-UFO people.

Moore reported on the UFO activities of avid military aircraft buff Lee Graham and Paul Bennewitz, a physicist living in Albuquerque, New Mexico. In return for these investigations, Moore was to be given inside information about UFOs and the alleged cover-up.

As Moore described it, the material started to flow in. By 1982, Falcon was providing so much inside information on UFOs that Moore could not handle it alone, so he brought Jamie Shandera in to help.[102]

The basis of the material that Moore would receive involved what became known as the UFO Core Story. Essentially, it is that aliens had made contact, and that bodies and a craft had been recovered from at least one crash. The concept of the Core UFO story was developed in a 1982 meeting at a Denny's Restaurant. The participants were Dr. Hal Puthoff, Dr. Kit Green, and Dr. Jacques Vallee. The idea was to answer the question, "What do we know for sure about UFOs?" This meeting occurred about the same time that Moore was obtaining much of his material from Falcon.[103]

Kit Green even pursued the Core Story while at the CIA, but was stopped. He told reporter Gus Russo, "I have been told by people more senior than me that there is some truth to it, but they told me time and time again to stop pursuing it with CIA people and other intel types. Two very senior officials told me they saw briefing books, [however] the only ones who would be cleared to know the story are the most senior Pentagon career officers."[104]

Doty would play the role of the public Falcon, to whom all researchers could point. That was part of the game intended to distract attention from the real Falcon. Researchers would be focused on Kirkland Air Force Base when the real story was happening elsewhere.

Doty began his public Falcon role in April 1983, by inviting acclaimed television producer Linda Moulton Howe to his office at Kirtland Air Force Base in Albuquerque, New Mexico. There he showed her putative "Presidential Briefing Papers." They described flying saucer crashes and recovered alien bodies.

During this conversation, Doty told Howe that he was Falcon, betting that she would repeat the Falcon story to the UFO community and thereby provide cover for the real Falcon, who was feeding Moore and Shandera government UFO secrets.

Howe outlined her association with Doty in an October 17, 1987 letter to *Just Cause*, and followed it up with a sworn affidavit, insisting that she would testify under penalty of perjury that the statements she had made regarding the meeting with Doty were true.

Doty responded to Howe's allegations in a March 4, 1988 letter to the UFO publication, *Focus*, that:

> She mentioned in her letter to Just Cause that I showed her a "Briefing Paper for the President of the United States" about the subject of unidentified flying vehicles. I can tell you, without a doubt, that I never showed her any such document. First of all, I was not in a position to obtain any presidential briefing documents. Secondly, I would not allow a person without a security clearance to see any such document. Lastly, she mentioned a document to me that was a "so-called" Project Aquarius briefing paper for the President of the United States. However, she brought up the subject, not me.

Doty went on in his letter to make some very definitive statements about the government's role concerning UFO information. According to Doty:

Finally, I know of no secret government investigation of UFOs. I have never heard of MJ-12 or any secret government agency that investigates UFOs. I am aware of Project Blue Book, which was an Air Force project that investigated UFOs from 1952 until 1969. To the best of my knowledge, the Air Force does not have any current program that investigates UFOs.

Doty chose his words very carefully. If the Briefing Document he showed to Howe was an altered version of a real document, then technically he was correct when he stated that he never showed her genuine documents. It was all part of a game that Doty would appear to continue to play for decades to come.

In the beginning, all the evidence seemed to point to Doty as being the real Falcon. In 1988, however, it started to become apparent that there were two Falcons and that Doty was simply a low level player in the game.

The real Falcon (who was represented on camera by a back-lit Doty) made some remarkable statements on the October 1988 television program, *UFO Cover-Up? Live!* In that program, Falcon told a national audience that there existed an agreement between the U.S. Government and extraterrestrials that permitted them to operate from an Air Force Base in Nevada called Area 51 or "Dreamland." Falcon went on to say that three different aliens had visited the USA since 1948-49, one of which was still a guest of the U.S. Government in 1988.

The authors, Cameron and Crain, have examined transcripts of telephone interviews with, and various letters written by, Doty. We have also conducted telephone interviews and corresponded with Linda Moulton Howe. Based on our investigation, it is our opinion that Linda Moulton Howe told the truth about what was presented to her by Doty.

Although Doty has denied any involvement in the MJ-12 affair, he was never willing to issue a sworn affidavit that Howe did not tell the truth. When asked by UFO researcher Robert Todd if he would issue a sworn affidavit to that effect,

Doty's response was simply, "I have no intention of sending you a notarized statement."

Further information pointing to two Falcons came from researcher Lee Graham, a friend of Moore, who stated in a letter of May 20, 1989 to Scott Crain that "Mr. William L. Moore has specifically given me permission to state that Mr. Richard C. Doty is not 'Falcon'!"

Graham, an electronics systems research technician at Aerojet Electro Systems from Monrovia, California, believed that Moore was telling the truth and that he was attempting to uncover government UFO secrets. Graham wrote:

> I, LEE MARVIN GRAHAM, BELIEVE that Mr. WILLIAM L. MOORE works With (I reiterate with) some agency of the United States Government that wants the American Public to believe that the "BRIEFING DOCUMENT: OPERATION MAJESTIC" is authentic.

Richard Doty did not play a big part in the release of UFO information. He did, however, have a large role in the story of Paul Bennewitz, which became one of the best known UFO stories of all time. This was also the story that led to the downfall of Bill Moore.

The Destruction of Paul Bennewitz

Why was Bennewitz selected to be monitored and neutralized by AFOSI? The reason seems quite simple. He had reported a series of UFO related events around Kirkland Air Force Base. More disturbing, he was using his scientific expertise to study what he was watching. "He was causing quite a problem," according to Moore, "headaches in high places."

In October 1980, Bennewitz reported to AFOSI he had filmed and photographed UFOs over the Manzano Nuclear Weapons Storage Area, east of Kirtland AFB. This set off alarm bells inside AFOSI. There were two possible reasons for the concern.

First, Bennewitz was watching some sort of secret Air Force

operation that he was mistaking for UFOs. Second, and the greater threat, was that Bennewitz was in fact watching UFOs over the nuclear weapons storage area (which was the biggest collection of nuclear weapons in the world at the time). Clearly, this would not be something that the Air Force wanted the public to know about or believe in.[105]

The claim by Bennewitz that UFOs would be found hovering over the nuclear weapons storage areas was an idea that was not generally accepted when Bennewitz first proposed it. Over the years, however, it has become commonly accepted by UFO researchers. Certainly, if there were UFOs over Manzano, it would have rated the highest level of classification and secrecy.

Bennewitz also reported that he was monitoring audio transmissions from UFOs with equipment he had created. He told AFOSI that his studies had convinced him that aliens were putting tiny devices into abductees in order to control them.

This idea was considered crazy at the time. Over the ensuring years, however, it has become more widely accepted. No one laughs anymore when there is a discussion of alien implants. Some of these tracking devices have even been removed for study by researchers such as Dr. Roger Leir and Derrel Sims.

It appeared that Bennewitz was on to something real. Moreover, he had the scientific resources to study what he was watching. He was in contact with a number of UFO research-ers, which meant the evidence he was gathering was about to spread. Soon everyone would know what was going on at Manzano. Bennewitz and his UFO discoveries had to be neutralized. AFOSI decided that Bennewitz needed to be misdirected with disinformation. The counterintelligence experts at Kirkland AFB were called in to run an operation against Bennewitz. He had become the enemy, and the counterintelligence experts would develop a plan to lead the enemy in another direction by providing those misdirecting dots

Moore acted as one of the go-betweens. He was familiar with Bennewitz's claims, as he was on the Board of Directors at APRO, which was receiving letters from Bennewitz. Moore was only involved with the AFOSI handling of Bennewitz, and during that time he provided him with a least one false document.[106] Moore knew the document was phony, as he had been shown the original. This was part of the game Falcon had warned him about. They would not break the law, but the material provided would be true and false. Bennewitz apparently believed the disinformation.

Moore said of his Bennewitz involvement:

> When you are approached and essentially recruited into something and you are given a choice—either you're in or you're out. You really don't know what you are getting into because they don't tell you very much about what you're getting into. It's sort of a step thing. It's one step at a time. You just get lured further and further into it, and at any point you can get out of it. And if you do, you do, you know...I was a little bit careful about how I did things. You are faced with a choice like that and someone says, "I would like you to involve yourself in this counterintelligence thing." That's basically what it was.[107]

According to Moore, J. Allen Hynek was also involved in this Bennewitz sting operation. He had provided a computer which was supposed to help track the aliens, when in fact it was tracking Bennewitz's actions. According to Moore, Bennewitz really went off the edge when he starting using this computer. If Moore's statement is true, Hynek like Moore was on the inside working with the government in exchange for information.

The disinformation campaign went beyond Bennewitz. AFOSI tried to mislead other UFO researchers with false information, as in the case of Linda Moulton Howe in 1983. In 1984, Moore himself was given false documents from AFOSI, at which point he withdrew his participation. Despite the fact that Moore pulled out in 1984, the story still circulates that

Moore's main boss was AFOSI, and that everything he did was part of an AFOSI operation to catch Russian spies.

Moore discussed his position in a 1993 interview with Greg Bishop:

> The whole story of Government/alien involvement, treaties with aliens, underground bases, a plot to take over the planet, implants, two different races of aliens, one hostile and one friendly, etc. was all cooked up by the counter-intelligence people for the purpose of discrediting Bennewitz. He bought it, and a lot of other people in the UFO community bought it, and they continue to buy it today. All of that stuff was cooked up as part of the operation against Bennewitz. Bennewitz was meeting with everybody who was anybody and telling that story to anyone who would listen, John Lear, and ultimately through him to Bill Cooper, Bill English, Wendelle Stevens . . . they all revolved around that information. It was the kind of paranoia that they wanted to hear. . . . Then I get up and tell them, "Folks, you've been had. And here's how I know. It isn't that I've heard it. I was part of it. I was there. I watched it happen. I knew who was doing it, and I was privy to it."

Doty discussed the Bennewitz case with the late Bob Pratt, a *MUFON UFO Journal* editor, in the early 1980s. Some of Pratt's taped transcripts and meeting notes appeared in the MUFON 2007 International UFO Symposium Proceedings in a paper prepared by Brad Sparks and Barry Greenwood.

Doty claimed that Bennewitz may have been onto something UFO-related that was of some interest to someone in the government, but he apparently did not know what it was. Nor did Doty. In any case, to discourage and discredit Bennewitz, OSI ran a disinformation and harassment campaign against him. Bennewitz was fed OSI-generated stories involving aliens ("Grays") who lived in underground bases that were conducting experiments to genetically change organs harvested from cattle and humans.

Coupling this information with the fact that Bennewitz was observing numerous strange lights over Sandia Labs and

Kirtland Air Force Base, he came to the conclusion that an extraterrestrial invasion was imminent, and he took his allegations public.

The terrorized Bennewitz eventually had a nervous break-down. Whether or not this had anything to do with the UFO material he was being fed is a matter of debate. Moore de-scribed a man who seemed to have some nerve problems. He was a chain smoker. Moore, however, confirmed that on at least one visit to Bennewitz's house that something strange was indeed going on.[108]

Bennewitz was being fed with material that was true and false, but so was every other researcher in the field. Not every other researcher has had a nervous breakdown. Bennewitz appeared to be at the forefront of many UFO discoveries that are now more generally understood and accepted. Because he was fed so much disinformation, we may never know the true extent of his real discoveries.

Sadly, the Bennewitz case also shows how easily the UFO community can be swayed to believe what the authorities want its members to believe. Bennewitz will probably always be remembered as a poor misguided soul who was destroyed by Moore, Doty, and the AFOSI.

Multiple Falcons?

In mid-1987, shortly after the release of the MJ-12 papers, Falcon suggested to Moore that they begin dropping subtle hints that Doty was "Falcon" to ensure the continued protec-tion of his identity. Although Moore used the date 1987, it appeared that the effort to paint Doty as the Falcon occurred much earlier. One example was in 1983 when Doty told Linda Moulton Howe that he was the Falcon.

The diversion was successful, especially following the national broadcast of the television show, *UFO Cover-Up? Live!*, in October 1988. After that documentary aired, many prominent UFO researchers became convinced that Richard

Doty was indeed Falcon. According to Moore, researchers writing to Doty for more information were writing to the wrong man. The man in control, the real Falcon, remained unidentified to all except those involved in Moore's project.

Can we believe Moore when he says that there was another Falcon? If so, what is the evidence?

Informed sources at the time hinted that this senior agent was connected with the DIA (Defense Intelligence Agency). William Moore confirmed in a telephone conversation with Grant Cameron on June 9, 1989, that "Falcon" was then in his 60s. Doty was 39 years old, or so he claimed in a May 24, 1989 letter to researcher Philip J. Klass.

Colonel Bill Coleman, former public spokesman for the U.S. Air Force Blue Book UFO program, told Florida reporter Billy Cox that the real Falcon was sitting in the audience during the broadcast of *UFO Cover-Up? Live!* Coleman added that "he knew Falcon" and was definitely with "the Agency." Coleman was surprised to see that this person was involved in UFOs.[109] Doty, on the other hand, in October 1988 when the documentary aired, had already left the Air Force and was at that time busy as a recruit in the New Mexico State Police Academy. Moore, in a June 9, 1989 telephone conversation with Cameron, refused either to confirm or deny that the real Falcon was in the studio audience at *UFO Cover-Up? Live!*, stating that it had been a small audience.

Other indications that there was a second Falcon are as follows:

Moore confirmed that the Falcon segment for the show was filmed the month before in Albuquerque. Coleman identified Falcon as being with the Agency, which would later turn out to be the CIA when Moore finally confirmed who the Falcon was.

The diversion to paint Doty as the Falcon on the documentary fooled most researchers. Even after Falcon was identified as a CIA official, many still insisted Doty was the one and only Falcon. It seemed like a case of textbook intelligence community misdirection.

The appearance by Doty on *UFO Cover-up? Live!* also set in motion a meeting the next day at CIA headquarters, supposedly to review Doty's acting debut. The meeting took place in the office of the CIA counterintelligence director. Those attending included USAF Colonel Barry Hennessey, head of Security for Air Force Special Projects; Colonel Richard Weaver, who later became famous for heading up the Roswell UFO crash investigation in 1993 ordered by the Clinton White House; Dr. Kit Green, who had responsibility for UFOs at the CIA from 1970 to 1983; and Dr. Ron Pandolfi, who took over the UFO responsibility when Green left the CIA.

Hennessey and Weaver denied any continuing connection to Doty, painting him as "nothing more than a petty criminal," and stating that he had failed a polygraph test before leaving the Air Force. After Pandolfi had left the room, Green produced a record showing that Doty had in fact passed the polygraph test. At this point both Hennessey and Weaver stormed out of the meeting.

This meeting occurred despite the CIA's public position that the Agency was not interested in UFOs. It also occurred despite a call from Bob Emenegger to his contact at the CIA just before the show started. Emenegger had been included in *UFO Cover-up? Live!*, in a segment describing how he and Allen Sandler had created a UFO documentary for the Pentagon. As part of that, the Pentagon had promised them an authentic film featuring a landing of aliens at Holloman Air Force Base in 1971.

Emenegger had learned through Michael Seligman, the producer of *UFO Cover-up? Live!* that Doty would appear in a backlit interview talking about the inner workings of the UFO cover-up, and about a live alien that had been hosted by the United States government.

In his call to the CIA, Emenegger warned that Doty would be claiming to be an intelligence agent who was going to tell all.

He was told by his contact that the CIA would "stand down" on the matter.

When the Falcon's CIA identity became known in 2012, it became apparent that the last thing the CIA was doing was "standing down" on UFOs being talked about on national TV. The fact that a senior CIA agent was sitting around watching a "supposedly" live UFO documentary being produced raises serious questions about how much of a role the CIA may have played in the documentary.

Add to this the fact that Seligman, the man in charge of the documentary, had worked for Grey Advertising, which is listed as one of 500 CIA front companies.[110] According to Air Force Captain Robert Collins, Seligman even attended a clandestine meeting hosted by Colonel Ernie Kellerstrauss. This is significant, since Kellerstrauss had worked at the Foreign Technology Division at Wright-Patterson Air Force Base before retiring in 1979. He possessed and shared a wealth of stories with Collins while he was stationed at there as a physicist. These were the same UFO Core Story material that Falcon was feeding to Moore.

Thus, Seligman was apparently communicating with Kellerstrauss in a meeting which was also attended by Doty and others. Among the topics of conversation was the "Yellow Book," supposedly written for the United States government in the early 1970s by EBE-2. EBE-3 was also openly discussed.[111]

Most importantly, the UFO documentary was anything but live. All of the people who appeared on the show were forced to read their stories from cue cards. These stories had been pre-written by someone who was never identified. Bob Emenegger was particularly annoyed at having to read someone else's version of his story from a cue card. At one point, while describing the aliens coming off the saucer in the film of his documentary, Bob playfully changed the words on the cue card in front of him. He said, "And the saucer door opened, and out walked Sasquatch." This caused someone to yell, "Stop, Stop. Read what's on the card!"

It was a carefully scripted production, with a top CIA official watching just off camera, and a meeting to discuss the whole event at CIA headquarters the next day. Also, in light of something Dr. Kit Green once stated in correspondence, perhaps Doty's acting role and the material released on UFO Cover-up? Live! should not have been much of a surprise, either. Once during a conversation, former CIA Director Richard Helms told Green, "Always believe what Richard Doty says about UFOs."

According to Moore, Doty had met with Falcon and knew what his role in the operation was. And, as Helms apparently told Green, he knew a few things about UFOs. His uncle, Edward Doty, had been involved in the 1947 Roswell incident and in UFO Project Twinkle.[112] His father, Charles, had attained the rank of Colonel in the U.S. Air Force. He was also involved in the Air Force's UFO investigations.

In January 1982, *National Enquirer* reporter Bob Pratt was contacted by Moore and Shandera to write a book based on material that Moore had been receiving from a surreptitious contact about government involvement in the UFO cover-up. This was about the same time Moore took on Shandera as a partner to handle the vast volumes of UFO material he was getting from Falcon.

The book's working title was *Majik-12*, but was entitled Project Aquarius. It was never published. Another person with the pseudonym "Ronald L. Davis" provided proof-reading. Pratt never met this person, but had a very interesting comment about him:

> Now it turns out that there was a third silent partner in this book, and Moore gave me the impression that this was Doty. The manuscript was submitted to him for approval. The manuscript came back with a lot of interesting technical details put into it such as weaponry and squads and things of that nature. This supposedly came from Doty. Whether it did or not I don't know.[113]

Years later it would be apparent that Pratt had been misdirected, along with the rest of the UFO community, about Doty. In fact, the material was actually coming from Falcon and other high level government sources—sources that may have included Henry Kissinger and former CIA Directors Richard Helms and Robert Gates.

Later in 1989, Pratt was allowed to view letters that Doty had sent to various researchers who were writing to him about his role in the cover-up. In view of phrasing, sentence structure, and grammatical errors in the letters, Pratt doubted that Doty was behind things. "He doesn't strike me as overly educated," Pratt wrote to researcher Robert Todd. "He doesn't sound like the brainy type who could create and carry out sophisticated disinformation programs." Moore maintained "Doty did indeed play a role in the project," but primarily as a liaison. Pratt went on to say that British researcher Timothy Good, who had released the MJ-12 Document in Britain as part of his best-selling book *Above Top Secret* in 1987, told him he knew the identity of Ronald L. Davis. It was not Doty, but "someone on the level of, say, a maintenance man on the Kirtland Air Force Base whose name was adopted by the 'real' agent."

Doty became very controversial and distrusted in the UFO research community. In a speech that Moore gave at the 1989 MUFON Symposium, he confirmed that Doty had met with a certain film producer (whom most researchers know to be Linda Moulton Howe) to mislead her. According to Moore, the counterintelligence people extended their disinformation campaign to include exposing this film producer to purportedly sensitive UFO government documentation that, to the best of Moore's knowledge, was all disinformation. The deception plan was effective, stated Moore, because that researcher (Howe) continued to believe the story.

Let us not forget that, in 1983, Special Agent Richard Doty of the Air Force Office of Special Investigations (AFOSI) at

Kirtland Air Force Base was an active agent representing the United States Government. In Howe's version of the story, Doty claimed that his superiors had instructed him to show her a document marked "Briefing Paper for the President of the United States of America." The document described recoveries of aliens, government UFO coded programs, and crashed UFOs.

Moreover, said Howe, Doty had promised her several thousand feet of historic film footage showing crashed discs, alien bodies, footage of a live extraterrestrial called "EBE," and scenes from a pre-planned meeting with extraterrestrials at White Sands, New Mexico, on April 25, 1964. She was under contract with Home Box Office at the time, and the footage was to be used in a UFO Special to be broadcast nationally.

There was a problem, however. Bridgett Potter of HBO wanted two things before production funds would be released: one, the film itself; and two, some confirmation (an official letter) from the President, the Secretary of Defense, the Secretary of State and the Joint Chiefs of Staff authenticating the film's content.

Doty failed to deliver the film, nor did he give a confirmation that the film existed. He claimed that, for "political reasons," the project was delayed. Later, he indicated to Howe that he was out of the project altogether and that another agent would assist her in her endeavors. Another agent did call, indicating that the team wanted to wait until after the November 1984 election before proceeding further. But Howe never got the film, and because of the delay her contract with HBO expired.

Some disturbing issues have been raised regarding the matter of Linda Moulton Howe and the U.S. Government. If Moore was correct in his estimate of what happened, then AFOSI Agent Richard Doty, his superiors, and others at AFOSI deliberately misled film producer Linda Moulton Howe, who at the time was representing HBO, and not herself, at the meeting. Therefore, the disinformation operation was directed at HBO. If HBO had aired a documentary without the written verification they wanted from the Defense Department (which they did not receive), millions of Americans viewers would have viewed a deceptive interpretation of the UFO phenomenon as supplied by the U.S. Air Force Office of Special Investigations.

During the October 14, 1988 broadcast of *UFO Cover-Up? Live!*, the silhouetted person known as "Condor" (identified by several researchers as U.S. Air Force Captain Robert Collins) shared the limelight with "Falcon." Condor reinforced Falcon's story that the U.S. Government had been communicating with extraterrestrial beings that were coming to Earth from another star system.

However, as with Falcon, both Collins and Moore have maintained that Collins is not the Condor. The implication is that like Doty, Collins was speaking on behalf of the real Condor when he appeared in show.

Leonard Stringfield, one of the foremost researchers on UFO crash and recovery operations carried out by the U.S. Government, was approached by Robert Collins in 1986 when Collins was stationed at Wright-Patterson Air Force Base. Collins described the help that he could provide to Stringfield in his research, including a meeting with a friend of his who had "a great deal of information." The informant proffered to Stringfield was a Colonel, and therefore not Richard Doty, who was a Master Sergeant.

The source was probably Colonel Ernie Kellerstrauss, who had been given the Aviary name "Hawk" by Moore.[114]

Collins also promised to provide Stringfield with a highly technical paper that dealt with UFOs and astronauts. The catch to all this help was that Stringfield would have to provide the names of all his sources that had given him information on UFO crashes and alien autopsies. When Stringfield refused to do so, Collins broke off the contact and moved on to a researcher on the Atlantic Coast.

Linda Moulton Howe indicated that in November 1987, Collins "desperately" wanted her to attend a meeting with him in Albuquerque, New Mexico. She attended the meeting, as did UFO researcher John Lear. At the meeting, Collins showed them a number of MJ-12-type documents, many relating to the purported live alien that was held in captivity by the U.S. Government. Howe said that Collins indicated that he had been working with Moore for years.

The bird contacts would continue into the 1990s. Bill Moore pulled back from research after 1989 so most of these contacts took place with Jamie Shandera.

One highlight briefly mentioned by Shandera was a failed initiative to bring about a UFO disclosure under George Bush Sr. in August of 1991. It was initiated and planned by the Parrot and the Raven. Negotiations took place and plans were set to brief Bush on the matter at his home in Kennebunkport, Maine. The plan however failed.

Shandera continued on until 1995 when he raced to Washington DC to meet with the third live alien that had been hinted at in 17+ pages of 'bird code.' This bird code was a series of riddles describing the government's role in UFOs and the bizarre 'Core Story' that three extraterrestrials had been guests of the United States at various times since 1947. It was put out by the Parrot.

Here is an example of the one bird code message sent in 1987/88 period which hinted at the three alien guests:

The Parrot Spoke Three Times

87/88: The Parrot three times spoke with the later. One in two parts and the Woodpecker taps this message. A few years after tens of thousands of birds flew over Europe: The Eagle acquired three rare birds. Unfortunately one died a few years after. Many years passed while Eagle learned to talk some rare bird: But mainly the rare bird learned to speak Eagle. These discussions are referred to in the book written in the forth repeat of the twin year the Woodpecker was born.

Screenshot from *UFO Cover-Up? Live!* showing an artist's depiction of the alien crystal.

Although the third live alien was no longer in the government safe house near the Washington Mall hinted at in the bird code (the story has it that the alien left in the early 1990s), Shandera was shown something that proved to him the existence of the ETs "beyond any doubt." He had seen what he wanted and, like Bill Moore before him, Shandera disappeared from the UFO scene.

When asked what Shandera had been shown that convinced him the ET situation was for real, Moore said he did not know for sure, as Shandera didn't tell him. However, he added that, if he were to guess, Shandera may have seen the crystal which was first described in the October 1988 *UFO Cover-up? Live!* show, where the Falcon was first introduced to the public.

The crystal was supposedly was hand-sized, and produced 3-D images and could show events in the past, such as the crucifixion of Jesus Christ.

As the 1990s arrived, except for Shandera's bird contacts in Washington, the bird story had ended. It appeared to be replaced by the appearance in 1991 of top CIA scientist Dr. Ronald Pandolfi. His interactions with the UFO community would bring a whole new type of UFO disclosure, one which continues to the present day.

Chapter 9
The Big Picture

A few years ago I lectured at the Hebrew Academy in San Francisco on a fairly regular basis. Many of the children in attendance are refugees from the Soviet Union. One afternoon, when no particular topic was planned, I asked the children what they would like to discuss. A young girl raised her hand and asked: "What can you tell us about UFOs?" I replied that all the sightings probably had some explanation in natural terrestrial phenomena. She remained unsatisfied and rephrased her question-several times. Finally, I asked her why she was so persistent. "Because," she said, "in Russia, they tell us UFOs don't exist, so, of course, they do, and now that I am in the United States I want to learn about them."
– Edward Teller

I
t is rather difficult to be definite about what is really going on here, but our research leads us to several conclusions about what the U.S. Government is doing with UFOs. Although the U.S. Government has, almost without exception, continually denied any involvement in UFO crash retrieval operations, there are bits and pieces of evidence that clearly indicate such involvement has occurred.

A pivotal point in our report concerns the purported meetings held at Wright-Patterson Air Force Base, at which flying saucer crash retrievals were discussed. If one can believe Dr. Robert Sarbacher—who clearly indicated in his November 23, 1983 letter that (1) UFO retrievals have occurred, (2) laboratories carefully analyzed the material from these crashes, and (3) these ships were controlled by alien pilots—then we have a working idea of the active involvement of the U.S. Government, and subsequent cover-up.

Dr. Eric Walker's initial telephone conversation with William Steinman confirmed that (1) those secret meetings at Wright-Patterson AFB really did take place, and (2) that the MJ-12 group really exists. One of Walker's letters—if legitimate—confirmed that aliens had been aboard a recovered UFO.

Canadian scientist Wilbert Smith's investigation into U.S. involvement led him to several discoveries. The most striking of these were that "flying saucers exist" and that their modus operandi was being studied by "a small U.S. group" (presumably MJ-12) headed by Dr. Vannevar Bush.

Based on the evidence that we have examined, it is our opinion that the U.S. Government has initiated a three-phase plan to handle UFOs.

Phase One: The U.S. government creation of quick-reaction intelligence teams to facilitate the recovery of crashed UFOs.

These intelligence teams, which operated in the field, were organized to collect and deliver, among other things, crashed or disabled UFOs to designated locations. If a UFO were to crash, military personnel would have to react quickly to a developing situation and follow a pre-planned set of procedures (concerned with photographs, mapping, interviews, securing the location, handling the press, etc.) all toward the end of securely transporting the evidence to a designated site for further study.

William Steinman offered an unsubstantiated example of an operation of this kind in his book, UFO Crash at Aztec. According to Steinman, when a UFO crashed, a special unit of U.S. Army Counterintelligence, known as the Interplanetary Phenomenon Unit (IPU), was placed on Red Alert. The IPU was part of the Army's Scientific and Technical Branch, and operated out of Camp Hale, Colorado. Although Steinman wrote that their purpose was to recover and deliver crashed flying saucers to secret locations, this has never been officially confirmed.

In response to William Steinman's letter of inquiry to the Department of the Army regarding the purpose and origin of the IPU, Lieutenant Colonel Lance R. Cornine, Director of Counterintelligence, responded with these comments in a letter to Steinman dated May 16, 1984.

> The "unit" was formed as an in-house project purely as an interest item for the Assistant Chief of Staff for Intelligence. It was never a "unit" in the military sense, nor was it ever formally organized or reportable, it had no investigative function, mission or authority, and may not even have had any formal records at all.

Lt. Col. Cornine's appraisal of the IPU to Steinman conflicted with the details released by Colonel William B. Guild, Director of Counterintelligence, Department of the Army, in a letter he wrote to researcher Richard Hall dated September 25, 1980. According to Guild, "all records pertaining to this unit were surrendered to the U.S. Air Force Office of Special Investigations in conjunction with Operation 'BLUEBOOK.'" Project Blue Book was an Air Force project to investigate UFOs. To date, the AFOSI has not released the files of the IPU.

It is interesting to note that General Douglas MacArthur and General George C. Marshall were both rumored to have been involved in establishing the IPU.

General Marshall served in the armed forces as the U.S. Army Chief of Staff in World War Two and as U.S. Secretary of State from 1947-49. Marshall also served as Secretary of Defense, a post that was originally held by James Forrestal, a designated Majestic-12 member. If the position of Secretary of Defense automatically made one a member of Majestic-12, then, obviously, it stands to reason that Marshall would have been privy to the recorded events regarding UFO retrievals.

Dr. Rolf Alexander claimed that he talked to General Marshall in 1951 about UFOs and their occupants. When asked about the landings, he said "Marshall admitted that there had actually been contact with the men in the UFOs, and that on three occasions there had been landings which had proved disastrous for the occupants." Marshall claimed that the Earth's oxygen-laced atmosphere had burned the visitors from the inside out.

Douglas MacArthur became a five-star general in the U.S. Army in 1944 and was one of America's military heroes during World War Two. During an interview in the mid-1950s, MacArthur was asked a question about the possibility of World War Three. According to the October 9, 1955 issue of the *New York Times*, MacArthur replied:

> The nations of the world will have to unite, for the next war will be an interplanetary war. The nations of the Earth must someday make a common front against attack by people from other planets.

MacArthur brought up the theme of interstellar invasions again during an address he gave at the 1962 graduating class at the United States Military Academy in West Point, New York. MacArthur said:

> We deal not only with things of this world alone, but with the illimitable distances and as yet unfathomed mysteries of the universe. We are reaching out for a new and boundless frontier. We speak in terms of harnessing the cosmic energy . . . of ultimate conflict between a united human race and the sinister forces of some other planetary galaxy.

Did MacArthur and Marshall share a secret they had learned at the IPU that still cannot be revealed?

Evidence that MacArthur maintained a detailed file on UFOs was reported in the August 7, 1982 edition of *The News World* (published in New York City). John R. Frick of Florida reported that MacArthur originally established the "Interplanetary Phenomenon Unit" while in Asia as early as 1945 after the general had had a close encounter with a UFO in April of that year.

According to Frick, Larry Bryant of "Citizens Against UFO Secrecy" (CAUS) was informed of MacArthur's Top Secret UFO file in October 1981.

MacArthur's ideas about an alien threat were voiced again by none other than former President Ronald Reagan shortly after he returned from a meeting in Geneva in 1985 with General Secretary Mikhail Gorbachev of the Soviet Union.

Reagan told his listeners at a December 4, 1985 speech he gave at Fallston High School in Maryland that he had told Gorbachev:

> ... how easy his task and mine might be in these meetings that we held if suddenly there was a threat to this world from some other species from another planet outside in the universe. We'd forget all the little local differences that we have between our countries ...[115]

On September 21, 1987, the President was speaking before the General Assembly of the United Nations when he remarked:

> I occasionally think, how quickly our differences worldwide would vanish if we were facing an alien threat from outside this world. And yet I ask, is not an alien force already among us?[116]

Then, on May 4, 1988, at Chicago's Palmer House Hotel, Reagan was answering questions after his speech and was quoted as having said:

> I've often wondered, what if all of us in the world discovered that we were threatened by an outer ... a power from outer space, from another planet.[117]

One cannot help but wonder if MacArthur and Reagan were speaking of the same alien threat—a threat they knew something about, and that we did not.

Although we could not prove that the Army's Interplanetary Phenomenon Unit was involved in retrieving downed UFOs, we did find substantial evidence that the U.S. Air Force's "Moon Dust" program was established for this very purpose.

Project Moon Dust

Researcher Robert Todd, in a letter he received from the Air Force on August 20, 1979, uncovered details of a U.S. Air Force "retrieval squad." Todd was inquiring about the Air Force's "Project Moon Dust," because references linking it to UFOs kept turning up in documents of the U.S. Defense Intelligence Agency and State Department.

Todd received in the mail an Air Force Intelligence document identified as "AFCIN-1E-Q," dated November 3, 1961. Although the text of the document had been partially redacted, there was enough left to give a glimpse of the purpose of the Moon Dust program.

On page one, the document reads:

> In addition to their staff duty assignments, intelligence team personnel have peacetime duty functions in support of such Air Force projects as Moon Dust, Blue Fly, and [Project] UFO, and other AFCIN directed quick reaction projects, which require intelligence team operational capabilities.

Project Moon Dust is described by the following excerpt:

> [As] a specialized aspect of its over-all material exploitation program, Headquarters USAF has established Project Moon Dust to locate, recover and deliver descended foreign space vehicles.

The document also stated that:

> These three peacetime projects all involve a potential for employment of qualified field intelligence personnel on a quick reaction basis to recover or perform field exploitation of *unidentified flying objects*, or known Soviet/Bloc aerospace vehicles, weapons systems, and/or residual components of such equipment. [Emphasis added by the authors.]

It is evident from the documents that the Air Force had developed a field team to handle crashed UFOs. According to the documents, "Blue Fly" was involved in the transportation of Moon Dust material which included, among other things, debris acquired from recovered UFOs.

It is interesting to note that UFO material has a separate listing from Soviet/Bloc aerospace vehicles, as if the Air Force considered UFOs a different area of investigation.

The documents stated that Moon Dust hardware and "other items of great technical intelligence interest" were forwarded to the Foreign Technology Division at Wright-Patterson Air Force Base in Ohio under the auspices of Operation Blue Fly.

That the Foreign Technology Division (FTD), which oversaw Project Moon Dust, was also the parent coordinator for Project Blue Book, the official Air Force program to investigate UFOs, appears to be more than happenstance.

Evidence indicating the existence of a Moon Dust link to UFO crash retrievals can be found in Donald Keyhoe's 1955 UFO book, *The Flying Saucer Conspiracy*. Here is one passage, for instance:

> Two days after this Lou Corbin called me to report another development. "Do you know anything about a crashed-object' program?" he asked me. "No. Whose project is it?" "It's an Air Force deal, unless somebody's trying to trick me. You've heard of the 4602nd Air Intelligence Service Squadron, of course?" "Yes. It's a hush-hush unit. They have investigators in all Air Defense Squadrons." "Well, I've been contacted by one of them. First I thought it might be some kind of hoax. But I've double- checked. He actually is with the 4602nd." "Sounds queer, Lou. They're not supposed to talk to anyone outside of Intelligence." "I know. But he may be under special orders. Anyway, he's against the secrecy policy. He told me the 4002nd has a special program called investigation of unidentified crashed objects."' "If it's true, that is big," I said. "It could mean they've actually got their hands on some flying saucers." "He wouldn't admit that," said Corbin. "But I got the impression they'd recovered some kind of 'objects'—probably something dropped from a saucer."[118]

And another example:

> At 2:00 P.M. on November 30 [1954?] a mysterious bright flash in the sky was reported simultaneously in Atlanta, Newman, and Columbus, Georgia; in Sylacauga and Birmingham, Alabama; and as far away as Greenville, Mississippi. This brilliant light was immediately followed by a series of strange explosions, apparently centered high in the sky above Sylacauga.
>
> Moments later a black object, six inches in diameter, crashed into the home of Mrs. Hewlett Hodges.
>
> Smashing a three-foot-wide hole in the roof, the shining black object tore through the living-room ceiling.
>
> Striking the radio, it bounced off and gashed Mrs. Hodges's arm.

Meanwhile, the mysterious explosions had caused a hurried Air Defense alert. A three-state search for fallen objects was immediately begun by squadrons of Air Force planes.

When word of the "Sylacauga object" reached the Air Force, Intelligence officers flew to the scene from Maxwell Air Force Base at Montgomery. Explaining that "the Air Force is required to examine such strange objects," they whisked it away to Maxwell Field from which it was flown immediately to ATIC (Air Technical Intelligence Center).

An hour or two later the object was labeled a meteorite.

As soon as this appeared in the papers, I received a call from Lou Corbin. "It's plain that this is part of the Air Force 'unidentified crashed-objects' investigation. They must believe the thing is linked with the saucers."[119]

Another example of an apparent Moon Dust / Blue Fly retrieval operation occurred on December 9, 1965, when a fiery, bright-orange UFO crashed in a wooded area near Kecksburg, Pennsylvania. Although local State Police officers set up road blocks and kept curiosity seekers out, local firemen that were called out to look for the object saw the downed vehicle before military officials arrived.

One local fireman described the object as metallic, tarnished silver or off-gold in color, approximately nine feet high and wide, with a "bumper" around the object. The bumper had what the fireman described as looking like "ancient Egyptian hieroglyphics" on it. Apparently, the acorn-shaped object had come down through the trees and carved out a trench five to six feet wide and twenty-five feet long before it came to a stop, half-buried in the ground.

The object's actual size and shape could not be well discerned, since it was difficult to tell how much was covered by dirt. The object was intact and had no windows, fuselage, wings, or seams on it.

Soon, military personnel moved into the area and compelled the firemen to leave the impact area immediately. According to Stan Gordon, Director of the Pennsylvania Association for the Study of the Unexplained, whatever fell in Kecksburg was of intense interest to the military.

> The Kecksburg Volunteer Fire Department had its truck station located only a short distance from the impact site. According to members of the local fire departments who were involved in the search efforts, the military set up a command post in that building. A lot of equipment was brought in, including one large radio unit. There seemed to be mainly Air Force personnel who manned the fire hall. The military reportedly asked the firemen to leave the fire hall. Armed guards were placed at the entrance. A large number of Army and Air Force vehicles were reported at different locations around the village during the evening. At least two flatbed trucks, one with military markings, another not marked and hauling a payloader or small crane were seen moving near the wooded area.[120]

According to Gordon, apparently the Blue Book staff had called the 662nd Radar Squadron in Oakdale, Pennsylvania, to investigate the crash. The radar facility dispatched a three-man team to investigate and retrieve the object that had landed. It is interesting to note that the Moon Dust documents state that "intelligence teams are comprised of three men each" and are activated to perform a Moon Dust operation.

Another witness to the recovery operation was Dr. Eric Walker. In a telephone interview on May 30, 1991, Henry Azadehdel interviewed Dr. Walker about the night a UFO fell out of the sky over Kecksburg. The impetus for the interview came from Cameron, who had put together two pieces of the puzzle. First, a 1990 interview with Stanton Friedman in which Walker said he had not been involved in UFOs for 25 years. In other words, since 1965, the year of the Kecksburg crash. Second, as the crow flies, Walker lived only 100 miles from the crash. Moreover, he had a pilot's license and plane. He could have been on the scene in an hour. Cameron therefore suggested that Azadehdel phone Walker and see if he would confirm being involved in the crash.

The interview originally appeared in the book *UFO Crash/Retrievals: The Inner Sanctum (Status Report VI)* by

Leonard H. Stringfield. It was published in July, 1991. What follows is an excerpt.

> HA: Doctor, I want to ask you about something that might not have anything to do with the UFOs. Would you mind me asking you?
>
> EW: What is that?
>
> HA: Doctor, it is about an incident which happened in the mid-60's. To be precise, on December 9, 1965, in Kecksburg. It was, one could say, almost in your back garden. Could you tell me something about it?
>
> EW: What about it?
>
> HA: Well, what did you find out about it?
>
> EW: You still have not given up.
>
> HA: Well Doctor, you would say I am like a turtle—you turn me over to get rid of me, I struggle for awhile in my shell, and eventually get back on my legs.
>
> EW: Well, we went there.
>
> HA: With the military?
>
> EW: Well, you see, two were from the military, but not on duty.
>
> HA: How about the others?
>
> EW: He was a fellow colleague of mine. [Who was the second military person LHS]
>
> HA: What did you find? Was it a—I know you are not going to like the word, but, was it a UFO?
>
> EW: I cannot comment on that. I cannot tell you.
>
> HA: Were you there for long?
>
> EW: Why?
>
> HA: Well, curiosity. I thought, maybe, there was a purpose in the sense of—maybe, preparing a report, or taking some notes.
>
> EW: We did not prepare any reports.

Stan Gordon went on to describe the retrieval operation:

> A number of onlookers witnessed a large flatbed military truck that was unloaded, moving in the direction of the impact area. It was late that evening when apparently the same truck came back down the road traveling at a high rate of speed [sic]. This time, however, a tarp covered over a large section of the flatbed. The vehicle, which had

numerous lights flashing on it, was being escorted in the front and rear by other military vehicles. One witness stated that the truck wasn't about to slow down for anyone, and seemed in a hurry to get out of the area. It was a short time later that word was passed on to the firemen, and circulated among the crowds, that the search operation was over. What was located was not a crashed airplane, but a meteorite according to military authorities.

Following the interview about Kecksburg, Cameron and Crain contacted Gordon to tell him that Walker had confirmed being on the scene. Gordon took it upon himself to contact Walker and see if Walker would help him with the details of what had occurred.

In November 1991, Gordon sent Walker a letter in which he outlined who he was and added that he was the chief civilian investigator for the crash. He asked if Walker could talk to him on or off the record about his involvement and provide information about what had crashed in 1965.

As with many researchers before, Walker did not throw the letter in the garbage. This would have been the simple thing to do, especially if he had not been involved. Instead, Walker returned the letter with a four-word hand-written notation: "wait for my book."

Walker had already published his autobiography, *Now It's My Turn: Engineering My Way*, in 1989. Therefore, taken at face value, Walker's comment indicated that there might be another book that would tell the story.

Gordon waited until 1995 before sending a follow-up letter. However, Dr. Walker had died on February 17, 1995, and the letter was never returned.

Returning to the Kecksburg object, it would appear that, based on observations and the times it was seen that night, it was traveling at roughly 5,000 miles per hour. (The speed of the slowest moving meteor that has yet been recorded is about 27,000 miles per hour.) Observers nearby claimed that the object looked to be about the size of a small plane and appeared to be gliding rather than plummeting as it made its slow descent towards Kecksburg. Whatever crashed at Kecksburg, it did not appear to be a meteorite.

Another suggestion has been made that the object was a failed Russian satellite. James Oberg, an expert on the Soviet space program, writing in *UFO Magazine* (Volume 8, Number 6, 1993), reported that the UFO may have been a classified Soviet Cosmos-96 satellite. Support for this conclusion came from a letter dated November 15, 1993, from Colonel Rodney S. Lusey, Deputy Chief of Staff, U.S. Space Command. The letter was a response to an inquiry made by Armen Victorian (a.k.a. Henry Azadehdel), and stated "Cosmos 96 was intended to be a Venus probe; however, a booster failure caused this satellite to decay after it's [sic] launch. Cosmos 96 was launched on November 23, 1965, and decayed on December 9, 1965, at 51.8 North latitude and 85.2 West longitude."

The re-entry date is the same as that of the Kecksburg crash. Cosmos satellites were bell-shaped in design, similar to witnesses' accounts at Kecksburg (and later by those who claimed see a bell-shaped craft in a hangar at Wright-Patterson Air Force Base in Ohio the next day). Eyewitness descriptions of seeing what appeared to be "ancient Egyptian hieroglyphics" around the rim of the object could have been Cyrillic characters.

Even so, there is strong evidence against the idea that the Kecksburg object was a Russian probe. Investigative journalist Leslie Kean, writing about the Kecksburg crash in the *International UFO Reporter* (Volume 30, Number 1), reported that Cosmos-96 re-entered the Earth's atmosphere over Canada at 3:18 a.m. This was over 13 hours before the Kecksburg incident. In 2003, Kean interviewed Nicholas L. Johnson, Chief Scientist for Orbital Debris at the NASA Johnson Space Center, about the Kecksburg UFO. "I can tell you categorically that there is no way that any debris from Cosmos 96 could have landed in Pennsylvania anywhere around 4:45 p.m.," Johnson said. Whatever crashed in Kecksburg does not appear to be a Russian probe.

If the object that fell in Kecksburg was neither a meteorite nor a Russian space probe, what was it?

Responsibility for Moon Dust documentation has been attributed to the Defense Intelligence Agency. Unfortunately, FOIA access to the files at the DIA on Moon Dust operations is denied, because access may reveal intelligence gathering methods, something that is automatically exempted under the Freedom of Information Act.

NASA is also linked to the Moon Dust program. According to a January 13, 1969 memo:

> The undersigned (Richard M. Schulherr) visited the Foreign Technology Division of the Air Force Systems Command, Wright-Patterson AFB, Ohio, 9 Jan. 1969. The purpose of this trip was to identify specific items of space debris which had been forwarded to NASA and to re-establish personal liaison with newly-assigned FTD Moon Dust personnel.[121]

To our knowledge, NASA is not exempt from FOIA. NASA personnel were reportedly at the crash site in Kecksburg. It would be reasonable to assume that they would have some knowledge of what was pulled out of the ground that night.

To find out, Leslie Kean sued NASA in 2003 for documentation relating to the Kecksburg crash. NASA eventually supplied a number of documents, but they were unresponsive to her request. U.S. District Judge Emmet Sullivan sided with Kean and, in March, 2007, rejected NASA's request to throw the case out of court. This led to an agreement with NASA to make a more comprehensive search of the archives for documents related to what happened that night in Kecksburg.

On September 13, 2010, Crain asked Kecksburg investigator Stan Gordon what NASA had found. Nothing related to the crash, replied Gordon.

Although the Air Force's Project Moon Dust and Blue Fly are supposedly no longer active, one can be sure that the Air Force still follows set procedures when an unknown vehicle lands on

U.S. soil, if only for reasons of national defense.

One has to wonder if MJ-12 helped formulate Project Moon Dust as a mechanism to retrieve UFOs in an effective manner.

Phase 2. Analysis of UFO Hardware (and Extraterrestrials) by Top-Level Scientists

Throughout this book, we have hinted that the IDA, DARPA, and Jason Group would very likely have been involved in any American recovery of a downed flying saucer. Over the years, these groups have held the highest of security clearances and have had access to some of the best scientific minds America has to offer.

According to Dr. Robert Sarbacher, meetings held at Wright-Patterson AFB involved "discussions associated with the reported recoveries," and he was sure "our laboratories analyzed them very carefully."

If so, who would be involved in analyzing recovered UFO hardware and its occupants?

One possible answer is indicated in the "Briefing Document: Operation Majestic 12," provided that the document is authentic. If so, then all the original MJ-12 members listed would have had a role either in the recovery or the analysis of a recovered craft. Others who would appear to be involved include Sarbacher's colleagues on the military's Research and Development Board in the early 1950s. This would include the Board's executive secretary, Dr. Eric A. Walker.

Dr. Vannevar Bush, former chairman of the R&D Board, appears to have headed up the original crash retrieval investigations. This is implied not only in the MJ-12 Document, but also by Canadian scientist Wilbert Smith in his November 1950 "Geo-Magnetics Memo."

According to the MJ-12 Document, the analysis of the "dead occupants" recovered at Roswell, New Mexico, was led by Dr. Detlev Bronk. Dr. Bronk, a physiologist and biophysicist of international stature, and his team referred to the creatures as

"Extra-Terrestrial Biological Entities" or EBEs until a later designation could be decided upon. The MJ-12 Document stated that it was:

> ... the tentative conclusion of this group ... that although these creatures are human-like in appearance, the biological and evolutionary processes responsible for their development have apparently been quite different from those observed or postulated in homo-sapiens.

According to William Steinman, one scientist who was involved in studying UFO hardware was Dr. Eric Henry Wang. In a September 8, 1987 letter to Grant Cameron, Steinman wrote:

> Dr. Eric Henry Wang headed up the Department of Special Studies at the old Wright Air Development Center at W.P.A.F.B. [Wright-Patterson AFB] from 1949-1956. The Department of Special Studies was moved to Kirtland Air Force Base/Sandia Labs Complex near Albuquerque, New Mexico, where Wang was in charge from 1956 until his death in 1960. I located Dr. Wang's widow, who confirmed to me that he was involved in an Above-Top-Secret project to analyze and subsequently duplicate the recovered flying saucers.

Steinman confirmed Wang's role with other sources, too. He detailed Wang's involvement in his book, *UFO Crash at Aztec*. One of the key discoveries made by Steinman about Wang's research is that, according to his widow, Mrs. Maria Wang, "[Henry Kissinger] is deeply involved in the Flying Saucer Program. . . . In fact, he was completely in charge of it at the time that Dr. Wang was still alive and involved with it." This is extremely significant as the conspiratorial side of the UFO community has long named Kissinger as a key member of MJ-12, possibly sitting as its head (MJ-1) at one point.

Steinman also claimed that Nobel Laureate Dr. Luis W. Alvarez was involved in the program. According to Steinman, Alvarez admitted to him in 1986 that he had been involved in a UFO recovery operation in the Sierra Madre mountain region in Mexico in November 1949. Steinman said that Dr.

Alvarez would not go into detail concerning the recovery, nor would he indicate who else was involved. Alvarez was a Jason member.

It appears from our research that a great quantity of UFO debris was originally sent to Wright-Patterson Air Force Base in Ohio for analysis. Examples include debris recovered from the Roswell UFO crash, as well as material retrieved from Moon Dust operations. To our knowledge, no useful government files have been unEarthed to describe an analysis of the debris.

However, some very interesting research on the Roswell crash debris has been carried out by Anthony Bragalia, a freelance investigator and UFO researcher. According to witnesses at the crash site, various types of debris was recovered, most of it not looking very other-worldly. However, one type of debris with some unusual characteristics did stand out. In the 2009 book, *Witness To Roswell*, authors Thomas J. Carey and Donald Schmitt describe this piece of flat aluminum looking metal as something "one could crumble a piece of it up in ones hand and then lay it on a flat surface, where it would quickly un-crumble itself into its original flat pristine condition without evidence of a crease. It also could not be scratched, cut, burned, or permanently deformed in any way." Known as "memory metal" we had nothing like it in 1947, and even today cannot reproduce all of its properties.

According to Bragalia, in a May 26, 2009 Internet article, the debris was originally sent to Wright-Patterson Air Force Base in Ohio, and was forwarded to Battelle Memorial Institute in Columbus, Ohio for analysis. Battelle scientists used the Roswell "memory metal" as a template to reproduce it. They came up with their own version of memory metal, calling it Nitinol, a mixture of nickel and titanium. Bragalia writes that Nitinol has the same properties as the crash debris reported at Roswell. Both are memory metals that remember their original shape, both are extremely lightweight. The materials are reported to have similar color, possess a high fatigue strength, and are able to withstand extreme high heat.

Interestingly, some files are missing. Bragalia writes he spent a year trying to obtain First and Second Progress Reports on memory metal, but they are missing, not only from Battelle, but also from the organization that contracted the work: Wright-Patterson AFB.

Bragalia writes that a graduate Chemical Engineer, Elroy John Center, "has stated that he analyzed metal from a crashed UFO when he was employed by the Institute." Center said it was understood he was working on debris retrieved by the U.S. Government of an earlier UFO crash. The research occurred in June 1960 and of course was classified. Center passed away in 1991.

It is possible that some types of analysis were conducted at Wright-Patterson Air Force Base. Researcher Lee Graham conducted an extensive investigation into the 1947 Roswell UFO crash after a coworker of his admitted that debris from the Roswell crash was still being stored there. While working at Hycon Manufacturing Co., an aerospace firm in Monrovia, California, a co-worker named Carl Johnson told him about the crashed saucer material stored there, Graham said. According to an article in the June 25, 1984 issue of the *San Gabriel Valley Tribune*, Johnson reportedly told Graham and others he had been privy to the Roswell artifacts while a field representative of Hycon at Wright -Patterson Air Force Base in Ohio in the 1960s.

Rumors surfaced that a secret room known as the "Blue Room" was maintained at Wright-Patterson AFB to store the remains of flying saucers. U.S. Senator Barry Goldwater asked to see it and was denied access. Goldwater (who was a reservist General in the U.S. Air Force) was refused admittance to this high security area of the base, because a "need-to-know" policy was in effect, and he did not need to know.

What happened to Goldwater is best described in the book

The Roswell Incident by Charles Berlitz and William L. Moore:

> According to Senator Goldwater, what actually happened
> was the following: while en route to California in the early
> 1960s, the Senator stopped at Wright-Patterson Air Base,
> where he visited his friend General Curtis LeMay. Senator
> Goldwater had heard of the existence of a room or section
> on the base referred to as the "Blue Room," where UFO
> artifacts, photographs, and exhibits were kept. The sena-
> tor, who as a longtime pilot, had more than a passing
> interest in UFOs, requested permission from General
> LeMay to visit the Blue Room exhibits. General LeMay's
> response was eminently succinct: "Hell, no. I can't go, you
> can't go, and don't ever ask me again!"

Graham wrote to Goldwater in order to get him to confirm or
deny the allegations made in the book. Goldwater responded
that he was denied access to the Blue Room.

In an earlier request for more information about the incident, Goldwater told Shlomo Amon of the UCLA Experimental
College that:

> About ten or twelve years ago I made an effort to find out
> what was in the building at Wright-Patterson Air Force
> Base where the information is stored that has been
> collected by the Air Force, and I was understandably
> denied this request. It is still classified above Top Secret.[122]

It is interesting to note that under Executive Order No.
12356 of National Security Information (April 1, 1982, 47 F.R.
14874), the first-level classification is defined as "Top Secret"
and is applied to information "the unauthorized disclosure of
which reasonably could be expected to cause exceptionally
grave damage to the national security."

UFO artifacts apparently rate the highest security classification.

William Moore inquired directly to Wright-Patterson AFB
about the rumored "Blue Room" in a FOIA request dated
December 30, 1980. He received several responses indicating
that neither the Foreign Technology Division nor the Aeronau-
tical Systems Division had any knowledge of "Project Blue

Room."

Although officially the U.S. Government denied the existence of the Blue Room, Lee Graham secured a document from Moore strongly implying it does exist.

In a letter dated July 25, 1988, Graham wrote to Representative Barbara Boxer describing the document entitled "Blue Room (Radar Scope)." Graham wrote:

> According to Mr. Moore, it was the testimony of the USAF individual who gave him this document that "RADAR SCOPE" of the "BLUE ROOM" had been a project to attempt to build an aircraft invisible to radar. Material from the 1947 crashed flying saucer had been stretched over a discoidally shaped target and towed behind an aircraft while being painted by radar. The return image was photographed on a Cathode Ray Tube (CRT), hence, "RADAR SCOPE."

Evidence that the Air Force had an interest in producing an aircraft invisible to radar is discussed below.

Lee Graham pieced together an interesting scenario about how events may have unfolded after the Roswell UFO crash. Again quoting from the June 24, 1984 issue of the *San Gabriel Valley Tribune*:

> For Graham, though, there's another possible explanation. He notes that Wright-Patterson has had a hand in the development of the Air Force's secret Stealth aircraft, the super-fast reconnaissance plane with properties allowing it to "hide" from enemy radar.
>
> "Consider this: perhaps the Air Force found the crashed saucer in 1947 and discovered it was made of a special material unknown on Earth," he hypothesized.
>
> "I can see a committee of scientists analyzing the material so that it could be manufactured, and Stealth is the result many years later."

The craft's remains, according to Jesse Marcel, who claimed to have touched it in 1947, were exceptionally light and similar to Kevlar—plastics which Graham suggested might be used on Stealth because of an ability to absorb or distort radar signals.

Whether or not Graham's ideas are correct remains a mystery.

Phase 3: Duplication of Alien Technology for the Development of a Strategic Military Advantage

This particular area of study is extremely speculative. And yet, bits and pieces of evidence fit into an interesting scenario. Could it be that the stealth fighter, whose prototype was developed by DARPA and whose test vehicle was developed by the U.S. Air Force, utilized technology exhibited by flying saucers?

The ability of UFOs to become invisible and perform with unusual flight characteristics was of immense interest to Air Force analysts, who duplicated some of these characteristics in the development of the Stealth aircraft. Early military interest in UFOs can be traced back to an "Air Intelligence Division Study No. 203" dated December 10, 1948, which outlines several UFO characteristics:

> Most of the objects were thin discs, round on top and flat on the bottom.
> A high rate of climb and ability to remain motionless for long periods was evident.
> Sizes ranged from a quarter [foot] to 250 feet.
> Speeds ranged from motionless to supersonic.

Initially, the Air Force did not take seriously cases where UFOs were observed at close range but were not detected on radar. But such reports continued. A number of cases are on file where airliner and military pilots reported seeing UFOs right off their wings, but with no radar detection.

For example, on April 27, 1950, a TWA DC-3 was flying over Goshen, Indiana, when crew members and passengers observed a disc-shaped object flying parallel to the aircraft. But when Captain Robert Adickes radioed Air Traffic Control about the UFO, radar observers reported that they had no other aircraft in the area on their radar screens.

A later case occurred on October 21, 1978, over the Bass

Strait in Australia. Pilot Fred Valentich reported a UFO flying right above his Cessna 182 aircraft. Again, radar observers detected nothing near Valentich's plane. Valentich and his plane vanished shortly thereafter.

An Air Force study (thought to be dated between 1948 and 1953) linked Air Force interest in the radar invisibility of UFOs to something they yearned to develop. The study was uncovered by investigator Robert Todd in the process of one of his Freedom of Information Act requests for UFO data in 1978. Todd was researching for UFO information in the files of the SSG ("Special Study Group") of Air Force Intelligence (later named SAG for "Special Advisory Group"). He received a number of documents from Major General James Brown, Assistant Chief of Staff, Air Force Intelligence. One undated report, entitled "Constraints," was released, and which elaborated on the development of aircraft that would avoid radar detection. According to the report:

> The only real possibilities of avoiding detection during these later time periods, therefore, require the development of vehicles that are either technically undetectable by radar, or of such unusual design that the radar signals they yield will be unrecognizable. The Cambridge Research Center has made a preliminary exploration of both of these possibilities for the Development Planning Office. They found that radar-absorbing materials could not be used in aircraft or missiles without sacrificing their aerodynamic qualities, and they concluded that the only vehicle that might confuse a radar net would be one in the shape of a flying saucer or a flying sphere. (Balloons might meet the latter requirements, but the altitudes they can achieve are such that they would be visible during the hours near dawn and sunset.)

It is clear from the "Constraints" report that Air Force Intelligence recognized (1) the potential of a radar-proof vehicle and (2) that the connection with a UFO or flying saucer design could be the mechanism to apply this technology to one of our own aircraft, viz. stealth.

The secret stealth aircraft developed by the U.S. Air Force

employ the advanced electronic technology, materials, and aerodynamic design to evade detection by radar and infrared sensors. Truly stealthy aircraft are practically invisible in flight. During the 1980s, Nellis AFB in Nevada was the place where this technology was being perfected. For years, stories surfaced from civilian and military personnel that stealth technology was developed with the assistance of insights gained from the analysis of alien technology.

In the October 1988 TV special, *UFO Cover-Up? Live!*, Robert Collins, a former Air Force officer stationed at Wright-Patterson Air Force Base and going under the name "Condor," speaking with a U.S. Intelligence officer known as "Falcon," told millions of viewers that there was an agreement between the U.S. Government and extraterrestrials that permitted them to operate from an Air Force Base in Nevada called Area 51 or "Dreamland."

Although no proof ever arose to confirm these allegations, there are stories in the press that implicated the U.S. Government as having stored debris and equipment from crashed UFOs at this facility.

Chapter 10
Dreamland

"Area 51" is an unofficial title that often refers to an area in southern Nevada containing United States Air Force (USAF) facilities. The USAF does not recognize owning or operating any facility regarded as "Area 51." They do recognize operations at the Nellis Range Complex which includes an Operating Location near Groom Lake, Nevada. However, much of the information regarding activities at these sites remain classified.
–March 27, 2008 Inventory letter to FOIA 2006-0527-F asking for files on Area 51.

W hat and where is Area 51? Shortly after it was publicized in 1989 and 1990, a description of America's most secret classified-operations base appeared in the *Las Vegas Review-Journal*. According to Christopher Beall:

> Lying about 85 miles northwest of Las Vegas, the base is an expanse of aircraft hangars, technical facilities and a 12,000 foot runway that rises above a dry lake bed in a desolate corner of Nellis Air Force Range. The place has no official name, although it is unofficially referred to as Area 51.

The base's radio call sign for the Nellis air-traffic controllers who maintain the highly restricted airspace overhead is "Dreamland."

Beall also noted that the stealth aircraft was developed there, and referred to the purported use of Area 51 as a storage location for UFO hardware. For example:

> Rumors about the base have variously attributed the Stealth bomber development program or President Reagan's "Star Wars" missile defense program to it. There are also people who believe the remains of an alien spacecraft are stored at the facility.

Area 51 was first constructed in 1955 and lies on the

outskirts of Nellis AFB in the northeast corner of Groom Lake, a dry lake; but most maps of the region do not even carry a reference to Area 51, nor do they give any indication that it even exists inside the test site's borders. The CIA controlled the base up until the early 1970s, when Air Force Intelligence took over.

To give the reader some idea of just how secret the aircraft are in Area 51, Ned Day, writing in the *Las Vegas Review-Journal*, reported:

> An insider tells of an airplane so secret that "whenever it comes out of its hanger, or when it comes in for a landing, a siren goes off and all personnel (except a select few) have to lie face down on their stomachs to make sure they don't look at it."

Clearly, the United States has had for many years a substantial capability to create new and usual aircraft. An article appearing in the February 1987 issue of *Gung-Ho*, a military magazine, shed some light on that question. Again, extraterrestrial assistance was implied. Under the heading "UnFunded Opportunities (UFO)," the article stated:

> As for "UnFunded Opportunities," these are programs dealing with technology levels so advanced that one Air Force officer involved in SR-71 development said: "We are flight-testing vehicles that defy description. To compare them conceptually to the SR-71 would be like comparing Leonardo da Vinci's parachute design to the space shuttle."

Other officers were similarly emphatic about the nature of these new systems: "We have things that are so far beyond the comprehension of the average aviation authority as to be really alien to our way of thinking," said one retired colonel.

Since the world first learned of Area 51, rumors circulated that some of these systems have involved force-field technology, gravity-drive systems, and "flying saucer" designs. Rumor further has had it that these designs have not necessarily been of Earth human origin. As far as who may have designed them or helped us do it, there is much less talk.

"Let's just put it this way," explained one retired Lockheed engineer. "We have things flying around in the Nevada desert that would make George Lucas drool [sic]."

It has been claimed that the Air Force has a unit at Nellis named Alien Technology Center. The center is rumored to have obtained alien equipment and, at times, personnel to help develop new aircraft and Star Wars weaponry. Could it be so?

Although *Gung-Ho* magazine credited Al Frickey as the writer of the article, researcher Lee Graham wrote to Crain that Frickey was a pseudonym for the real writer, James C. Goodall, a renowned aviation author and photographer.

Goodall is an expert on stealth technology. While doing his research, he changed his opinion of UFOs from that of skeptic to believer. Why? Because he had talked to experts who knew what kinds of aircraft were being test-flown at Groom Lake.

In May 1990, Goodall was interviewed by KLAS-TV in Las Vegas for George Knapp's series of reports on UFOs. Goodall told Knapp that he had talked to an engineer at Lockheed Aircraft Corporation's Advanced Systems Division, better known as Skunk Works, which tested machines at Area 51. When Goodall asked about UFOs, the engineer replied, "Absolutely, positively, without a doubt, they exist."

But is the technology extraterrestrial?

Goodall put exactly that question to a master sergeant who claimed to have done three tours of duty at Groom Lake. Goodall reported:

> He says the United States Government and the military has things that are out there, you can't describe them as airplanes, that are literally out of this world. And he emphasized, out of this world. And he says they're alien to anything that you've ever seen.

Goodall, tried to press the source for more details, but the source replied that he had said too much already.

KLAS-TV also interviewed Ben Rich, the man who was running Lockheed's famous Skunk Works Division at the time, and who was the mastermind behind such advanced aircraft as the U-2, the SR-71 "Blackbird," and the Stealth Fighter (F-117-A). When Rich was asked if alien technology was being used at Area 51, he replied, "No, it isn't . . . it's just good American ingenuity." However, Rich wrote to a long-time friend that he was a "believer" in both man-made and extraterrestrial UFOs.

It is no secret that unusual aircraft have been secretly flown for years at Nellis AFB. But, is it true, as some suspect, that Area 51 has been a complex also used to study and perhaps fly recovered UFOs?

UFO investigator Tom Adams, publisher of *Stigmata*, uncovered some remarkable information involving pilots who had accidentally flown over "Dreamland." We quote from Adams's report:

> 1st Lt. Parrish, 27th TFW (Tactical Fighter Wing)/522 TFS (Tactical Fighter Squadron); Cannon AFB, New Mexico. Lt. Parrish and pilot accidentally flew over Dreamland by 3 miles. Ground radar picked up [an] F111D aircraft and sent up interceptors. Parrish followed instructions from ground and interceptors and landed his F-111D on [the] desert floor. He and his pilot were picked up and detained for three days in which he was asked what and how much he had seen. He was later debriefed and let go, as was his pilot. Parrish refused to say what he saw.
>
> Capt. Nunnallee, 27th TFW /522 TFS, Cannon AFB, New Mexico. Capt. Nunnallee tells a story of knowing an individual who guarded a certain hangar at a place in the desert known as Dreamland. This individual told him that the hangar held a cosmic type aircraft [the likes] of which he had never seen before. He disclosed that all area lights were shut off when the hangar doors were to be opened. On one occasion he saw the doors open during the night and saw an unusual object come out and take off straight up. The aerial craft was disc-shaped with dull tone lights. He said rumors were about of a strange new aircraft design given to the United States from a superior group which was taken to be aliens because of the advances and overall security hush-hush.
>
> Security Policeman, 27th TFW, Cannon AFB, New Mexico. SP (name not given) told me that he was assigned

out in an area named Dreamland, at which he guarded a specific hangar. He said that he never knew what he was guarding and was never told. The object inside was considered above TOP SECRET.

If there have been captured disks near Area 51 at Groom Lake, have pilots also been there? It is interesting to note that in the July 1988 issue of the *Nevada Aerial Research Newsletter*, it stated that the U.S. Air Force was asked point-blank if there were aliens on the Nevada Test Range. The newsletter stated that the Air Force "could neither confirm nor deny the presence of aliens on the range, which is tantamount to saying 'yes' as far as most people are concerned."

There are other stories that seem to confirm that the military has been test-flying a saucer-shaped object at Area 51 or Dreamland

The October 1, 1990 issue of *Aviation Week & Space Technology* averred that:

> Advanced secret aircraft developed at highly classified government facilities in the Nevada desert over the last decade are demonstrating and validating new technologies for the U.S.'s future fighters, bombers and reconnaissance platforms. . . . Several vehicles, though, appear to incorporate technologies that outstrip those now employed by engineers charged with developing more traditional, current generation aircraft. . . . there is substantial evidence that another family of craft exists that relies on exotic propulsion and aerodynamic schemes not fully understood at this time.

The publication also stated that at least two, perhaps more, types of vehicles were being test-flown in Nevada, one of which is "a triangular shaped, quiet aircraft . . ." and another "high-speed aircraft characterized by a very loud, deep, rumbling roar reminiscent of heavy-lift rockets." Officials who were closely tied to "classified programs at several Nevada test sites" reported "there are bigger and better things out there," referring to aircraft based at the Nevada test locations.

In another article in the same issue, it was reported:

Workers who were assigned to one or more of the classified Nevada locations in the past agreed the triangular shape of the reported aircraft "has been around a long time" and is a platform familiar to those associated with that community. . . . One of the earliest accounts of such a vehicle was reported by Timothy B. Reynolds, a computer system manager in Houston Texas, who saw a triangular-shaped aircraft parked in an Ellington AFB hangar in the late 1960s. The aircraft had an estimated 30-40 ft. wingspan, no visible cockpit, no vertical tail and tricycle landing gear. Two 4 x 12 in. rectangular openings in the wing leading edge, one on each side of the nose, appeared to be engine inlets, although no cowlings or engine pods were visible. The vehicle was relatively thin, measuring about 4-5 ft. thick at the center and tapering to each wingtip. Reynolds described the aircraft as "very rounded—with a molded look—and gray-colored."

The science writer David L. Dobbs of Cincinnati, Ohio, reported in a letter dated April 5, 1980, that a secret operation was conducted at Area 51 called "Project Red Light." He stated that a "UFO" was flown there from Edwards Air Force Base. Dobbs's story was corroborated somewhat by a radio technician named "Mike" who performed radar maintenance work at the test site.

Although "Mike" had a "Q" clearance with the Atomic Energy Commission and an inter-agency Top Secret clearance, he had to be investigated again for a special Air Force Top Secret clearance to work at Area 51. While working there, he claimed, he saw a number of large crates with the words "Project Red Light" and a stenciled "Edwards AFB" painted or stamped on them.

Because "Mike" thought these crates were connected with a possible UFO crash he had read about, researcher Bill Moore contacted Nellis Air Force Base, Edwards Air Force Base, the Defense Intelligence Agency, the Defense Logistics Agency, and other departments for possible identification of "Project Red Light." To our knowledge, no official files were located.

Robert Lazar and the Area 51 Story

In 1995, President Bill Clinton gave a lecture for members of an investment firm in Hong Kong. During the question and answer that followed, Clinton was asked whether lists of secrets are ever passed from one President to the next, such as "what really happened at Roswell?"

He replied that he had looked into the Roswell crash story, but that most in his administration had concluded it did not represent a crash of an extraterrestrial spacecraft. The same members of the staff did, however, believe that there had been alien technology and possibly an alien a base in Nevada. Clinton admitted that the belief had become so strong that he had actually sent someone to the base to find out of the rumor was true.*

A key source for the belief in a secret presence of alien technology—or even an actual alien—at a Nevada base was Robert P. Lazar, a putative former government scientist. Lazar claimed that the U.S. military possessed and was test-flying recovered UFOs at the Nevada test site. According to Lazar, at least nine flying saucers were being tested at "S-4," ten miles south of Area 51, and "they were not built by humans." Lazar said that he worked on the project there that involved back engineering the saucer's technology.

Lazar first publicly revealed his involvement in an interview with award winning anchorman George Knapp of Eyewitness News, which was broadcast in May, 1989, by Channel 8 KLAS-TV, Las Vegas, Nevada. The story eventually won Knapp the "Individual Achievement by a Journalist" award from the United Press International.

Starting on November 10, 1989, Knapp aired a series of news

---

* It is not known who visited the base for President Clinton, but the person came back to the White House stating that there was no alien or alien technology at Area 51. The only thing there, the report stated was advanced aircraft technology tests that the USAF did not want the public to see. It would seem to put the alien story to rest, except that the rumored alien activities were supposed to be at S-4, 10 miles south of Area 51. Therefore the USAF could have made the truthful statement of no alien activities at Area 51, even through there were alien activities going on.

reports about Lazar, UFOs, and the UFO cover-up. Knapp reported the allegations of Lazar, who claimed that the technology being tested at the S-4 sector of the base was of an alien, i.e. extraterrestrial, origin.

As Knapp later put it, within months, the Area 51 story "moved like a giant tsunami around the world." Every major network in the world came to Nevada to investigate Area 51. Bus tours of interested citizens got as close as possible to the base. Area 51 quickly became one of the best-known and famous places in the world.

Knapp stated that the station first became involved with UFOs in mid-1987.[123] UFO investigator John Lear, whose father had invented the Lear jet, brought the subject of UFOs to the attention of Ned Day, managing editor at KLAS. Day would have nothing to do with UFOs, but Knapp overheard the conversation and asked to see what Lear had. Lear described a vast government cover-up, FOIA documents related to UFOs, and the recently released MJ-12 documents.

Lear was held in high regard inside KLAS-TV. His importance arose from the fact that he had been snooping around Area 51 for years, and he had been providing his information to the TV station.

Lear had first learned of the existence of Area 51 years before when a friend of his who flew for CarCo (the predecessor for Special Projects) told Lear that he had just flown a General up to a place on the test site called Groom Lake. Some months later, while soaring with a friend at Pahrump, Nevada, the friend said he had been to the test site but "no Area 51 stuff." Lear assumed that Area 51 was Groom Lake, which turned out to be true.

Lear did have track record with KLAS: he had provided the station with the story of the F-117A stealth jet fighter that was being tested at Groom Lake. As early as 1981, Lear had alerted Ned Day, then a newspaper reporter, about it. Based on Lear's information, Day ended up breaking the F- 117A story after he moved to KLAS-TV. This led to the eventual release of the Stealth story by the American government during the first Iraq war. It also led to the station getting into some trouble with the military[124]

As a result of this, the Air Force could not have been happy with Lear. In addition to the stealth leaks, Lear had caused further trouble when, in 1977, he snuck onto the Groom Lake Bed and photographed a MIG-21 sitting outside of a hanger. The Air Force had acquired Russian airplane technology and was testing it in secret.

By 1987, Lear was very interested in UFOs. He had given lectures about his understanding of the UFO cover-up, including one for the local chapter of the Association of Former Intelligence Officers. Information about Lear was spreading throughout Las Vegas, which was home for most of the workers for Area 51 and other secret facilities on the Nevada Test and Training Range.

The phone calls began pouring in. It became so bad that Lear's wife disconnected his phone and took way his UFO files. On December 29, 1987, Lear released what came to be called the Lear Paper, outlining his view of the cover-up. It was posted to an early Internet bulletin board called the Paranet BBS system. The controversial paper described an alliance with the aliens, a deal allowing the aliens to abduct people, aliens mutilating livestock along with the occasional human, crashed saucers, underground bases, and a group called MJ-12 that was in change of the whole UFO cover-up. He stated that the aliens had provided advanced alien technology to the U.S. military. Lear also presented a grim view of the aliens, and ended by saying, "if you see a UFO - RUN LIKE HELL."

While Ned Day had turned down Lear and his wild UFO claims, Knapp had shown interest. After viewing his material, Knapp interviewed Lear on a 6:00 A.M. Sunday show called "On the Record." Although the show normally had a small audience, the audience numbers for the Lear show were huge, and the station took many calls. Lear's second appearance brought even larger numbers, followed by a third show with UFO witness Bill Cooper, which drove the numbers even higher. After the third show, Knapp asked Lear what they could do for an encore. Lear mentioned that he had a friend who had just been fired after working on the flying saucers up at Area 51.

This led to a May 1989 back-lit interview that Knapp did with Lazar, who used the pseudonym Dennis (a name Lazar chose because his boss's name at the site was Dennis Mariani). Within days, the story had exploded worldwide. Lear believed it would lead to worldwide disclosure, which did not happen.

However, it did inspire Knapp and KLAS-TV to began an eight month investigation. This led to a November 1989 series of stories on UFOs at Area 51. It became the most-watched special news story ever broadcast in Las Vegas.

If the military thought that Lear had caused problems with the F-117A story, or the MIG-21 photo, they now had to deal with a new revelation that dwarfed anything Lear had done in the past. Scores of people headed to the base perimeter to see for themselves. President Clinton's Air Force Secretary, Sheila Widnall, was forced to request control of nearly 4,900 acres of Bureau of Land Management holdings just outside the base perimeter, in an effort to move people farther away from the base.

The Knapp investigation showed that Lazar had claimed to have previously worked as a physicist at Los Alamos National Laboratories in 1982 and 1983. His wife Tracy's father had also worked there. The Los Alamos officials, however, were denying the connection to Lazar. Knapp's investigation seemed to support the fact that Lazar had indeed worked there and that the government was lying. He discovered Lazar's name in the Los Alamos phone book, and was able to find a 1982 newspaper article that referred to Lazar as working at the lab. Later, Lazar took Knapp and a TV crew on a tour of the facility. It led

Knapp to believe that Lazar was telling the truth. Knapp recalled the tour given by Lazar:

> I was stunned during that visit to Los Alamos. Bob took us into several buildings and labs. He ran through the innards of some of them like a rabbit zipping through its own burrow. He waved at the employees, including security, and they waved back. No one even questioned us, even when my photographer fired up his camera and started shooting video (most of which has never been made public.)
> The question for hardcore critics is—what did Lazar do at Los Alamos? They think he was a low level flunky. Even if the lab's security was ridiculously lax, I tend to doubt that a flunky could take a TV crew wherever we wanted to go without any interference. Maybe I'm wrong.
> People who don't want to accept the story will discard this entirely. That's their right. I was there—they weren't, and I know what I saw. A lot of it is recorded for posterity on videotape.[125]

Lear and Lazar had met through a chance encounter. In the summer of 1988, Gene Huff, a local real estate appraiser, had seen Lear's "On the Record" interview with Knapp. He contacted Lear and asked him for copies of all of his UFO papers. Lear was not interested until he learned that Huff was an appraiser, at which point he offered to exchange the UFO material for an appraisal on his house in Las Vegas.

When Huff showed up, he was accompanied by Bob Lazar, who was holding the measuring tape for him. Huff had known Lazar since late 1985, and knew that he had worked at Los Alamos, a place Lear had described as one of the focal points of the UFO cover-up.

Lazar had left Los Alamos to go on his own. Moving to Las Vegas, he owned a brothel in Northern Nevada and a business that provided photos for all the real estate appraisals done in Las Vegas.

As the appraisal was taking place, Huff and Lear were talking UFOs. Lazar listened but was unimpressed. In his thinking, the subject was crazy. Lear was vocal in his opinion that the U.S. Government had already retrieved twenty to thirty saucers, that the U.S. Air Force possessed between thirty and forty alien beings in cold storage, and that the U.S. military had secured agreements with live aliens to conduct activities here in exchange for technological information.

Lear then discussed accounts of UFO activities at Los Alamos Lab. Here, Lazar spoke up. He had worked there, he told Lear, and had held a "Q" clearance. If this UFO stuff were true, he said, he would have heard about it.

Lear insisted he was correct, and gave Lazar three things to investigate, with the help of his former co-workers at Los Alamos. These included the Top Secret Excalibur missile, the classified library for Project Grudge, and YY-11, a facility at Los Alamos where a live alien was allegedly being housed.

Lazar accepted the challenge. He confirmed the existence of the Excalibur program. In September 1988, he wrote a report on it for Lear. Lazar also discovered that a facility known as YY-11 did exist, and it was at a level beyond which he could learn anything about it. As a result, Lear challenged Lazar to get a job up at Groom Lake, where he believed work was being done on UFO technology.

Lazar sent out a series of resumes in an attempt to get back into science. One went to Dr. Edward Teller, known as the father of the hydrogen bomb. In his letter to Teller, he reminded him of a chance meeting they had at Los Alamos on June 28, 1982, when Lazar had worked there. Teller was there to lecture on the SDI program and Lazar had gotten permission from his boss to attend the lecture. Teller was outside the auditorium reading the newspaper, which happened to have a story about Lazar and a jet engine car he had built. As Lazar related the story:

> I had built a jet car, and they put it in the local newspaper on the front page. As I walked up to the lecture hall, I noticed Teller was outside sitting on a brick wall reading the front page. I said, 'Hi, I'm the one you're reading about there.' He said, 'That's interesting.' I sat down and had a little talk with him.

Teller had been involved in UFOs since 1948, when he attended a secret "Conference on Aerial Phenomena" held at Los Alamos. The point of this conference was to discuss UFOs, in particular the so-called 'green fireballs' which were then being widely reported in the area. The project created to investigate the so-called fireballs was known as "Project Twinkle."

By the late 1980s, when Lazar wrote to Teller, Teller was rumored to be a member of the MJ-12 group in care of he UFO cover-up. Finally, the scientist phoned Lazar in November 1988, asking him if he would rather work at Lawrence Livermore National Laboratory in California or within the Nevada area, where he lived. Lazar said he would prefer to work at Groom Lake.

Lear recounted to Cameron in a March 1, 1990 letter how Lazar ended up at S-4:

> Bob Lazar did not believe any of this at the beginning. Several months later his application was being processed at EG&G and (he) was beginning to think that maybe some of the things I was saying may have basis in fact, he specifically requested to be assigned work at Area 51 with EG&G. He requested this to Dr. Teller . . .

In late November and early December 1988, Lazar had three interviews at EG&G for a job at the Nevada Test Site. Each of the interviews involved technical questions, and Lazar claimed that he aced them.

The only difficulty during the process was posed by the first question during the second interview: "Do you know John Lear?" And then: "What do you think of John Lear?" Lazar replied that he knew Lear, but added that Lear was a guy who stuck his nose in where it did not belong. (In recounting the story later to Lear, Lazar probably wisely neglected to mention that last statement).

This event, missing in most accounts of the Lazar-Area 51 story, is critically important. Its importance lies in the fact that right from the beginning, the officials at Area 51 knew that John Lear, the long-time snoop who had caused the Air Force several headaches already, was closely connected to someone who was trying to get a job at Groom Lake.

Most probably, the Lear/Lazar friendship was discovered because of Lazar's request to people at Los Alamos (who had security clearances) about such items as Excalibur and YY-11. In all likelihood, someone reported that Lazar was trying to obtain information on Lear's behalf. If the UFO stories at Los Alamos were true, the security bells would have gone off.

The Trip To Nowhere

The next thing that happened is probably the most important part of the whole Area 51 story. With security officials aware that Lazar and Lear were friends, and with Lear now openly promoting UFO conspiracies, Lazar was hired on December 6, 1988. His assignment: the test site at S-4, a site 10 miles south of Area 51. Lazar's story would make S-4 the primary place for recovered UFO technology in the United States—for UFO believers.

What is critically important about the hiring is that there were thousands of non-UFO-related jobs at Groom Lake and in areas around the base. Most were connected with advanced jet aircraft, which would have suited Lazar. He had, after all, built a car with a jet engine. But, instead, Lazar was hired for the one UFO-related job that had become available.

Lazar would record December 6th on his wall calendar as "Trip to nowhere." An important part of his job at S-4, according to Lazar, would be to report on John Lear and his UFO activities.

Lazar stated that he was phoned and told to report to the Key Flight terminal near McCarran airport. He was then flown to Groom Lake via Janet Airline, which took workers to the Tonopah Test Range, Edwards AFB (North Base), and other "spook" areas.

Once on the base, he took a bus with blacked-out windows to

S-4, and was then brought inside the base. This base, incidentally, looked like "part of the desert" from the outside because the hangar doors were camouflaged by sand.[126] Lazar speculated that he had been hired to work on the advanced propulsion systems that the U.S. military was developing there.

From December 1988 to early April 1989, Lazar worked at S-4 a mere handful of times. He was on call, and only went when called. The first few days that Lazar went to the site were spent reading classified documents about "Project Galileo" (which dealt gravity and propulsion) and "Project Looking Glass" (which involved the physics of looking back in time). Lazar was led to believe that he would be working on the gravity and propulsion project.

The activities at the base surprised and amazed Lazar. He noticed pictures of flying saucers posted all over. More importantly, he noticed real flying saucers there. The project there was called "Majestic," he said, and the personnel wore badges labeled "MAJ," although the badge of Dennis, Lazar's supervisor, said "MAJESTIC." Lazar said that he had heard the stories about "Majestic Twelve" and the MJ-12 Document, but that he had no idea if any of it was related to the project at the base.

Although Lazar only worked there a short period of time, he said he was brought up to speed quickly. So quickly, in fact, that he began working immediately. Lazar said that he was educated about what had been learned up to that point about the alien spacecrafts, including the work that had been done on the "anti-matter reactor," which he said powered the disks. This created its own gravitational field, a technology that "doesn't exist on Earth."

In an ongoing effort to "back-engineer" the disks—that is, to see how they worked—some of them were being taken apart and others test-flown. He had no idea how they had gotten there. Progress in reproducing the technology was moving slowly, Lazar said, because they were having a hard time substituting alien materials with Earthly ones.

Lazar Begins to Talk

An important part of the story, and one which is often left out in the retelling, is that Lazar began to tell Lear all about S-4 from the time of his third visit, when he was allowed to see a disc.

Lazar showed up at Lear's house as Lear was writing checks and declared, "I saw a disc today."

"A disc?" replied Lear. "Theirs or ours?"

"Theirs," said Lazar.

"You went to Groom Lake?" Lear asked.

"Yeah," said Lazar.

Lear exclaimed, "What are you doing here? Obviously they're going to follow you. Why didn't you just, you know, work there for a while and then come and tell us what happened?"

Lazar replied, "Because I've seen you take so much crap over the past six months about this. I'm telling you it's real. I saw it, I touched it."[127]

At that point Lazar made a statement that Lear found funny and which he was never able to explain. Yet, it is critical to understanding what really happened in the Bob Lazar story.

"I can't tell you anything," Lazar told Lear. "I can only answer your questions."

Lazar never did explain who had said that he could only answer questions about the Top Secret UFO work at S-4, or whether it was was part of the agreement he had with S-4 security to report on John Lear and his UFO activities. The idea that he could answer questions was revealing.

Lear took the opportunity to ask questions, and for two hours Lazar answered. This conversation took place despite the fact that Lear knew his phone was tapped and that his house was probably being monitored.*

---

* Lear had become aware of the phone tap from a technician who was rewiring phones for Lear's two daughters. He traced the tap back to the main frame and discovered that there was paper work. When he asked about it, the technician was

Lazar related how the craft was propelled, how the levels of security worked, what he had read in classified briefings, who was running the program, and how they were able hide the program from the public.

A month later, in January 1989, Lazar came to Lear's house again and said he had something new to tell. He motioned with his head that they should talk outside. Despite the cold and windy weather conditions, both men went out behind the house, by a stable, to talk. Lazar stated, "John, you will never know what it's like to see your first alien."

Lazar told Lear that while walking down a hallway at S-4 he had walked by a door with a 12-inch windowpane which had wires running through it. In the window, he had seen two men in lab coats facing him. Facing the two men, and with his back to Lazar, there appeared to be a small grey alien. When Lazar returned down the hall later, the alien was gone.

This was one of three times that Lazar had an encounter with an alien while he worked at S-4.

Lazar's claim of a live alien at S-4 is only one of a rash of such stories that were circulating within the UFO community at the time. The most dramatic story, and the one mostly closely linked to the Lazar encounter, came from George Knapp (described later) who had tracked down what he believed was a highly credible witness. After months of meetings talking about Area 51, this man began to talk about a live alien who was there.

At around this time, researchers Bill Moore, Jamie Shandera, Whitley Strieber, and Linda Moulton Howe had all been offered an interview with a live alien. All of the interviews failed to materialize for one reason or another. In late October, just before Lazar was hired, a major two-hour documentary, *UFO Cover-Up? Live!,* was broadcast from Washington, D.C. On this show, much-discussed already in this

---

told if he did not like it he could quit. All this was reported to Lear in December 1988.

book, Condor and Falcon talked about a live alien that was a guest of the United States.

Bob Emenegger, who had done a UFO documentary following a request from the CIA/Pentagon during the early 1970s, participated in *UFO Cover-up? Live!* He had no faith in the stories being told by Falcon and Condor, particularly their remarks about the live alien who liked strawberry ice cream.

Yet in a conversation with Cameron, Emenegger was asked, "Did you not get an invitation at this time to interview a live alien?"

He confirmed that yes he did get an invite to take a film crew to meet a live alien and that the offer had come from a highly reliable source: Norton AFB Defense Audiovisual Agency (DAVA) security manager, Paul Shartle.

The final live alien story which tied into Lazar's own claim came in a rumor, one related to President Ronald Reagan. Reagan had a strong interest in UFOs, and had hinted at the UFO reality in several of his speeches. During his first term in office, two of his appointees had contacted Emenegger, stating that there were military UFO films they wanted the public to see, and asking him if he would make another UFO documentary. During those pre-Internet days, there were nevertheless many rumors of a UFO disclosure led by Reagan himself.

The great rumor, however, that consumed the UFO community in December 1988 and January 1989 was that Reagan's final act as President would be to appear on TV with a live alien at his side. Reagan, of course, left office in January 1989, the month that Lazar claimed to see the live alien.

Element 115

Bob Lazar had many claims about activities inside S-4. He stated, for example, that the Majestic project was being run by the U.S. Navy.

Certainly one of his most intriguing claims had to do with the existence of Element 115. This, he said, was the substance that fueled the anti-matter reactor in the flying disks. It does not appear on most periodic tables, but does appear on extended periodic tables in Group 5, along with Nitrogen, Phosphorus, Arsenic, Antimony, and Bismuth. According to the International Union of Pure and Applied Chemistry (IUPAC), the name of Element 115 is "Ununpentium," and is represented by the symbol Uup.

Although the element cannot readily be produced on Earth, Lazar continued, the government possesses about five hundred pounds of it. One kilogram of it, he went on, has the capacity to produce the equivalent of "46 ten-megaton hydrogen bombs." Surely, that would be one thing to account for the tight security: the substance is extraordinarily dangerous.

Indeed, claimed Lazar, back in April 1987 there had been an accident at the Nevada test site area which killed two people. Although the explosion was explained as an "unannounced nuclear test," Lazar said that it had something to do with Element 115 and the anti-matter reactor. Lazar stated further that he had been told he had been hired to replace one of the victims of the accident.

Lazar said that he had seen all nine saucers being stored at S-4. He became so familiar with them that he named them. In an interview with George Knapp that aired on November 13, 1989, Lazar said:

> I gave everything names—the Top Hat one and, you know, the Jello Mold [one] and, uh, the Sport Model operated without any hitches at all. I mean, it looked new . . . if I knew what a new flying saucer looked like. One of them looked like it was hit with some sort of a projectile. It had a large hole in the bottom and a large hole in the top with the metal bent out like some sort of, you know, large caliber 4 or 5-inch [projectile] had gone through it.

After his first glimpse inside the craft, Lazar suspected that the saucers were from "elsewhere." He told Knapp:

> I got to look inside, and it had really small chairs. I think that was the first confirmation I had. That was just a

shocking thing because every time before that, I was able to label it. This is just a little advance that a group of scientists had formed and, you know, they're keeping it secret, and yeah, we could have built a big disc like that, and yeah, that's no problem, and, you know, we could have adapted the use [?] to make it fly, but why does it have little furniture inside? [garbled] And things began to click together just all too fast.

Some of the disks being stored there were fully operational, Lazar said. He described to Knapp how one of the ships took off:

The bottom of it glowed blue and began to hiss like any, like high voltage does on a round sphere. It's my impression that the reason that they're round and have no sharp edges is to contain the high voltage like, uh, if you've seen a high-voltage system's insulators—things are round or else you get a corona discharge. In either case, it began to hiss as in high voltage and it lifted off the ground quietly except for that little hiss in the background, and that stopped as soon as it reached about 20 or 30 feet.

The discs made no sound at take-off or while in flight.

As exciting as all this might seem, Lazar told Knapp that he became disenchanted with the government's saucer program. The progress moved "at a snail's pace." He attributed this to the extreme caution and intense secrecy surrounding the project. According to Lazar:

It's just unfair, outright, not to put it in the hands of the overall scientific community. There are people much more capable of dealing with this information and by this time would have gotten a lot farther along than this small select group of people working out in the middle of the desert. They don't even have the facilities, really, to completely analyze what they're dealing with. . . . I did not believe that this should be a security matter. Some of it, sure. But, just the concept that there's definite proof, and uh, we even have articles from another world, another [star] system, you just can't not tell everyone. A lot of people don't believe that. But I do.

The Fishing Trips

Lazar had a hard time keeping the story of what was going on at S-4 to himself. To support his claims, he predicted the time and location of the UFO test flights. The tests took place on Wednesday nights at 9:00 P.M., which was when there was the least activity around the base. According to five witnesses, Lazar's predictions proved to be correct.

The fact Lazar was able to predict the test flights of what appeared to be an object with UFO characteristics was, as reporter Knapp described it, "a big deal." It showed that Lazar, no matter what people would later say about him, was able accurately to describe the time and location of test flights of what appeared to be a UFO.

There were three nights involved in all.

First was March 22, 1989. The day before, Lazar was at Lear's house making a "doggie death-ray." This was an amplifier that could broadcast a high-pitched sound to keep Lear's dogs out of his wife's flowers. While working on this, Lazar asked Lear if he wanted to go and watch them run a test of the saucer. He told Lear that they could access the base by a road on the north-east that would allow them to see the test over S-4 and yet not be on the base. Lear agreed to go.

The witnesses were Lazar, Lazar's wife Tracy, Gene Huff, and Lear. They traveled to the base in Lear's motor home. According to Huff, the real reason Lazar wanted to go up to the site to watch the test was to impress his wife, as they were going through a difficult time. Huff insisted that if that situation had not existed, then neither he nor Lear would have been invited that night.

They arrived at the border of the base, and Lear set up his 8-inch Celestron telescope. Right at 9:00, P.M., just as Lazar had predicted, an object rose above the mountain range. Lear scrambled to focus the object in his telescope. There was so much excitement that no one bothered to record the event with the video camera they had brought along.

As the object stopped rising and hovered in the western sky, Lear managed to capture the object in the telescope. He stated that it took up the entire field of vision. He saw a saucer-like disc oriented at a 30 degree angle, 45 degrees to the horizon. It was radiated a "yellowish-goldish stuff." He moved to allow Huff to watch and hooked the tripod leg as he did. There was not enough time to locate the object in the telescope a second time before it dropped down again below the mountains.

The second night was exactly one week later, on March 29, 1989. The witnesses that night were Lazar, his wife, Gene Huff, and Jim Taliani, an aviation worker at the Tonopah Test Range. Lear was on a flight to Minneapolis and not present. He did, however, phone Lazar the night before. "What are you doing tomorrow?" he asked. "Going fishing," came Lazar's reply.

This time the group remembered the video camera. As the object rose over S-4, they began recording it. According to Huff, the object came much closer this night, so close in fact that at one point they "backed up behind the trunk lid, because it glowed so brightly we thought it might explode."

Later, KLAS-TV played the videotape for the world to see. Unfortunately, darkness and distance ensured that the video showed no distinct shapes or reference points. It was virtually impossible to determine from the videotape just what the object was or what it was doing.

The videotape made history. It turned out to be costly for some of the witnesses, however. Taliani, who could be heard on the tape saying "Oh neat! Oh neat!" was called into work and fired. A few months later, in July, John Lear, then a L-1011 captain for America Trans Air, was called into work by the Vice President of Operations. He asked Lear if he really believed all that UFO stuff. When Lear replied that he did, he was fired with the line, "Well John we can't have a Captain at America Trans Air flying a L-1011 who believes in UFOs."

Lazar's third and final fishing trip to S-4 was on April 6,

1989. The witnesses were Lazar, his wife, his wife's sister, Lear, and Huff. Despite Lear's warning not to go too far, the group continued onward. Suddenly, farther down the road, two sets of car headlights turned on.

With their lights turned off, the group tried to elude the two security vehicles. They stopped the car, however, when they realized they would not succeed. Lazar ran off into the desert with a 9mm gun. Lear and Huff quickly set up the telescope.

The security guards asked the group what they were doing. Looking at the stars, they said. The guards replied, why then did you try to run after first being spotted? To this, no one had an answer. After checking social security numbers and holding them for 30 minutes, the group was allowed to go.

The guards appeared to leave, but actually just went a hundred meters down the road and turned their lights off. With night vision equipment and a parabolic microphone, they continued to watch the four. Lazar reappeared from the desert, and the group joked about flying saucers and what had just happened.

As they arrived back at the highway, the five were met by flashing police car lights and Lincoln County Sheriff Deputy Sergeant, Doug Lamoreaux. The five were ordered out of the car. By loud speaker, they were told repeatedly to place their hands on the car.*

Lamoreaux only had two questions. Why are there now five people when there were only four when they were at the edge of the base? And, where is the gun? It was apparent that he had received information from the security people who had

---

* Lamoreaux later became notorious for seizing film from television crews that journeyed to the edge of Area 51. On one occasion in 1994, he seized all the film that had been shot by KNBC-TV of Los Angeles. Although the Groom Lake security could not arrest people, Lamoreaux could, and arrested onlookers such as Area 51 activist Glenn Campbell after Campbell refused to turn over his film. Lamoreaux did admit that "everyone and their dog has pictures of the base." See "Campbell arrested in second TV seizure," *The Groom Lake Desert Rat.* Issue #12. July 20, 1994. See also Donovan Webster, "Area 51," *The New York Times Sunday Magazine*, June 24, 1994.

stopped them, and they knew most of what had happened.

The next day, Lazar was driven not to work but to the Area 51 security center at Indian Springs Air Force Base. There he was debriefed. The military reminded him of his security oaths, then threatened him with bodily harm by automatic weapons. Although Lazar said that he was called back to work, he decided that because of what had happened, it would not be in his best interests to return to such an isolated place in the desert, where his employers could take any action against him that they wished.

Lazar said that by speaking out and going public, he hoped his employers would be less inclined to "terminate" him.

Analysis

Lazar's amazing allegations about extraterrestrial vehicles being test-flown at S-4 set private investigators, television stations, and UFO researchers off tracking down leads. Hopefully, these would either substantiate his claims or show him to be a fraud.

After two decades, the evidence collected has been mixed. Those looking into the Lazar affair include KLAS-TV news commentator George Knapp, Tony Pelham, a journalist who once worked for the *Las Vegas Bullet* newspaper, Scott McKenzie, a private investigator from San Diego, California, Stanton Friedman, a nuclear physicist from Canada, and many others.

Knapp was the closest to the Lazar story and did six to eight months of investigation into the story. Although Knapp found no one to corroborate the details Lazar had given him regarding specific activities at S-4, he did interview roughly two dozen other insiders from Groom Lake who provided various levels of corroboration of Lazar's story.

This included one witness that Knapp tracked down as someone who would have known whether Lazar's claims were true or false. He had been at the test site from the early days.

After months of clandestine meetings with this high-level person, the man finally admitted that, yes, there was reverse engineering of alien craft going on at the test site. The man went on further to admit that there was a live alien there (just as Lazar had claimed). It had taken them quite a while to learn how to communicate with the creature, and there was always a fear that the alien would escape.

In at least six instances, witnesses were visited and intimidated within hours after agreeing to be interviewed. All six withdrew their offers to be recorded on video, citing fear for their safety.

As early as the November 13, 1989 installment of the KLAS-TV series on UFOs, Knapp said he interviewed a technician who had worked in a very sensitive position and who reported that it was "common knowledge among those with high security clearances that recovered alien disks are stored at the Nevada test site."

Knapp also told of a former military man who was stationed at the test site, who claimed that he had once inadvertently seen an aerial disc make a landing outside the boundaries of Area 51. Security personnel arrived at the scene, and he was taken away and debriefed for several hours.

A technician who once worked at Groom Lake told Knapp that he had once accidentally walked into the wrong hanger and seen what appeared to be a disk-shaped object under a tarp; men wearing lab coats had been examining it.

Because Lazar had claimed that he had been told that the U.S. Navy was in charge of the project at S-4, KLAS-TV made Freedom of Information Act requests to four separate Navy offices for information. All denied having any information on such a project.*

Major questions in this case centered on whether or not

---

* However, the Navy also denied having any files on a UFO filmed over Trementon, Utah, in 1952, a case they had previously admitted having spent hundreds of hours examining. So much for FOIA requests.

Robert Lazar actually worked at S-4 and whether or not his educational and employment records checked out. Results here have been decidedly mixed.

KLAS-TV called Los Alamos National Laboratory to confirm Lazar's previous employment there. Public relations people said that they did not know him. KLAS-TV also called Massachusetts Institute of Technology (MIT), where Lazar said he had gone to school. People there said that they had no record of him. Even Lazar's birth records were missing: KLAS-TV found that they had "disappeared." Lazar said that when he discovered that the transcripts from the schools he had attended were "disappearing" and records of his birth "no longer existed," he realized the government was trying to turn him into a "non-person." He might be next to disappear. He decided, therefore, to go public and appear on KLAS-TV.

But then some confirmatory evidence appeared. Knapp and his associates uncovered newspaper articles at Los Alamos clearly showing that Lazar had worked there. In a January 21, 1990 interview with Cameron, Tony Pelham said:

> The thing we did verify was at Los Alamos. When I met Lazar, I asked, "How did you get up there?" He said, "I worked at Los Alamos," and he said [that] Dr. Teller was the one who had given him the job. He said, "Well, there was a front-page story of me in the Los Alamos paper." He said, "Dr. Teller was lecturing there, and we just happened to strike up a conversation." I wound up getting a copy of that article, and that checked out. I tracked down the reporter over there in Phoenix, to talk to him, and the reporter said, "Yes, seven years ago I went out and interviewed this physicist Bob Lazar and his wife. He had a VW, and he [had] put a jet engine in it, and it was sort of an unusual thing. I checked his speeding record at the police department there in Los Alamos. He had a half dozen typical 60 mph speeding tickets.

Although a spokesman at Los Alamos National Lab claimed that Lazar had never been employed by them, they found it difficult to explain why Robert Lazar's name appeared in the 1982 Los Alamos Lab internal phone book. Knapp went to Los

Alamos Lab and talked to some of Lazar's colleagues. They said that he had indeed worked there.

Pelham found it hard to believe that Lazar's school records at MIT would be erased; surely there would have to be records if he had been enrolled there.

Lazar called Stan Friedman and mentioned that he had also attended Pierce College and California State University Northridge, in San Fernando Valley, California. In a January 17, 1990 letter to Cameron, Friedman wrote: "there is a Robert Lazar born in 1959 who took a number of electronics courses at Pierce [College] ending in 1976. . . . I will check more."

Friedman found it unusual that Lazar was not a member of the American Nuclear Society or the American Physical Society. He also called MIT and Cal Tech, and found no records on Lazar.

Cameron asked John Lear why investigators were having such a hard time finding school transcripts of Lazar. Lear wrote back, "I can't help you with that other than to say I know what the story is, it's personal on Bob's part, and it's part of the reason that no records are coming up from MIT or Cal Tech."

Interestingly, it appears that Knapp did find one or more person who confirmed that Lazar did indeed work at S-4. According to Tony Pelham, "Knapp claims that he did talk to someone at Los Alamos who had worked with [Lazar] there, and remembered [Lazar], and he also claims that he talked to another person out there at Area 51, or S-4, who remembered Lazar out there."

More on Element 115

During a radio broadcast of Billy Goodman's "Happening" program, Lazar made statements regarding Element 115 which may have had national security implications. This problem was brought to light by Lee Graham, an electronics research technician and employee of Aerojet Electro Systems.

Graham was familiar with government security agreements because he had access to material classified as Secret. He had been asked by his firm to sign a "Classified Information Non-Disclosure Agreement," Form 312, which would have committed him to a binding agreement to obey Executive Order No. 12356.

Executive Order No. 12356 "prohibits the unauthorized disclosure of information in the interest of national security." Standard Form 312 has a section in it listed as DoD 5220.22-M, which states, in part:

> Whoever, being entrusted with, or having lawful possession or control of, any document, writing, code book, signal book, sketch, photograph, photographic negative, blueprint, plan, map, model, instrument, appliance, note, or information, relating to the national defense, through gross negligence permits the same to be removed from its proper place of custody or delivered to anyone in violation of his trust, or to be lost, stolen, abstracted, or destroyed, or having knowledge that the same has been illegally removed from its proper place of custody or delivered to anyone in violation of his trust, or lost, or stolen, abstracted, or destroyed, and fails to make prompt report of such loss, theft, abstraction, or destruction to his superior [etc.] shall be fined not more than $10,000 or imprisoned not more than ten years, or both.

Because of the nature of the work Lazar was engaged in at S-4, it was assumed that Lazar would have had to sign similar security agreements before he was permitted to work there.

Graham recorded Lazar's comments made on the radio program and sent them to Mike Majowicz of the Defense Investigative Service (DIS) of the Department of Defense. In his February 1, 1990 letter to Majowicz, Graham wrote:

> Mr. MAJOWICZ, Sir, on the enclosed tape Mr. BOB LAZAR states that he has a "Q" level clearance and that he was in possession of an element #115 of extraterrestrial origin, which had ostensibly been entrusted to his care while being employed for the United States Government at an area he calls "S-4" located at "Papoose Lake" about "10

miles south of Groom Lake (Area-51)," Nevada. Mr. LAZAR further states that this element #115 was his proof that he had worked for the U.S. Government as a physicist back-engineering an anti-matter reactor from an Alien extraterrestrial flying Disc which employed this element #115 in said reactor in connection with 3 gravity amplifiers to create gravity waves for the purpose of interstellar travel.

Mr. LAZAR, however, indicates that this element #115 was stolen/removed from him, thus violating the above indicated DOD ordinance.

Whether the U.S. Government knew it or not, apparently Lazar had Element 115 at his home and even experimented with it. John Lear told Cameron in a letter dated March 1, 1990, that:

The 115 was kept in Bob's laboratory at his house for about 3 or 4 months. It was stolen back by the government the 3rd night of the Knapp UFO special as it appears, in its lead casing, in the background of one of the video shots of Bob. We did several experiments with it, which we have on videotape. These include putting the 115 in a cloud chamber and passing radioactive particles across the 115 to demonstrate the attraction (deflection). I held the lead-encased 115 many times. We also had a number of other items from the saucer, which were stolen back also. [Asked in 2011, Lear did not offer to explain what other "items from the saucer" Lazar had.]

There were three pieces of the orange colored element 115 in Lazar's possession. Although Lazar at the time said the material had been smuggled out of S-4, the pieces had actually been given to Lazar by the technician at Los Alamos National Labs (apparently given the code name LA1000). They machined cone-shaped pieces of 115 into two inch-long triangle segments, which were allegedly used to propel the saucer at S-4. Each of the smaller pieces weighed 233 grams.[128]

As Lear described it, someone stole back the 115 after it appeared in an interview shot of Lazar on the KLAS-TV special, but they only got two of the three pieces. One was being stored in a separate location.

The pieces at Lazar's house became part of experiments in the summer of 1989 which were seen by many people. The main experiment, conducted by Lazar and Joe Vaninitti, was to see whether or not Element 115 could divert the course of an Alpha particle. John Lear and George Knapp were observers, which Knapp video-recorded.

Dry ice was placed at the bottom of a bell jar. The Element 115 (which had been stored "in a hockey puck sized lead container that was cut in half and hollowed out slightly") was then placed on top of the dry ice. A Coleman lantern mantel was used as a radioactive source to produce alpha particles, which would be tracked in the mist created by the dry ice. The Coleman lantern mantel was tied to the inside of the top of the bell jar, hanging down about a third of the way, putting it about 6 to 8 inches above the Element 115. The bell jar was placed over the dry ice, with the 115 on top.

Knapp started the video camera while the fog began to form. Lear wrote that it was his understanding, because he was looking away at the time, "that one alpha particle, radiated out from the mantel did a u-turn into the piece of 115."

Lear described what happened on the abovetopsecret.com website:

> As the bell jar fogged up you could see the alpha rays leaving the radioactive mantle headed out into space at a high rate of speed with a few (not many) doing a u-turn back into the 115. A video tape was made of the experiment and I believe Bob still has the original tape.[129]

George Knapp told Angelia Joiner on her radio show in January 2011 that he also saw Lazar do the cloud experiment with the 115 at the house. Knapp described the same bending effect and stated he had also taped it but added, "Darned if I can find the tape."

According to Lear, the third piece of 115 was eventually hidden by Lazar somewhere in downtown Las Vegas. Lear still refuses to say exactly where it was hidden. All he would say is that it was "under 6 inches of concrete. Me, Gene Huff, George

Knapp and Bob's father are the only ones who know where it is."[130]

More Evidence Uncovered

Lazar underwent four polygraph tests, and although he did not fail any of them, the results were mixed on some. Although Lazar had vivid recollections about the flying saucers and alien technology, his mind was hazy about other things, such as the briefing papers he claimed he was shown and large blocks of time on work days during which he could not remember what he had done.

Consequently, Lazar sought out a licensed hypnotherapist named Layne Keck to help him recall various details and remember what else may have happened during his brief stint at S-4. Lazar suspected that his employers used "mind-control techniques" to prevent him from remembering too much about S-4. Keck apparently agreed, saying that it appeared that chemicals might have been used on Lazar.

After he was caught on Groom Mountain that night watching a test flight, Lazar claimed to have received many threatening phone calls, and even to have been shot at by someone on the freeway.

On February 15, 1990, researcher Tom Mickus circulated a file, on an early Internet system called UFONET I, containing a purported release by the U.S. Government regarding Lazar's allegations. According to the file:

> NOTE: This file was received anonymously here at my Fidonet address, from a mailer using an unlisted Fidonet number of (1:999/999). The file was sent along with a short msg, which I will reproduce here:

> "DEAR FRIEND: HERE IS A FILE THAT YOU MIGHT BE INTERESTED IN. I SUGGEST YOU LOOK AT [IT] VERY VERY CLOSELY. IT CONTAINS MORE THAN WHAT IS EASLY (sic) READABLE."

> SUMMARY REPORT

Sub: Robert Lazar 2 Feb 1990
Scope: Background and personality

1. The purpose of this report is to detail the available background of Mr. Robert Lazar. Since his recent exposure to the media and the attention it has placed on the activities in the test range this will function as an internal document for staff briefings on the matter.

2. The subject has been employed by a DoD contractor to service and maintain ECM simulator sites in the test complex. At no time has he been admitted to the advanced systems test. Contractor personnel are familiar with [the] area thru the peer gossip that occurs. As far as can be determined Mr. Lazar has not had access to any current programs in the area nor does the contractor support team he was associated with have clearance for these projects.

3. After a review of his background it is highly likely that the subject seeks recognition thru the spotlight of the media. Mr. Lazar has been featured on a local TV program as well as visits to radio talk programs. All indications are that he is highly intelligent but is not satisfied with his level of achievement in his current profession. Checks with his coworkers backup this assessment.

4. All inquiries about Mr. Lazar should be handled thru the Nellis AFB Public Affairs office. No further action is recommended or required. As of this date Mr. Lazar has not released any sensitive or classified information for which he may have had access.

In a telephone interview on June 14, 1990, KLAS-TV news commentator George Knapp told Crain that he had called Nellis Air Force Base for officials either to confirm or deny the release. The officials replied that they did not write it and "that's for sure." It appears that someone was using the computer network to disseminate false information.

According to the September/October 1990 issue of *UFO Magazine*, Lazar had obtained his W-2 form from U.S. Naval Intelligence, which ostensibly confirmed his former employment with them.

When the W-2 form was released, various researchers began researching it. John Andrews, plastic kit division manager of the Testor Corporation, found out that the U.S. Postal Service sends mail with the ZIP code NIC-01, the code on Lazar's W-2 form, to Naval Intelligence Command in Maryland. Researcher Bob Oechsler, formally with NASA, discovered that the E6722MAJ stood for the Department of Energy, Kirkland Air Force Base, with MAJ as the point of origin.

The W-2 showed that it was not the Air Force, but the Navy that may well have been the big player in the UFO back-engineering program. For years, other researchers have also contended this. Some examples:

- The Navy (unlike the Air Force) existed as an independent agency when the flying saucer flap began just after WWII. Moreover, it controlled most of the research and development funds being handed out by the government for weapons research. Any intelligence that was being collected by the Navy would have gone through the Department of Naval Intelligence, which appears on Lazar's W-2. The Air Force did not come into existence until September 1947. As early as 1948, the Office of Naval Intelligence co-authored Air Intelligence Division No. 203, titled "Analysis of Flying Objects in the U.S.," which circulated among the top intelligence agencies.
- Contacts around Canadian government engineer Wilbert Smith stated that Smith's main contacts in the United States providing him information were Navy. Robert Sarbacher, for example, stated the conversations he had overhead about the UFO crash briefing being held at WPAFB took place in an office in the Navy building.
- Vannevar Bush, who was rumored to have done the first Top Secret study into UFOs in following WWII was a Navy man.
- Dr. Eric Walker did research for the Navy during the war and later ran one of the main Navy laboratories.
- During the television show *UFO Cover-Up? Live!*, information was put out that the Navy was a key element and that the headquarters for MJ-12 was at the Naval Observatory in

Washington, D.C.
- When, in the 1980s, Representative Christopher Dodd attempted to track down the famous Holloman alien landing film, he was told that it was being held by the Navy. One of the more respected members of the Aviary was quoted as saying that a main reason why the government cooperated on the 1970s documentary, *UFOs, Past, Present, and Future*, was that the Navy was hoping it would encourage scientists to look at the UFO phenomena.
- CIA UFO record keeper Ronald Pandolfi told researcher Dan Smith that "every flag officer in the ONI" (Office of Naval Intelligence; Commander and above) had been briefed on the alien visitors.
- Bill Clinton, in a statement in 2005, stated that he had sent someone to Area 51 looking for the UFO and the alien that many people in his administration believed was there. The answer came back that the only thing going on was Top Secret research on new aircraft being developed by the Air Force. However, Lazar had stated clearly that there were no saucers or saucer research going on at Area 51. The UFO research and the possible live alien were at S-4, south of the Air Force Groom Lake base, and that it was controlled by the Navy.

Lazar's life became subject to intense scrutiny and even surveillance. In a May 1990 interview with a journalist from *Inside Report*, physicist Dr. Edward Teller was asked if he knew Robert Lazar. (As previously mentioned, Lazar stated that Teller had helped him to get his job at S-4.) What appeared on the television account is that Dr. Teller initially indicated that he did not know Lazar, or at least did not remember him. After much prodding, he remarked: "Maybe I know him . . . maybe I helped him somewhere along the line."

In another story confirmed by several sources, Lazar was offered $7,500 to appear on a UFO television special in Japan. Apparently, Lazar had planned to go, until he received a threatening phone call from someone (according to KLAS-TV, it was Lazar's former boss at S-4) to the effect that if he went to Japan, he wouldn't be coming back to the U.S. Lazar appears not to have gone.

Lazar was also implicated in a prostitution ring. According to the June 3, 1990 issue of the *Las Vegas Review-Journal*, Lazar was indicted and was in danger of facing a sentence of up to five years in prison. He pled guilty to one charge of pandering in the prostitution ring. Regardless, the charges had nothing to do with his employment at S-4 and his claims about what he saw there.

A Las Vegas researcher looking into Lazar's case told Cameron that the reason investigators had such a hard time confirming Lazar's background was that he had gone by a different name earlier in his educational career. We did not uncover the reason for this, but, as Lear explained in a letter to us, Lazar's reasons were "personal."

During Billy Goodman's radio talk show on KVEG in Las Vegas, a listener called in who identified himself as "Yellow Fruit" (whose first name we were told is Buck). This person claimed he had worked at the test site as a security officer, and that Area 51 contained underground bases and tunnels concealing the activities of secret U.S. Government projects dealing with aliens. William F. Hamilton, Director of the UFO Research Center for ET Studies, met with "Yellow Fruit" at Rachel's Bar & Grill (now the Little A Le Inn) near the test site. According to the informant, there was a conflict brewing at the underground base between the "benevolent ones" and another group of small gray aliens called "EBEs."

According to Hamilton's article "Aliens in Dreamland" appearing in the July 1990 issue of *UFO Universe*, an informant claimed that the name "Yellow Fruit" was the designation for the first level of security at Area 51. There was also a second level of security, one which rated much harsher security measures, and it was known as "Seaspray."

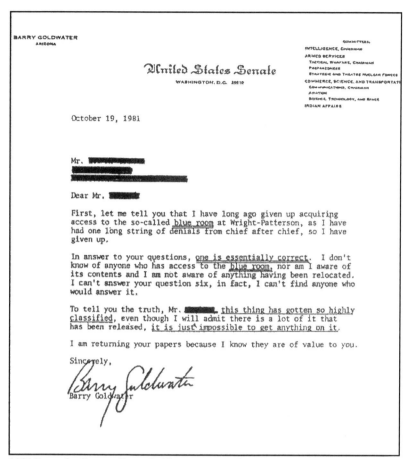

1981 Letter by Senator Barry Goldwater to constituent.

Interestingly, these titles have significance within the U.S. Intelligence community. *Philadelphia Inquirer* reporter Tim Weiner wrote a series of articles between February 8th and 10th, 1987, entitled "The Pentagon's Secret Cache." These described funds for intelligence agencies, as well as secret spending for classified projects (e.g. secret weapons). He revealed that the "black budget" in 1987 totaled $35 billion, or about 11% of the Pentagon's total budget.

According to Weiner, "Yellow Fruit," "Seaspray" and "Delta Force" all reported their activities to a group known as the Intelligence Support Activity (ISA). According to Congressional investigators, the ISA "was a secret spy squad, with a corps of at least 250 officers, that the Pentagon created in 1981 behind Congress's back . . ." Little is known about the activities of these groups. If Hamilton's informant told the truth, they were working at Area 51 during the 1980s and perhaps beyond.

KLAS-TV's Follow-Up UFO Investigation

In May, 1990, journalist George Knapp of KLAS-TV anchored a series of reports entitled *UFOs: The Best Evidence?* In it, Knapp covered a wide range of UFO-related topics, including cover-up possibilities, and a special emphasis on Lazar. Unfortunately, Knapp's follow-up investigation was hampered by purported government agents who reached informants before they talked to him.

One example included a former police officer named Terry Tavemetti, who had performed a polygraph test on Lazar. It was his opinion that Lazar answered the questions truthfully. When it was made public that Tavemetti was involved in the Lazar probe, his current employer was contacted. Tavemetti learned that a government agency had contacted the corporate office, wanting to know why he was mixed up in the Lazar case. Tavemetti asked which agency was initiating the inquiry, but he was not given an answer.*

Another instance was that of Roy Byron. November 1989, Byron, a resident of Las Vegas, contacted KLAS-TV, claiming to have information about Area 51. Byron said that he had helped several employees who worked at Groom Lake with their tax returns. Less than twenty-four hours after making the call, he was visited by two men claiming to be Secret Service agents. According to Byron, they "just wanted to lean on me a bit."

In still another case of obvious government pressure, a former employee of the military contractor, Holmes and

---

* Tavemetti retained Lazar's interview data and polygraph test, and found it more than a coincidence that his home was burglarized in January, 1990.

Narver, claimed that she had been privy to high-level discussions about crashed saucers, their pilots, and alien technology. She had sat in on a meeting with the USAF where ET-type material was being moved from Wright Patterson AFB to Area 51 (this has been believed by many to have occurred in the early 1980s). This Las Vegas resident, who was then working in local government, agreed to supply KLAS-TV with details about what she knew. But less than two weeks before KLAS-TV started airing its new series on UFOs, she was visited by a man who claimed to be a government agent. He told her that if she released information about UFOs, there would be trouble. The agent was aware the woman did "a lot of traveling." He warned her that "accidents can happen," and that harm could also come to her family. The woman decided not to supply the details to KLAS-TV.

Despite the pressure on various witnesses, Knapp continued to find corroborative support for Lazar. For instance, Lazar had claimed that for his job at S-4, as well as his earlier job at Los Alamos, the FBI had investigated him for his security clearance. For months, Nevada Congressman Jim Bilbray tried to learn about these security clearance records. Bilbray's staff contacted the Navy, the CIA, the FBI, and other agencies for Lazar's files. Their response was not that the agencies in question did not have the files; rather, that they could not find them and were still checking. The FBI allegedly searched their files for five months without finding files on Lazar

But Lazar had also said that one of the three FBI agents to visit his home was named Mike Thigpen. Although the Las Vegas FBI office claimed Thigpen never worked there, an informed source at the FBI told KLAS-TV that a "Thigpen" had done a job out of that office, but was attached to another division of the Bureau. The source did not know what Thigpen had been doing there.

KLAS-TV investigators uncovered that Thigpen actually worked for the Office of Federal Investigation (OFI). This

MASTER ARCHIVAL REFERENCE RECORD									
IDENTIFICATION NUMBER USAF 23775		TITLE BLUE ROOM (RADAR SCOPE), WRIGHT-PATTERSON AFB, OHIO, 1955							
PROJECT NUMBER 7307									
CROSS REFERENCE NUMBERS		CLASSIFICATION Secret	SOURCE OF CLASSIFICATION Form 42						
		TYPE OF MATERIAL							
1	REELS 35MM 53	FOOTAGE	EDITED X	D & W X	SILENT X	Fair	QUALITY	
	REELS 16MM	FOOTAGE X	UNEDITED	COLOR	SOUND no	CAPTIONS OR DATA		
Covers time lapse photography of aircraft beacon targets on radar scope.									
		REFERENCE DATA							
ANALYZED BY Field		DATE 9 Apr 65	EVALUATION Perm/Electr/Radar		DATE 7 Mar 57			
RECEIVED FROM Engineering Div, WPAFB			PRODUCED BY						
SHOT BY Engineering Div, WPAFB			REQUESTED BY USAF						
REMARKS									
1350 FORM SEP 61 25	PREVIOUS EDITIONS OF THIS FORM MAY BE USED.				AF-WP-O-FEB 65 50(				

Despite denials from the USAF about a "Blue Room" where UFO bodies and hardware were kept, and to which Senator Barry Goldwater was denied access, here is a document indicating that such a room did exist at WPAFB in 1955.

organization was responsible for security clearance work for Area 51. Such a revelation provided strong support for Lazar's claim that he worked at Area 51. After all, how else could Lazar have come up with the name Mike Thigpen as the person doing his security check?

Unfortunately, the organization could not be found in the phone book. When Knapp contacted its Washington office, it refused to help him determine not only whether or not Thigpen investigated Robert Lazar, but even if Thigpen worked for the OFI at all. Later, Knapp actually tracked Thigpen down and questioned him about his work on Lazar's security clearance. Thigpen said he could not remember.

After all his work on the Lazar case, Knapp remained impressed with the Lazar story, despite the inconsistencies. In a letter dated April 16, 1990, George Knapp wrote to Crain:

> I'm sorry that you feel some details about Lazar's background "don't click." I have spent nearly a year trying to verify or dispute his story and have found no evidence that he is lying, despite almost daily meetings and conversations with Lazar, his associates, and various independent

sources of my own. I am not in a position to say that I can prove everything that he says, but I haven't found anything that discredits him in my mind. Bob has consented to allow me to delve into his background but is somewhat reluctant to turn over details about his private life to people he doesn't know. This is the main reason he hasn't sent a copy of his resume to Stan Friedman or anyone else other than me. Let me assure you that even if you had a copy of it, it wouldn't do you much good since very little of it can be verified without a great deal of effort.

Chapter 11
Conclusions

The information collected in this book would seem to suggest that certain U.S. Government agencies have gathered intelligence on UFOs, and that the intelligence gathered, which can receive the highest of security classifications, includes physical "items."

Some items are so sensitive that they are not even classified. This means they can escape the laws created to bring the classified black world back into the white world and to the knowledge of the taxpayers who paid for the program. One example of this is the famous Holloman alien landing film, which was said to have recorded an interaction between aliens and the U.S. military in May, 1971. More than one statement by those who were involved say that the film was never classified. Therefore, no one knows where to look for it.

Another statement supporting the widespread nature of secrecy was made by Ben Rich is a 1993 presentation to the alumni of the UCLA Engineering School, not long before he died. There, Rich spoke of government UFO technologies which were "locked up in black projects and [that] it would take an act of God to ever get them out to benefit humanity." Many have concluded that control over the paper trail lies with not with the government, but with private industries.

Moreover, UFO researchers, in the course of trying to discover at least the purport of that intelligence via the Freedom of Information Act and other means, have become a target for counterintelligence efforts to protect classified UFO evidence.

Also, by unleashing a steady flow of UFO "fact and fiction" through putative "government informants," counterintelligence efforts have successfully obfuscated the truth, thereby creating confusion, controversy, doubts, and sensationalism among UFO researchers, as well as within the general public.

Despite the continuing controversy regarding the authenticity of the MJ-12 Document, there is nonetheless compelling evidence to support the notions that a shadowy group known as "MJ-12" actually exists or existed, and that a UFO crashed near Roswell, New Mexico, in 1947.

Unconfirmed leaks may possess grains of truth, but are covered by a cloak of disinformation. Confronted with truth mixed with untruth, investigators are left either to accept or dismiss specific cases in their entirety or to try separating fact from fiction through careful research.

The facts indicate that Dr. Robert I. Sarbacher had intimate knowledge about UFO crashes and alien beings, that Wilbert B. Smith handled UFO hardware supplied to him by the Americans, and that Dr. Eric A. Walker was aware since 1947 of a group known as MJ-12 and of secret U.S. government research on UFOs.

The 1980s appearance of space-visitor movies casting extraterrestrials in a benign light could have been part of an overall plan to educate—and perhaps, acclimate—the public to the idea that "not necessarily pernicious" aliens are here now.

This could very well be just one part of a long-range government indoctrination program. Indeed, its roots may have originated in a 1960 NASA study, in which experts tried to predict the effects on society if contact were made openly between an alien civilization and us "Earthlings." The report concluded that contact would cause anarchy—destroying the very fabric of society and disrupting institutions, religion and governments—unless it were presented to the public gradually, conditioning the public over a period of time to accept it.

If this is the game plan, it appears to be working.

According to the April 9, 1990 issue of *Newsweek*, studies by Jon Miller, director of Northern Illinois University's Public Opinion Laboratory, indicated, "fully 40 percent of the nation's adults think alien creatures have visited Earth."

Twenty-two years later, that number appears to have grown. A Sci Fi Channel/Roper Poll conducted in 2002 showed that 56 percent of the American public believed UFOs were something real and not imaginary. Nearly as many (48 percent) believed that UFOs have visited Earth in some form.[131]

More recently still, a 2011 poll by National Geographic showed that while 36% of respondents "believed" in UFOs, only 17% did not, and a whopping 77 percent of Americans believed there are signs that aliens have visited Earth.[132]

Meanwhile Victor Stenger, a scientist, skeptic, and pope for the "New Atheist" movement, has complained bitterly that a 2010 Gallup poll showed that only 16% of the American public believed in strict random mutation evolution, that is Darwinian evolution without theistic intervention, despite the fact that this is how American children are taught in schools. The *ETs Are Here* theory, banned from schools, is doing much better.[133]

Meanwhile, the advanced scientific and technological activity occurring at government facilities in the Nevada desert suggests that we may be developing the new technologies at least partially by means of what we have learned from recovered alien craft.

Despite U.S. government public statements to the effect that

UFOs are not real, there appears to be a clandestine group within the government infrastructure that knows the truth about their existence. That group appears to be buying time until it can figure out what to do with the technology before dealing with how to tell the public the truth about "visitors from the stars."

Afterword

Every major power wants to be able to build its own flying saucers to use as weapons in the worldwide power struggle taking place on this planet. Any useful measurements, crashed UFOs, artifacts, pilots, etc. would be held in the highest secrecy and not shared.

–Stanton T. Friedman "A Scientific Approach to Flying Saucer Behavior" in *Thesis-Synthesis-Antithesis*, American Institute of Aeronautics & Astronautics

Keeping a secret doesn't mean that there aren't lots of people who know about it—only that it is not publicly discussed outside of the sometimes very large group of people involved in the particular program.

–Stanton T. Friedman

D r. Walker circumvented our questions regarding his participation in secret government UFO meetings. So, we wondered what his reaction would be if a media source contacted him for an "on-the-record" statement. An opportunity presented itself on September 4, 1990, when a staff writer for *The Daily Collegian* met with Crain to write an article about our report. (The newspaper is published by students at Penn State, University Park, Pennsylvania, and has a wide circulation on campus and in downtown State College, Pennsylvania.)

After writing the article, the reporter called Dr. Walker to get his reaction to our allegations. She asked Dr. Walker about the secret meetings at Wright-Patterson Air Force Base, about what he knew about MJ-12, and about conversations he had allegedly had with Crain and Steinman.

Walker had always seemed to be unable to hang up the phone. When researchers phoned him about UFOs, he typically continued talking, trying as it were to walk around the question. Not this day, however.

When the reporter called him, Walker simply responded that he had no idea what she was talking about. He denied everything, and claimed he did not know who Crain or Steinman were. The reporter went on to ask Walker about a conversation that he had had with William Steinman in August 1987. At that point Walker abruptly interrupted her, saying there was someone at his door and that he could not talk now. Good-bye. The reporter said she had never had a response like that before.

For the record, to the press, Walker had always denied any involvement in government UFO activity. However, the phone conversations and correspondence with William Steinman, Henry Azadehdel, Tom Mickus, and Scott Crain tell a different story. We are not surprised by Walker's reaction and hope that someday the whole truth about his and others' purported involvement with UFOs will be disclosed.

Appendix I:
The Chase Brandon Roswell Claims

There is clearly an endless supply of such stories, and they are always volunteered to people who are prone to believing them but have no ability to check them.
– Jacques Vallee

In a July 8th story run in the *Huffington Post,* Chase Brandon, a 35-year CIA veteran (plus 5 years under contract) spelled out for reporter Lee Speigel how he came to learn that the 1947 Roswell crash was an extraterrestrial event. He stated that he learned this while walking through an area at the Langley headquarters.

"It was a vaulted area and not everybody could get in it," Brandon told Speigel. "One day, I was looking around in there and reading some of the titles that were mostly hand-scribbled summations of what was in the boxes. And there was one box that really caught my eye. It had one word on it: Roswell."

"I took the box down, lifted the lid up, rummaged around inside it, put the box back on the shelf and said, 'My god, it really happened!'"[134]

At first, the story sounded good. Brandon turned out to be exactly the CIA agent he represented himself to be. It appeared that a long-time CIA official had confirmed the Roswell story, and disclosure was right around the corner.

Well not quite. As the old saying goes "If it seems too good to be true, it probably is." There are many problems with the story.

The main one deals mostly with the "Roswell box" that Brandon claims he saw. This is simply not how things are done in government archives, and the CIA is part of the government.[135] Large organizations like the CIA have very complex and complete filing systems; they must, in order to keep track of the vast amount of material they process, and then to access them quickly when the time is right.

Anyone who has conducted research at government and non-government archives knows that there are no boxes with hand-written summations on them. A government archives box is going to have date, file number, agency, and a host of other things. There is a great deal of money for this kind of operation, and the archivists working there are well-paid professionals.

Moreover, the UFO topic is the most highly classified subject in the United States. It will therefore be controlled by Top Secret Special Access. This means that the materials will be compartmentalized on a "need to know" basis. The photos will be with the photo people, the metal with the metallurgists, and so on. Each person working on the crash of a UFO, for instance, will only be given access to what he or she needs to do their job. At no time would all the material in a "Roswell box" where everyone can see what everyone else is doing.

An important point about Brandon's claim is what he said was in the box, "Some written material and some photographs, and that's all I will ever say to anybody about the contents of that box." Brandon said that he could talk about the box but not give specifics about the pictures and written material inside. "I'm not reluctant to talk about it," he said, "I won't talk about it."

Combine this information with the fact that Brandon seemed to be saying that he was not violating his security oath: "to not say anything about sources, methods, classified information having to do with working for the Central Intelligence Agency."

"We all sign a secrecy agreement," Brandon explained, "that says we understand we are forbidden to do that by law, and that is an inherent part of keeping and safeguarding what we do, how we do it, why we do it, out of national security concerns."

Brandon said he could talk about finding the box but "won't

talk" about the items in the box. How can this be so?

Let us take a guess.

As archives do not file material in boxes with hand-written Roswell markings on the side, the box does not exist. Brandon, or more accurately the CIA, invented this part of the story. There is no box. Therefore, it is not classified, and he can talk about it.

On the other hand, Brandon spelled out that the specific items he saw related to Roswell are things he "won't talk about" and referenced his oath to guard classified information. The Roswell pictures and written material is classified. If Brandon mentioned a specific document or picture he would be in violation of his security oath.

Ironically, at the time of Brandon's claims, the U.S. Congress was investigating President Obama and the White House for leaks of classified material related to bombings done by U.S. drones, as well as a computer hacking attack against Iran. If they can investigate the President, there certainly would not be a "get out of jail free" card for Brandon.

The Brandon story was told on the 65th anniversary of Roswell. Indeed, it harkened back to a similar story told on the 50th anniversary of Roswell. At that time, U.S. Army Colonel Phillip Corso told the world he too had found Roswell material. Corso's Roswell discovery came not in an archives box, but in a filing cabinet in his Pentagon office. Like Brandon, Corso took oaths to guard classified material that he had been entrusted with during his long military career.

The big question is, how were Corso and Brandon given a pass when the President of the United States does not seem to have immunity?

The obvious answer begins with there being no filing cabinet and no Roswell box. If the story is not true, then it cannot be classified. If it is not classified, one cannot be prosecuted for talking about it. Well then what about the material in the box? It's classified and Brandon isn't talking.

Starting to make sense?

Does this mean that Corso and Brandon bad guys running a scam to sell books? There is another interesting possibility.

In September 1980, UFO researcher Bill Moore was contacted by a high-level CIA agent. Moore recounted the event,

> In early September, 1980, I was approached by a well-placed individual within the intelligence community who claimed to be directly connected to a high-level project dealing with UFOs. This individual told me that he spoke for a small group of similar individuals who were uncomfortable with the government's continuing cover-up of the truth and indicated that he and his group would like to help me with my research into the subject in the hope and expectation that I might be able to help them find a way to change the prevailing policy and get the facts to the public without breaking any laws in the process.

The key part of the statement was Moore's informant, the man known as Falcon and now identified to have been Harry Rositzke, who said that a high-level group wanted to help "without breaking any laws in the process." Moore was told that the material he would be given would be a mixture of true and false information. Moore would have to separate the wheat from the chaff.

Corso and Brandon both appeared to the world during major anniversaries of Roswell. Perhaps the government decided to replay the operation that Falcon began with Bill Moore many years ago. A message is conveyed to the public that Roswell was real, but is packaged as a collection of Roswell goodies found in an archives box or a filing cabinet.

It is not fair to question whether Corso made a deal to tell his story, allowing for certain details to be changed by government officials—he is not alive to defend himself. We do have some evidence, however, that supports the thesis that this was exactly what Brandon did.

When Brandon went public, he had just had contact with the CIA. He was being a good boy and had taken his upcoming fictional book, which dealt in part with extraterrestrials, to be reviewed and cleared by the CIA. During such a process, the Agency would have removed anything Brandon wrote that was classified.

Following this process, Brandon appeared on *Coast to Coast AM,* where he dropped the bomb that Roswell was an extraterrestrial crash, complete with bodies.

That incident inspired Robbie Graham, a Ph.D. candidate whose expertise is Hollywood's historical representations of UFOs and extraterrestrial life, to write a letter to the CIA (to which Cameron is a signatory). Graham described to the CIA what Brandon had said and asked for an explanation of what was going on. The CIA Public Affairs representative, Ian Tuttle, replied, "Off the record, we will look into your questions and get back to you as quickly as possible."

In order to "look into" this query (assuming they actually had an intention to search) the CIA would have had to pull the *Coast to Coast AM* audio to hear what Brandon said. Then, in order to look for the records in the Historical Intelligence Collection at Langley, where Brandon said he found the box, they would have to talk to Brandon and ask him where in the HIC he found it.

If Brandon had made up the story, thereby implying that the CIA had lied about its disinterest in UFOs since 1953 (as is its claim), the CIA certainly would have shut him up. That did not take place.

What did take place is that Brandon immediately ran out and talked to another major media outlet for UFO coverage, *The Huffington Post.* At the same time, he stopped taking questions from one UFO researcher who was in contact with him. In the *Huffington Post* interview, he added that he wouldn't be specific about any of the items of evidence he saw.

Eventually, the CIA stated that the Agency had looked in the HIC for the material Brandon had talked about, but found nothing. As predicted, they neither defended Brandon nor called him a liar.

Assuming that the CIA, and not Brandon, was behind the story, people should not be surprised. This is exactly what the group of researchers who wrote to the CIA with questions on Brandon had predicted. The story was out and making the rounds. The job was done. The CIA could now go back to its standard line that it has not been interested or involved in UFOs since 1953.

What Brandon did is something that is done all the time at the CIA. There are parts of CIA history that, though they may be classified for one reason or another, still want to be told.

Consider a CIA agent who wants to write a book about his career so that his grandchildren will know that he was a James Bond figure who saved the western world from imminent disaster. What happened to the agent is classified. Because no one wants to go to jail, such classified material cannot be told—unless it appears in a fictional novel mixed in with invented material, e.g. disinformation. The CIA agent then writes his story as a fictional tale, leaving his grandchildren to wonder what is true and what is not.

This is what Brandon did. It is also the same process Falcon used to tell Moore the stories of UFO cover-up: Falcon warned that he would mix true and false material together. Moore was left to do his best to sort out was true and what was not.

The agent gets to tell his heroic tale, the Agency gets to tell the CIA story without violating security, and everyone is happy. Bill Moore got his insights into the world of UFOs and the government. His story, however, did not have a happy ending. Once he revealed that he had cooperated in the government's game, he was no longer respected in the UFO community and walked away from the UFO field.

So it was with the 65th anniversary of Roswell. Like the 50th anniversary when Corso came out, the CIA wanted to give the American people the message that Roswell was real. It was sort of a birthday present.

That is the way it has to be done. They cannot simply come

out and say "it's real." Such a statement would force disclosure of material that is still classified. The CIA also does not want to reveal it because its senior members probably do not want to be dragged through the streets by an angry mob, like Muammar Gaddafi.

Hence Brandon has not been prosecuted for lying about the CIA. Hence the CIA did not call him a liar. The Roswell box story is a made-up story with no breaches of security. Brandon and the CIA are a team. This is why nothing was done by the CIA, and nothing will be done.

The game played by Brandon and the CIA is not new. They have been doing this kind of disclosure for at least 40 years and there are piles of examples that can be sited.

Kit Green, a CIA analyst from 1969-1983, spoke about how this gradual UFO disclosure works. He should know. He has long been rumored to have been in control of the "UFO desk" during his time at the CIA. He has also been rumored to be a person who has briefed the President on UFOs. Researcher Bill Moore, who called Green the "Bluejay" in his Aviary, described Green as "a person close to the President of the United States, capable of checking on information to determine its reliability."

Green indicates that what the government is trying to get across is the "Core Story." Green, along with researcher Jacques Vallee and scientist Dr. Hal Puthoff, came up with the Core Story concept in 1987 after sitting down and trying to establish what they knew to be true among all the thousands of UFOs stories that had been told. As Green described the Core Story"

> The ETs came here, maybe once, maybe a few times. Either through accident or by design, the U.S. government acquired one of their craft. The only problem was that the physics that powered the craft were so advanced that for decades we humans have struggled to understand it or replicate it.[136]

Green also described the problem that the United States government and the CIA face in trying to get the story out to the public in the least damaging way.

> If something really strange in the area of UFOs is true,
> then what do we do about conveying that information to
> the public? First we must consider what may be the basic
> facts. If you were to give them the Core Story right off the
> bat, they'd get sick, so you do it slowly over ten or twenty
> years. You put out a bunch of movies, a bunch of books, a
> bunch of stories, a bunch of Internet memes about reptilian
> aliens eating our children, about the crazy stuff we've seen
> recently in Serpo (a bizarre series of e-mails that appeared
> on the Internet claiming that there had been an exchange
> of people between the aliens and the US military—These
> e-mails apparently were watched closely by many high
> government people). Then one day you say, "Hey, all that
> stuff is nonsense, relax, it's not that bad, you don't have to
> worry, the reality is this" and then you give them the real
> story.[137]

The conclusion of the story is that there are really no bad guys. The government is facing a challenge of protecting classified material related to the technologies involved, and of informing the population of what is going on. It is not disinformation to throw people off, but information to acclimatize people just in case something happens that the government cannot control and the UFO cover-up unravels.

Disinformation is not necessary and does not make sense. This was pointed out by Jacques Vallee many years ago when he said, "Something does not make much sense here. Why would someone in Washington mount a disinformation effort if the only result is to confuse members of the UFO research community, which is a very small group without much influence over the public at large?"

In 1969 the United States government shut down Project Blue Book, officially putting itself out of the UFO business. The U.S. government could simply have stayed quiet and would never have to face the UFO question again. If it faced a question, its spokesperson could simply say, "Don't know. Not interested. Not involved."

That, however, is not what the United States government

has done.

The pattern did not begin with Chase Brandon and the CIA failing to do anything to stop him from running to major media outlets claiming that the government is lying and covering up the fact we have been visited by extraterrestrials. Even in 1973, the U.S. government gave indications that it was still interested and the alien rumors were true.

It was in 1973 that member of the U.S. military signed a contract in the Pentagon for Bob Emenegger and Allen Sandler to create a documentary on UFOs. They provided them with the story that the CIA had channeled an alien in 1959 which flew by the window of one of the most Top Secret CIA facilities in Washington, D.C. They provided them film of a landing of aliens at Holloman Air Force Base, and film of UFOs tracking a missile launch out of Vandenberg AFB.

Yes, the government, and especially the CIA, started telling such tales in 1973, and has been telling them to various researchers in various ways almost every year since. The Brandon "Roswell is Real" tale is only the latest in a long stream of planned government leaks.

The CIA runs a great risk in doing this. Sooner or later, something is going to go wrong. Sooner or later, the walls of Jericho will come crashing down. If they do, the President will go with them, because they work for him and he is responsible for what happens at the CIA.

That is important in light of the Brandon story. In a tough election year, where Obama struggled to stay up in the polls, the CIA operatives needed to be very sure they knew what they were doing. Perhaps, having played this game before, they were expert enough at it. An interesting point to note, however, is that the CIA does not simply go off and do what it wants, especially in an election year. As Brandon cannot just go and talk to the media the CIA cannot simply run a UFO scam to see how it might work.

This means that the Brandon story had to have a green light

from the White House. The CIA takes direction from the White House. The risks are too high, and the damage to Obama, if it failed, would have been too great.

It may be that Obama wanted this message sent to the American people for Roswell's 65th anniversary. Like Clinton before him, Obama has been talking about UFOs more than most Presidents before him. Without prompting, he brought it up in a trip to New Mexico saying "we will keep our secrets on Roswell." No one had asked a question related to UFOs. In the same way, he openly played with Will Smith's son at the White House saying, "I can neither confirm nor deny the existence of aliens." Why would Obama keep talking about extraterrestrials and Roswell knowing that at any moment some Congressman or Senator, or some major news agency might press the point of what is going on?

Did Obama order this Brandon Roswell confirmation? Did he send a message on the 65th anniversary of Roswell, much like a UFO friendly Bill Clinton may have done on the 50th anniversary in 1997? Like everything else in the UFO world, it is impossible to prove. It is nice, however, to think that we might just have a friend in the White House.

Appendix II:

The Majestic 12 Document

[Notes: page seven is not reproduced here, as it is an otherwise blank title page for "Appendix A," which is the Truman Executive Order.]

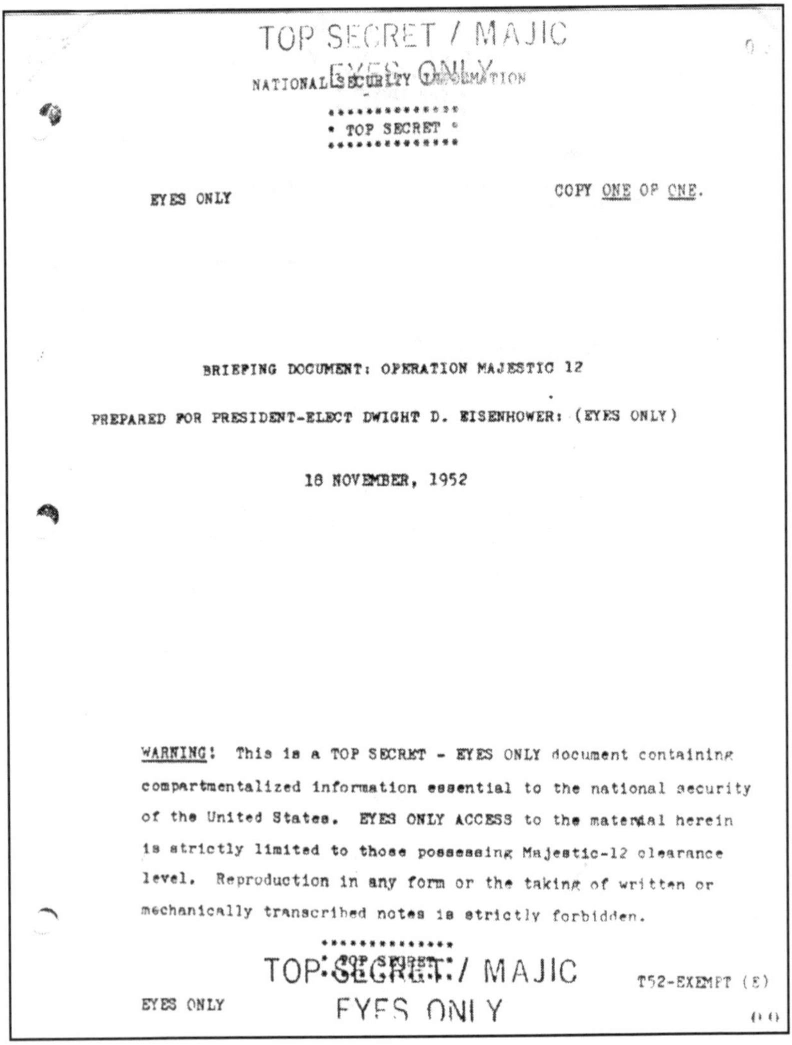

TOP SECRET / MAJIC
EYES ONLY
* TOP SECRET *
••••••••••••

EYES ONLY

COPY ONE OF ONE.

SUBJECT: OPERATION MAJESTIC-12 PRELIMINARY BRIEFING FOR
PRESIDENT-ELECT EISENHOWER.

DOCUMENT PREPARED 18 NOVEMBER, 1952.

BRIEFING OFFICER: ADM. ROSCOE H. HILLENKOETTER (MJ-1)

NOTE: This document has been prepared as a preliminary briefing
only. It should be regarded as introductory to a full operations
briefing intended to follow.

• • • • • •

OPERATION MAJESTIC-12 is a TOP SECRET Research and Development/
Intelligence operation responsible directly and only to the
President of the United States. Operations of the project are
carried out under control of the Majestic-12 (Majic-12) Group
which was established by special classified executive order of
President Truman on 24 September, 1947, upon recommendation by
Dr. Vannevar Bush and Secretary James Forrestal. (See Attachment
"A".) Members of the Majestic-12 Group were designated as follows:

> Adm. Roscoe H. Hillenkoetter
> Dr. Vannevar Bush
> Secy. James V. Forrestal*
> Gen. Nathan F. Twining
> Gen. Hoyt S. Vandenberg
> Dr. Detlev Bronk
> Dr. Jerome Hunsaker
> Mr. Sidney W. Souers
> Mr. Gordon Gray
> Dr. Donald Menzel
> Gen. Robert M. Montague
> Dr. Lloyd V. Berkner

The death of Secretary Forrestal on 22 May, 1949, created
a vacancy which remained unfilled until 01 August, 1950, upon
which date Gen. Walter B. Smith was designated as permanent
replacement.

••••••••••••••
* TOP SECRET *
TOP SECRET / MAJIC
EYES ONLY

EYES ONLY

T52-EXEMPT (E)

0 0 2

A-3

TOP SECRET / MAJIC
EYES ONLY

* TOP SECRET *
****

003

EYES ONLY

COPY ONE OF ONE.

On 24 June, 1947, a civilian pilot flying over the Cascade
Mountains in the State of Washington observed nine flying
disc-shaped aircraft traveling in formation at a high rate
of speed. Although this was not the first known sighting
of such objects, it was the first to gain widespread attention
in the public media. Hundreds of reports of similar objects
similar objects followed. Many of these came from highly
credible military and civilian sources. These reports resulted in independent efforts by several different elements
of the military to ascertain the nature and purpose of these
objects in the interests of national defense. A number of
witnesses were interviewed and there were several unsuccessful
attempts to utilize aircraft in efforts to pursue reported
discs in flight. Public reaction bordered on near hysteria
at times.

In spite of these efforts, little of substance was learned
about the objects until a local rancher reported that one
had crashed in a remote region of New Mexico located approximately seventy-five miles northwest of Roswell Army Air
Base (now Walker Field).

On 07 July, 1947, a secret operation was begun to assure
recovery of the wreckage of this object for scientific study.
During the course of this operation, aerial reconnaissance
discovered that four small human-like beings had apparently
ejected from the craft at some point before it exploded.
These had fallen to earth about two miles east of the wreckage
site. All four were dead and badly decomposed due to action
by predators and exposure to the elements during the approximately one week time period which had elapsed before their
discovery. A special scientific team took charge of removing
these bodies for study. (See Attachment "C".) The wreckage
of the craft was also removed to several different locations.
(See Attachment "B".) Civilian and military witnesses in
the area were debriefed, and news reporters were given the
effective cover story that the object had been a misguided
weather research balloon.

****
* TOP SECRET *
****

EYES ONLY TOP SECRET / MAJIC
EYES ONLY

T52-EXEMPT (E)

003

TOP SECRET / MAJIC
R-4
EYES ONLY

004

* TOP SECRET *

EYES ONLY

COPY ONE OF ONE.

A covert analytical effort organized by Gen. Twining and Dr. Bush acting on the direct orders of the President, resulted in a preliminary concensus (19 September, 1947) that the disc was most likely a short range reconnaissance craft. This conclusion was based for the most part on the craft's size and the apparent lack of any identifiable provisioning. (See Attachment "D".) A similar analysis of the four dead occupants was arranged by Dr. Bronk. It was the tentative conclusion of this group (30 November, 1947) that although these creatures are human-like in appearance, the biological and evolutionary processes responsible for their development has apparently been quite different from those observed or postulated in homo-sapiens. Dr. Bronk's team has suggested the term "Extra-terrestrial Biological Entities", or "EBEs", be adopted as the standard term of reference for these creatures until such time as a more definitive designation can be agreed upon.

Since it is virtually certain that these craft do not originate in any country on earth, considerable speculation has centered around what their point of origin might be and how they get here. Mars was and remains a possibility, although some scientists, most notably Dr. Menzel, consider it more likely that we are dealing with beings from another solar system entirely.

Numerous examples of what appear to be a form of writing were found in the wreckage. Efforts to decipher these have remained largely unsuccessful. (See Attachment "E".) Equally unsuccessful have been efforts to determine the method of propulsion or the nature or method of transmission of the power source involved. Research along these lines has been complicated by the complete absence of identifiable wings, propellers, jets, or other conventional methods of propulsion and guidance, as well as a total lack of metallic wiring, vacuum tubes, or similar recognizable electronic components. (See Attachment "F".) It is assumed that the propulsion unit was completely destroyed by the explosion which caused the crash.

* TOP SECRET *

EYES ONLY TOP SECRET / MAJIC T52-EXEMPT (E)

EYES ONLY

004

TOP SECRET / MAJIC
EYES ONLY
005

```
••••••••••••••
* TOP SECRET *
••••••••••••••
```

EYES ONLY   COPY ONE OF ONE.

A need for as much additional information as possible about
these craft, their performance characteristics and their
purpose led to the undertaking known as U.S. Air Force Project
SIGN in December, 1947. In order to preserve security, liason
between SIGN and Majestic-12 was limited to two individuals
within the Intelligence Division of Air Materiel Command whose
role was to pass along certain types of information through
channels. SIGN evolved into Project GRUDGE in December, 1948.
The operation is currently being conducted under the code name
BLUE BOOK, with liason maintained through the Air Force officer
who is head of the project.

On 06 December, 1950, a second object, probably of similar
origin, impacted the earth at high speed in the El Indio -
Guerrero area of the Texas - Mexican boder after following
a long trajectory through the atmosphere. By the time a
search team arrived, what remained of the object had been almost
totally incinerated. Such material as could be recovered was
transported to the A.E.C. facility at Sandia, New Mexico, for
study.

Implications for the National Security are of continuing importance in that the motives and ultimate intentions of these
visitors remain completely unknown. In addition, a significant
upsurge in the surveillance activity of these craft beginning
in May and continuing through the autumn of this year has caused
considerable concern that new developments may be imminent.
It is for these reasons, as well as the obvious international
and technological considerations and the ultimate need to
avoid a public panic at all costs, that the Majestic-12 Group
remains of the unanimous opinion that imposition of the
strictest security precautions should continue without inter-
ruption into the new administration. At the same time, contingency plan MJ-1949-04P/78 (Top Secret - Eyes Only) should
be held in continued readiness should the need to make a
public announcement present itself. (See Attachment "G".)

TOP SECRET.MAJIC
EYES ONLY

EYES ONLY   T52-EXEMPT (E)

TOP SECRET / MAJIC   006
EYES ONLY

****
* TOP SECRET *
****

EYES ONLY   COPY ONE OF ONE.

ENUMERATION OF ATTACHMENTS:

*ATTACHMENT "A".........Special Classified Executive
                        Order #092447. (TS/EO)

*ATTACHMENT "B".........Operation Majestic-12 Status
                        Report #1, Part A. 30 NOV '47.
                        (TS-MAJIC/EO)

*ATTACHMENT "C".........Operation Majestic-12 Status
                        Report #1, Part B. 30 NOV '47.
                        (TS-MAJIC/EO)

*ATTACHMENT "D".........Operation Majestic-12 Preliminary
                        Analytical Report. 19 SEP '47.
                        (TS-MAJIC/EO)

*ATTACHMENT "E".........Operation Majestic-12 Blue Team
                        Report #5. 30 JUN '52.
                        (TS-MAJIC/EO)

*ATTACHMENT "F".........Operation Majestic-12 Status
                        Report #2. 31 JAN '48.
                        (TS-MAJIC/EO)

*ATTACHMENT "G".........Operation Majestic-12 Contingency
                        Plan MJ-1949-04P/78: 31 JAN '49.
                        (TS-MAJIC/EO)

*ATTACHMENT "H".........Operation Majestic-12, Maps and
                        Photographs Folio (Extractions).
                        (TS-MAJIC/EO)

****
* TOP SECRET *
TOP SECRET / MAJIC

EYES ONLY   EYES ONLY   T52-EXEMPT (E)
                                                        006

TOP SECRET

EYES ONLY

THE WHITE HOUSE

WASHINGTON

September 24, 1947.

MEMORANDUM FOR THE SECRETARY OF DEFENSE

Dear Secretary Forrestal:

As per our recent conversation on this matter,
you are hereby authorized to proceed with all due
speed and caution upon your undertaking. Hereafter
this matter shall be referred to only as Operation
Majestic Twelve.

It continues to be my feeling that any future
considerations relative to the ultimate disposition
of this matter should rest solely with the Office
of the President following appropriate discussions
with yourself, Dr. Bush and the Director of Central
Intelligence.

Harry Truman

TOP SECRET

EYES ONLY

Appendix III
The Aquarius Briefing Document

According to William Moore, he was permitted exactly 19 minutes with which to photograph this 11-page document. He believe it to be "a transcription of notes either intended for use in preparing a briefing, or taken down during one and typed later."

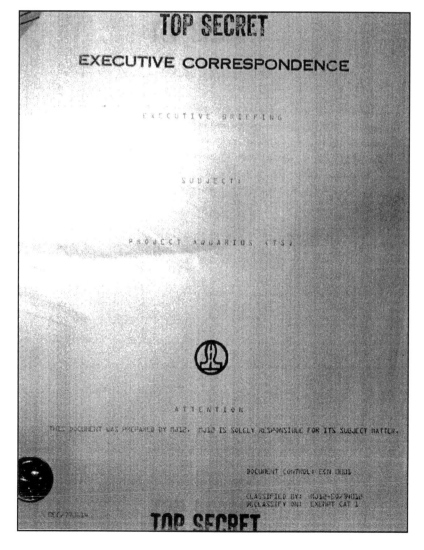

TOP SECRET

CLASSIFICATION AND RELEASE INSTRUCTIONS

(TS/ORCON)   The information contained in this document is classified TOP SECRET with ORCON. (Only the originator may release the information) Only MJ12 has access to Project Aquarius. No other government agency, to include the military, has access to the information contained in this briefing. There are only two copies of Project Aquarius and the location is known only to MJ12. This document will be destroyed after the briefing. No notes, photographs, or audio recordings, may be made of this briefing.

PAGE 1 OF 2

TOP SECRET

TOP SECRET

PROJECT AQUARIUS

(TS/ORCON) (PROWORD: DANCE) Contains 16 volumes of documented information collected from the beginning of the United States Investigation of Unidentified Flying Objects (UFOs) and Identified Alien Crafts (IAC). The Project was originally established in 1953, by order of President Eisenhower, under control of NSC and MJ12. In 1966, the Project's name was changed from Project Gleem to Project Aquarius. The Project was funded by CIA confidential funds (non-appropriated). The Project was originally classified SECRET but was upgraded to its present classification in Dec 1969 after Project Blue Book was closed. The purpose of Project Aquarius was to collect all scientific, technological, medical and intelligence information from UFO/IAC sightings and contacts with alien life forms. This orderly file of collected information has been used to advance the United States Space Program.

(TS/ORCON) The proceeding briefing is an historical account of the United States Government's investigation of Aerial Phenomenas, Recovered Alien Aircrafts and Contacts with Extraterrestrial Life Forms.

PAGE 1 OF 19

TOP SECRET

TOP SECRET

EXECUTIVE BRIEFING

(TS/EXEC) ... In the 1940's a civilian pilot flying over [...] mountains of [...] State reported a "Flying disc." [...] referred to [...] of the Aerospace Defense Intelligence Center of the [...] Air Force ... [...] aerospace companies as a [...]. [...] was the beginning of the United States [...] into "UFO investigations." In 1947 an aircraft of extraterrestrial origin crashed in [...] New Mexico. The craft was recovered by the military. Four Aliens (designated as EBE's) were recovered from the wreckage. The Aliens were found to be not only not related to human beings (Atch 1). In late 1940's another Alien aircraft crashed in the United States and was recovered partially intact by the military. The source of extraterrestrial origin survived the crash. The survivor [...] referred to itself, "EBE". The Alien was thoroughly interrogated by military intelligence personnel at a base in New Mexico. The Alien's language was translated by means of picturegraphs. It was learned the Alien came from a planet in the Zeta Reticuli star system, approximately 40 lights years from Earth. EBE lived until Jun 18, 1952, when he died fo an unexplained illness. During the time period EUE was alive, he provided valuable information regarding space technology, origins of the Universe, and exobiological matters. Further data is contained in Atch 2.

TOP SECRET

TOP SECRET

(TS/ORCON)   The recovery of Alien aircrafts lead the United States on an extensive investigative program to determine whether these Aliens posed a direct threat to our national security. In 1947, the newly created Air Force initiated a program to investigate incidents involving UFOs. The program was operated under three different code names: Grudge, Sign and finally Blue Book. The original mission of the Air Force program was to collect and analyze all reported sightings or incidents involving UFOs and determine whether the information could be interrupted as having any bearing on the security of the United States. Some information was evaluated with the idea of using the gained data to advance our own space technology and future space programs. 90 percent of the estimated 12,000 reports analyzed by the Air Force, were considered hoaxes, explained aerial phenomenas or natural astronomical objects. The other 10 percent were considered legitimate Alien sightings and/or incidents. However, not all UFO sightings or incidents were reported under the Air Force program. In 1953, Project Gleem was initiated by order of President Eisenhower, who believed the UFOs presented a threat to the national security of the United States. Project Gleem, which became Project Aquarius in 1966, was a parallel reporting system for UFO sightings and incidents. Reports collected under Project Aquarius were considered actual sightings, of Alien aircrafts or contacts with Alien Life Forms. Most reports were made by reliable military and defense department civilian personnel.

PAGE 3 OF 9

TOP SECRET

TOP SECRET

(TS/ORCON)   In 1958 the United States recovered a third Alien aircraft from the desert of Utah. The aircarft was in excellent flying condition. The aircraft was apparently abandoned by the Aliens for some unexplainable reason, since no Alien life forms were found in or around the aircraft. The aircraft was considered a technological marvel by United States Scientists. However, the operating instrumentations of the aircraft were so complexed that our scientists could not interrupt their operation. The aircraft was stored in a top security area and analyzed throughout the years by our best aerospace scientists. The United States gained a large volume of technological data from the recovered Alien aircraft.

A detailed description and further information regarding the aircraft is explained in Atch 3.

TOP SECRET

TOP SECRET

(TS/ORCON)   Several independent scientific investigations, at the request of the Air Force and CIA, were initiated during the era of Project Blue Book. MJ12 decided that officially, the Air Force should end their investigation of UFOs. This decision was arrived at during the MJ12 meeting (Atch 9) in 1966. The reason was twofold. Firstly, the United States had established communication with the Aliens. The United States felt relatively sure the Aliens exploration of earth was non-aggressive and non-hostile. It was also established that the Aliens presence did not directly threaten the security of the United States. Secondly, the public was beginning to believe that UFOs were real. The NSC felt this public feeling could lead to a nationwide panic. The United States was involved in several sensitive projects during this time period. It was felt that public awareness of these projects would have jeopardized the future space program of the United States. Therefore, MJ12 decided that an independent scientific study of the UFO phenomena would be needed to satisfy public curiosity. The final official study of the UFO phenomena was accomplished by the University of Colorado under Air Force contract. The study concluded that sufficient data did not exist that would indicate UFOs threatened the security of the United States. The final conclusion satisfied the government and allowed the Air Force to officially step out of the UFO investigating business.

TOP SECRET

TOP SECRET

(TS/MCID) When the Air Force officially closed Project Blue Book in Dec 1969, Project Aquarius continued operation under control of NSC/MJ12. The NSC felt investigations of UFO sightings and incidents had to continue in secrecy without any public knowledge. The reasoning behind the decision was this: If the Air Force continued its investigation of UFOs, eventually some uncleared and unbriefed Air Force or defense department civilian officials would obtain the facts behind Project Aquarius. Obviously (for operational security reasons) this could not be allowed. In order to continue the investigation of UFO sightings and incidents in secrecy, investigators from CIA/DCD and MJ12 were assigned to military and other governmental agencies with orders to investigate all legitimate UFO/IAC sightings and incidents. These agents are presently operating at various locations throughout the the United States and Canada. All reports are filtered either directly or indirectly to MJ12. These agents are collecting reports of UFO/IAC sightings and incidents occurring on or near sensitive governmental installations. (NOTE: Aliens have been extremely interested in our nuclear weapons and nuclear research. Many reported military sightings and incidents occur over nuclear weapons bases. The Alien's interest in our nuclear weapons can only be attributed to the future threat of a nuclear war on earth. The Air Force have initiated measures to assure the security of the nuclear weapons from Alien theft or destruction). MJ12 feels confident the Aliens are on an exploration of our solar system for peaceful purposes. However, we must continue to observe and track the Aliens movement until it is determined that the Alien's future plans contain no threat to our national security or the civilization of earth.

PAGE 2 OF 9

TOP SECRET

TOP SECRET

(TS/ORCON)   Most governmental documents pertaining to UFO sightings, incidents and governmental policies, including Project Blue Book, have been released to the public under FOIA or under various other release programs. MJ12 felt the remaining documents and information (not relating to Project Aquarius) relating to technological facts regarding Aliens medical matters, the fact that an Alien was captured alive and survived for three years under secrecy, can not be released to the public for fear the information would be obtained by SHIS. There was other information obtained from CIR that was deemed sensitive and not releasable to the public. Notably, Project Aquarius Volume IX, which pertains to tracing the Aliens first visitation of earth back some 5,000 years. CBE reported that 2,000 years ago his ancestors planted a human creature on earth to assist the inhabitants of earth in developing a civilization. This information was only vague and the exact identity or background information on this homo-sapien was not obtained. Undoubtfully, if this information was released to the public, it would cause a worldwide religious panic. MJ3 has developed a plan that will allow release of Project Aquarius, Volumes I thru III. The release program calls for a gradual release of information over a period of time in order to condition the public for future disclosures. Atch 5 of this briefing contains certain guidlines for future public releases.

TOP SECRET

TOP SECRET

(TS/ORCON)   In the 1976 MJ3 report (Atch 6), it was estimated the Alien's technology was many thousands of years ahead of United States technology. Our scientists
speculate that until our technology develops to a level equal to the Aliens, we cannot
understand the large volume of scientific information the United States has already
gained from the Aliens. This advancement of United States Technology may take many
hundred of years.

PAGE 8 OF 9

TOP SECRET

TOP SECRET

SUB PROJECTS UNDER PROJECT AQUARIUS

1. (TS/ORCON)   PROJECT BANDO: (PROWORD: RISK) Originally established in
1949. Its mission was to collect and evaluate medical information from the sur-
viving Alien creature and the recovered Alien bodies. This Project medically
examined and provided United States medical researchers with certain answers
to the evolution theory. (OPR: CIA) (Terminated in 1974).

2. (TS/ORCON)   PROJECT SIGMA: (PROWORD: MIDNIGHT). Originally established
as part of Project Sleem in 1954. Became a separate project in 1976. Its mission
was to establish communication with Aliens. This Project met with positive sucess-
when in 1959, the United States established primitive communications with the
Aliens. On April 25, 1964, a USAF intelligence officer, met two Aliens at a prearranged location in the desert of New Mexico. The contact lasted for approximately
three hours. Based on the Alien's language given to us by EBE, the Air Force
officer managed to exchange basic information with the two Aliens (Atch 7). This
project is continuing at an Air Force base in New Mexico. (OPR: MJ12/NSA).

3. (TS/ORCON)   PROJECT SNOWBIRD: (PROWORD: CETUS). Originally established
in 1972. Its mission was to test fly a recovered Alien aircraft. This project
is continuing in Nevada. (OPR: USAF/NASA/CIA/MJ12)

4. (TS/ORCON)   PROJECT POUNCE: (PROWORD: DIXIE) Originally established
in 1968. Its mission was to evaluate all UFO/IAC information pertaining to space
technology. PROJECT POUNCE continues. (OPR: NASA/USAF)

TOP SECRET

Endnotes

1. Larson, Phil. "Searching for ET, But No Evidence Yet" https://petitions.whitehouse.gov/response/searching-et-no-evidence-yet
2. "In Obama's Words," *Washington Post*, March 21, 2012; http://projects.washingtonpost.com/obama-speeches/speech/973/
3. Speigel, Lee, "Roswell UFO Was Not Of This Earth And There Were ET Cadavers: Ex-CIA Agent Says" *Huffington Post*, July 8, 2012; Waugh, Rob, "'It was a craft that did not come from this planet': CIA agent speaks out on 65th anniversary of Roswell 'UFO' landings," *Daily Mail* (UK), July 9, 2012; Eversley, Melanie, "Ex-CIA agent: Roswell, N.M., incident really happened" *USA Today*, July 10, 2012.
4. In 1967, the Canadian Defense Department made a move to move the UFO files to the National Research Council, a largely scientific organization. Dr. Peter Millman, the head of the Dominion Observatory learned that his section of the NRC council would be getting the documents. Millman was involved with the UFO phenomena from the beginning but maintained a skepticism about the subject. When he heard that the files were coming his way, he stated that he would not accept any classified files, as there was nothing to UFOs, and because he believed scientific organization like the NRC must maintain an open and unclassified stance on evidence. Therefore, a declassification of the evidence was forced. Even with that order, the Top Secret memo remained classified, and the declassifying officer attached a note that "a no time should this be made available to the public." Asked years later Millman stated he had never ever seen the Top Secret memo himself.
5. Creighton, Gordon. "Top U.S. Scientist Admits Crashed UFOs," *Flying Saucer Review*, Vol. 31, No. 1, October 1985.
6. Walker, Eric A., *Now It's My Turn: Engineering My Way*, Vantage Press (1989), p. 146.
7. Telephone conversation between Stanton Friedman and Grant Cameron, December 1989.
8. Walker, Eric A., "Approaching the Benign Environment," in *Franklin Lectures in the Science and Humanities*, First Series (1970), "Lectures, April 1969 at Auburn University."
9. William Steinman, letter to Grant Cameron, dated September 8, 1987.
10. "Astronaut Edgar Mitchell Sets Record Straight About E.T. Beliefs," Blog Talk Radio, July 24, 2008. http://blog.blogtalkradio.com/blogtalkradio/dr-edgar-mitchell-sets-the-record-straight/
11. Kevin Randle, "Edgar Mitchell and Roswell," *A Different Perspective,* July 26, 2008.
12. Tim Good, *Alien Update*, Avon, Books 1995, pp. 208 and 211.
13. Audio source: "Goldwater to Inman on UFOs" http://yourlisten.com/channel/content/131384/Goldwater_to_Inman_on_UFOs#./Goldwater_to_Inman_on_FOs?&_suid=13566565595320 6258235384802753
14. Exempt from Disclosure, Robert M. Collins, 2005-2008 Peregrine Communications.
15. Brian Parks, "former Truman Administration Official Confirms MJ-12" 2008, http://www.ufoconspiracy.com/reports/truman-stuart-mj12.htm
16. Greg Bishop, "Jamie Shandera and Proof of UFOs," *UFO Mystic*, February 1, 2007.
17. Letter from Timothy Good to Lee Graham, May 19, 1988.
18. Peter Hough, Jenny Randles, *The Complete Book of UFOs: An Investigation into Alien Contacts and Encounters*, Piatkus, 1997.
19. Klass, Philip J. "The Klass Files Volume 56," *The Skeptics UFO Newsletter*, March 1, 1999. http://www.csicop.org/specialarticles/show/klass_files_volume_56
20. Sider, Jean, Bullard, Thomas E. (trans.), "Majestic & Moore: Not Guilty!" *MUFON UFO Journal,* August 1989, No. 256, pp. 14-16.
21. Robert G. Todd, Mark Rodeghier, Barry Greenwood, and Bruce Maccabee, "A forum on MJ-12," *International UFO Reporter*, May/June 1990, Vol. 15, No. 3.
22. Scott Crain did two interviews with the source - August 3, 1990 and August 8, 1990.
23. "Thomas Coleman Sheppard's 1976 Encounter with Navy Alien Information." *Imaginative Worlds Forum.* http://imaginativeworlds.com/forum/showthread.php?5538-Thomas-Coleman-Sheppard-s-1976-Encounter-with-Navy-Alien-Information
24. "Will the Real Scott Jones Please Stand Up" http://www.tricksterbook.com/ArticlesOnline/ScottJonesWhitePaper.pdf
25. Graham stated that Bill had been instructed by Falcon to watch three people involved in UFOs: Paul Benniwitz, Clifford Stone, and Lee Graham.

26. Graham has filed over 5,000 letters and FOIAs with the various government agencies related to UFOs.

27. Letter Areojet ElectroSystems to DISCO, dated August 23, 1985.

28. This Unclassified stamp had been put on by researcher Ron Regher who also worked at Aerojet. The document was not actually declassified, although an "Unclassified" did appear on the DIA investigation report of Graham that was released in 1990.

29. ibid.

30. Also stamped Unclassified was a letter to Lee Graham from John Andrews and the text of the 1989 MUFO speech given by Bill Moore except page 15 which outlined his conclusions.

31. Lee Graham quoting the GOA in an FOIA to the "Information Security Oversight Office, April 30, 2006.

32. He was the boss for Special Agent Richard Doty who has been fingered by many researchers as the source of much of the disinformation that has been fed into the UFO community.

33. Letter—John Andrews to Lee Graham September 16, 1987.

34. Graham FOIA Appeal to the Secretary of the Air Force July 8, 1989.

35. Telephone conversation with Lee Graham June 7, 2012.

36. Moore, William. "UFOs and the U.S. Government: Part IV," *Focus*, March 31, 1990 .

37. Moore, William L. and Shandera, Jaime H. "The MJ-12 Documents: An Analytical Report," Fair Witness Project, 1990.

38. Walker, Eric A., *Now It's My Turn*, p. 146.

39. Information provided by researcher William Moore.

40. Russo, Rus. "The Real X-files: Is Uncle Same a Closet Ufologist." *American Chronicle Website*, June 12, 2007.

41. Pilkington, Mark. *Mirage Men: An Adventure into Paranoia, Espionage, Psychological Warfare, and UFOs*, Skyhorse Publishing, New York (2010), p 279.

42. Crain, T. Scott."UFO Informant Dies," *MUFON UFO Journal*, March 1995.

43. Dickson, Paul. *Think Tanks*, Ballentine Books (1972), p. 141.

44. Dickson, Paul. *Think Tanks*, Ballentine Books (1972), p. 141.

45. *Science*, May 17, 1968, p. 744.

46. Dickson, Paul. *Think Tanks*, Ballentine Books (1972), p. 144-145.

47. *Science*, May 17, 1968, p. 745.

48. Institute for Defense Analyses, *Report on a Decade of Challenge and Change, 1977-1986*.

49. Dickson, Paul. *Think Tanks*, Ballentine Books (1972), p. 142.

50. Bamford, James, *The Puzzle Palace: Inside the National Security Agency, America's Most Secret Intelligence Organization*, Penguin Books, 1983.

51. Smith, Bruce, *The Rand Corporation*, Harvard University Press, Cambridge, MA (1966), p. 5

52. IDA, "Report on a Decade of Challenge and Change, 1977-1986," p. 1-2.

53. Keyhoe, Donald, *Aliens from Space: The Real Story of Unidentified Flying Objects*, Doubleday & Company, Inc. (1973), p. 39-40.

54. Fawcett, Lawrence & Greenwood, Barry. *Clear Intent*, Prentice-Hall, Inc., (1984), p. 8.

55. *The War Physicists*, edited by Bruno Vitale, Instituto di Fiscia Teorica, Napoli, Italy.

56. Possony, Stephen & Pourelle, J. E. *The Strategy of Technology—Winning the Decisive War*, Cambridge University Press (1970), p. 100.

57. Possony & Pourelle. *The Strategy of Technology*, p. 78.

58. Klass, Philip. *UFOs: The Public Deceived*, Prometheus Books (1983), p. 35.

59. Fawcett & Greenwood, *Clear Intent*, p. 125.

60. Keyhoe, Donald. *Flying Saucers from Outer Space*, Henry Holt and Company (1953), p. 143.

61. Possony & Pourelle. *The Strategy of Technology*, p. 100.

62. North, David M. "U.S. Using Disinformation Policy to Impede Technical Data Flow," *Aviation Week & Space Technology*, March 17, 1986.

63. Marchetti, Victor. "How the CIA Views the UFO Phenomenon" *Second Look*, May 1979 .

64. Cook, William. *U.S. News & World Report*, December 26, 1988/January 2, 1989.

65. Gonsalves, Tony. "The Secret Version of 'Stealth,'" *UFO Magazine*, November/December 1990.

66. ibid.

67. York, Herbert. *Making Weapons—Talking Peace, A Physicist's Odyssey from Hiroshima to Geneva*, Basic Books, (1989). p. 138.

68. York, Herbert, *Making Weapons—Talking Peace*, p. 153.

69. *The War Physicists*, p. 39.

70. *The War Physicists*, p. 36.

71. Telephone conversation between Grant Cameron and William Steinman, February 1989.

72. Klare, Michael T. "The Secret Thinkers," *The Nation*, April 15, 1968.

73. York, Herbert. *Making Weapons—Talking Peace*, p. 153.

74. Hersh, Seymour. *The Price of Power: Kissinger in the Nixon White House*, Simon & Schuster (1984), P. 150.

75. An IDA spokesman.

76. Howe, Linda Moulton. *An Alien Harvest* (L. M. Howe Productions, 1989), p. 212.

77. *The War Physicists*, p. 59

78. Gary Bekkum, "Knowing the Future: CIA, 9/11, UFOs, and the Extraterrestrial Presence Part 10, June 6, 2009 (http://weirddesk.blogspot.com/2009/06/knowing-future-cia-911-ufos-and.html)

79. Franklin, H. Bruce . "A Weapon to End all Wars," *Bulletin of the Atomic Scientist*, November 1989.

80. Schnabel, Jim, *Remote Viewers: The Secret History of America's Psychic Spies*, Dell, (1997), pg 347.

81. Carter, Jimmy. *White House Diary*, Farrar, Staus and Gireau, (2010), p. 313.

82. Waller, Douglas. "The Vision Thing," *Time*, 11 December 1995, p. 45.

83. Rense, Jeff. "Jim Marrs On Remote Viewing, ET Agenda,JFK, Illuminati," May 19, 2000, http://www.rense.com/general/enchilada.htm.

84. Bekkum, Gary. "NSA alleged to have tested psychics against Iranian targets." http://www.starpod.org/news/1107282.htm

85. Komarek, Ed. "Ron Enters Navy and Source A's Arena" http://www.ufodigest.com/news/0309/arena2.php

86. James Smith interview on radio show "Strange Days Indeed" with Errol Bruce Knapp, March 6, 2002.

87. Schwarz, Berthold "UFO Dynamics—Book 2" Rainbow Books, New Jersey: , 1983 p. 535.

88. Press release, Controller of Telecommunications Ottawa, Ontario, August 10, 1954.

89. Bondarchuk, Yurko. *UFO: Sightings, Landings, and Abductions*, Methuen Publishing, Toronto, 1979, p. 103.

90. Keyhoe, Donald, E. *Aliens from Space: The Real Story of Unidentified Flying Objects*. Doubleday & Company, Inc. 1973., p. 52.

91. Grant Cameron has never been contacted by anyone in the Canadian government offering inside information or documents. Moreover, even though he has been involved with the President and high level intelligence organizations that might be involved with UFOs, in 37 years he has only been provided with one classified document related to UFOs, and that document was related to an event that was only partly related to the U.S. government role in UFOs.

92. "U.S. News and World Report—Washington Whispers Column," April 18, 1977

93 During the four years of the Carter administration, the CIA, FBI, NSA, State, Army, USAF and the Navy department released thousands of pages of UFO documents.

94. E-mail, Robert Collins, "Re: UFO Mystery: Was Prez CARTER Ever Briefed on UFOs? 5 Controversial Viewpoints!," May 27, 2011.

95. ibid.

96. As an interesting highlight to this document, Grant Cameron received an e-mail from one of the more respected members of the Aviary, asking what he thought of the UN story. Cameron replied that it had all the hallmarks of the previous setups, and he therefore wasn't spending much time looking at the story. It struck Cameron, however, that this person, who never e-mailed questions in the past, was so interested in something that seemed on the surface to be an obvious hoax.

97. Project Serpo is the name of an alleged top-secret program between the United States government and an alien planet called Serpo. The story first surfaced in a UFO email list maintained by UFO researcher Victor Martinez. Kit Green stated in an e-mail to Ron Pandolfi

that he had been told by Col. Richard Weaver (who was in charge of the 1995 USAF Roswell investigation) that "the essence of the SERPO story was true."

98. http://www.starpod.org/news/1201181.htm

99. For a more on the CIA aspect and how it tied into material provided by Falcon, the reader should refer to "Hocus Pocus: The Story of Falcon" at http://presidentialufo.com/articles-a-papers/439-ufo-hocus-pocus-the-story-of-the-falcon

100. There were indications at the time that the Falcon was a DIA officer and Moore in fact hinted at it, so the name Harry Rositzke may just be another cover. From inside the Aviary, Grant Cameron was given the name of Admiral Edward A. Burkhalter as being the Falcon. Cameron was told that it was Burkhalter who was actually the man who mailed the MJ-12 documents to Jamie Shandera. The documents, created to catch Soviets spies, were recovered from the files of CIA counterintelligence director James Angleton's files, and released as a disclosure move.

101. Moore interview with Greg Bishop, "Radio Mysterioso Show," December 4, 2004.

102. Some have questioned why Moore teamed up with Shandera instead of his friend Stanton Friedman, who had helped him break the Roswell story. Years later, it now makes sense that Shandera was chosen, as he had intelligence connections that Friedman lacked.

103. As one of the participants of the 1982 meeting told Caryn Anscomb, "It is the smallest set of elements for which the three of us at that time agreed had scientifically sound evidence. Since that time, we have briefed it dozens of times..." Asked if contact had been made with aliens Anscomb was told, "Yes I most assuredly do. And I do not believe that contact has been metaphysical, or ethereal, or n-dimensional in the context of the CORE STORY. I am silent as to those possibilities, also, however -- but leave to the metaphysicians to say if that also had been a form of contact. The 'contact' of which I speak I believe has been real in a traditional sensory, physics, and time & space sense. In short, what you may have seen in the original writings in 1987 of what the three inventors of the CORE STORY said the three of us, at that time believed. We three have never changed our minds."

104. http://www.bibliotecapleyades.net/ciencia/ciencia_flyingobjects10.htm

105. UFOs over nuclear weapons storage areas are actually quite common in UFO literature. The most prominent of the reports include the shutdown of all the nuclear missiles at the Malmstrom missile base in 1967. In 1975 NORAD filed reports of UFOs over nuclear weapons storage areas at Loring AFB, Wordsworth AFB, and Minot AFB. Then there is the well publicized story of UFOs over the nuclear weapons at a RAF Bentwaters base in the United Kingdom during the famous Rendlesham Forest UFO incident.

106. Bill Moore has stated repeatedly that he only passed one document to Bennewitz that he knew to be phony. Moreover, he had warned Bennewitz not to publish it.

107. Moore interview with Greg Bishop, "Radio Mysterioso Show," December 4, 2004.

108. New Mexico police officer Gabe Valdez also told Greg Bishop that he could confirm some of the weird things Bennewitz was claiming. One of these were alien faces that would appear on an oscilloscope that Bennewitz was using to monitor the UFOs. In Moore's case, Bennewitz was demonstrating his UFO detectors when he suddenly told Moore that the aliens knew he was in the room, that they knew who he was and why he was present, and that they had just scanned Moore. He showed a seismograph-type instrument that had just gone right off the scale. Bennewitz stated "If they do it again you'll feel it." At that point, Moore stated that he suddenly got a hot flash and felt very dizzy, lightheaded, and warm. "Did you feel that?," Bennewitz asked him. Moore confirmed that he had felt something. "I never knew," said Moore, "what to make of that experience."

109. After Falcon was identified as CIA agent Harry Rositzke, Greg Bishop tried to get Coleman to confirm or deny that this was the man he had run into during the *UFO Cover-up? Live!* production. Both attempts to get friends of Coleman to ask him failed.

110. http://www.thepeoplesvoice.org/TPV3/Voices.php/2009/06/11/the-cia-500

111. According to Robert Collins: "The Yellow Book was said to be written in the years 1972-1973 by EBE-2 (female) who is reportedly the 'Alien' Ambassador to the United States: There are three copies of the Yellow Book, one is kept by EBE-2 and the other two are kept in a 'Vault' near the Mall in Washington DC." He continued, "Second meeting with Ernie in 1988. Executive Producer Seligman (UFO Cover-up Live) was present. Ernie was retired at the time but had Det 22, OSI security personnel with him at this meeting. Rick was present. EBE-3 was Female Alien. Yellow book discussed."

112. http://muller.lbl.gov/teaching/physics10/Roswell/USMogulReport.html

113. http://www.presidentialufo.com/ufo-disclosure/250-disclosure-pattern-1980-85

114. In Robert Collins' 2005 book, *Exempt from Disclosure*, he tells of meetings starting in 1986 that involved Kellerstrauss, Moore, Shandera, John Alexander, Richard Doty, Hal Puthoff, and Kit Green (two of the originators of the Core story idea) to discuss "UFOs and the alien subject" along with MJ-12, which was just referred to as "the committee."

115. Reagan, Ronald. White House transcript of "Remarks of the President to Fallston High School Students and Faculty," December 4, 1985.

116. Reagan, Ronald. Speech to the United Nations General Assembly, Forty-second session, "Provisional Verbatim Record of the Fourth Meeting", September 21, 1987.

117. Hovni, A. "The Shocking Truth: Ronald Reagan's Obsession With An Alien Invasion," *UFO Universe*, September 1988.

118. Keyhoe, Donald. *The Flying Saucer Conspiracy*. Henry Holt, 1955. p. 214-215.

119. Keyhoe, Donald. *The Flying Saucer Conspiracy*. Henry Holt, 1955. p. 231-232.

120. Gordon, Stan. "The Military UFO Retrieval at Kecksburg, Pennsylvania," *Pursuit*, No. 80 (Fourth Quarter 1987).

121. *Just Cause*, June 1986

122. Letter, Senator Barry Goldwater to Mr. Shlomo Arnon, UCLA Experimental College, March 28, 1975.

123. George Knapp, interview with Chuck Harder, "For the People" radio show on the Sun Radio Network, November 17, 1989.

124. George Knapp interview with Tim Binnall,"Binnall of America radio talk show, November 23, 2008.

125. George Knapp, "George Knapp: Breaking the Bob Story" Abovetopsecret.com, October 8, 2006 http://www.abovetopsecret.com/forum/thread218963/pg1

126. Camelot interview with John Lear, "John Lear Tells All - Part 2" April 2008 http://www.bibliotecapleyades.net/sociopolitica/sociopol_lear03b.htm

127. Camelot interview with John Lear, "John Lear Tells All - Part 2" April 2008 http://www.bibliotecapleyades.net/sociopolitica/sociopol_lear03b.htm

128. Letter - John Lear to Grant Cameron, March 1, 1990.

129. http://www.abovetopsecret.com/forum/thread272252/pg22

130. John Lear, June 1, 2008, Bob Lazar Debunked for Good, www.abovesecret.com.

131. http://www.syfy.com/ufo/roper/05.html

132. http://abcnews.go.com/Technology/ufos-exist-americans-national-geographic-survey/story?id=16661311#.UNtBnG99KrY

133. Alex Tsakiris, Dr. Victor Stenger Slams Parapsychology, Calls Dr. Stanley Krippner Charlatan, October 30, 2012. http://www.skeptiko.com/victor-stenger-slams-parapsychology-calls-stanley-krippner-charlatan/

134. Speigel, Lee, "Roswell UFO Was Not Of This Earth And There Were ET Cadavers: Ex-CIA Agent Says" *Huffington Post*, July 8, 2012

135. There are other problems with details in the story. These include Brandon's statement that there is a small lady with blue hair and tennis sneakers who runs the Historical Intelligence Collection (HIC). This seems much more an expression of an old stereotype about librarians that anything that happened in reality. Another key problem with the story is Brandon's statement that people are not allowed in the HIC unescorted. In the same sentence, however, he states that he was in the room alone. Finally, in a later story, that seemed to be told to direct attention away from claims that the CIA was therefore covering up the Roswell event, Brandon told a story that the material in the book was probably just material that had been cleared out of some desk during a move. This new story seemed to want to convey the message that someone in the CIA knew but he was not directed by the CIA.

136. Grant Cameron, "John Alexander, UFOs, Myths, Conspiracies, and Realities: The Rest of the Story" http://presidentialufo.com/articles-a-papers/359-john-alexander-ufos-myths-and-conspiracies-and-realities-the-rest-of-the-story

137. Grant Cameron "The True Story of Area 51: A Look at the Actual Evidence" http://presidentialufo.com/articles-a-papers/379-the-true-story-of-area-51-a-look-at-the-actual-evidence/

Index

About the Authors

Grant Cameron became involved in ufology in May 1975 with personal sightings and an investigation of a large flap of UFO sightings in Carman, Manitoba, about 25 miles north of the Canada-US border. He produced a manuscript called "Tales of Charlie Red Star" that detailed the three-year investigation.

He moved on to research the work of the early 1950s Canadian government flying saucer investigations, and the related involvement of former Penn State University President Dr. Eric Walker in the United States.

In the past few years, Cameron has turned his research interests to the involvement and actions of the President of the United States in the UFO problem. A highlight of his research produced almost 2,500 pages of UFO files from the Clinton administration.

Cameron has researched the paranormal/UFO files of the late Senator Claiborne Pell, collected all of Senator Barry Goldwater's UFO letters from his Senatorial papers, and gathered a complete collection of files of the late head of the Canadian flying saucer investigation, Wilbert Smith.

He hosts the President's UFO, Hillary Clinton UFO, and Barack Obama UFO websites. He has lectured widely in Canada, Europe, and the United States and is the recipient of the 2012 Great Britain Exopolitics International Researcher Award.

T. Scott Crain received his B.S. degree in Marketing from the Pennsylvania State University in 1976. Having studied UFOs since 1966, he began writing UFO research articles for Ray Palmer's *Flying Saucers* magazine in 1969.

In 1977, Crain became a State Section Director for the Mutual UFO Network, and also served as a technical consultant for Sun Classic Pictures, researching UFO crash retrievals.

Over the years, he has written dozens of articles for varous publications, notably *Search Magazine, Flying Saucers Magazine*, Info-Paranet computer newsletter, and the Mutual UFO Network. His articles have also appeared in Argentina"s *UFO Press, The International UFO Reporter, The Cambridge UFO Research Group Newsletter* in Canada and England's *Flying Saucer Review.*

23249662R00166

Made in the USA
Lexington, KY
10 June 2013